GREAT HABITS,
GREAT READERS

GREAT HABITS, GREAT READERS

A Practical Guide for K–4 Reading in the Light of Common Core

Paul Bambrick-Santoyo
Aja Settles
Juliana Worrell

Foreword by Norman Atkins

JB JOSSEY-BASS™
A Wiley Brand

Cover design: Michael Cook & Adrian Morgan
Cover image: © iStockphoto/Thinkstock; Bambrick photo by Dennis Conners; Worrell photo by Jacob Krupnick.

Published by Jossey-Bass
A Wiley Brand
One Montgomery Street, Suite 1200, San Francisco, CA 94104-4594 — www.josseybass.com

Jossey-Bass books and products are available through most bookstores. To contact Jossey-Bass directly call our Customer Care Department within the U.S. at 800-956-7739, outside the U.S. at 317-572-3986, or fax 317-572-4002.

Wiley publishes in a variety of print and electronic formats and by print-on-demand. Some material included with standard print versions of this book may not be included in e-books or in print-on-demand. If this book refers to media such as a CD or DVD that is not included in the version you purchased, you may download this material at **http://booksupport.wiley.com**. For more information about Wiley products, visit **www.wiley.com**.

All video clips copyright © 2013 Uncommon Schools, Inc.

Library of Congress Cataloging-in-Publication Data has been applied for.

ISBN 9781-1-181-4395-7 (paper)
ISBN 9781-1-184-1926-7 (ebk.)
ISBN 9781-1-184-2104-8 (ebk.)
ISBN 9781-1-185-4020-6 (ebk.)

Printed in the United States of America
FIRST EDITION
PB Printing   10 9 8 7 6 5 4 3 2 1

Contents

DVD Contents

Main Folder	Sub Folder	File Name
Top Resources	One-Pagers	Lesson Types in the Reading-by-Habit Model
		Keys to Effective Habits of the Classroom
		Habits of Discussion Scope and Sequence
		Read Aloud: Key Guidelines to Remember
		Comprehension Skills Framework
		Phonics Instruction Framework
		Guided Reading Lesson Planning
		Independent Reading: Guidelines to Remember
	Guided Reading Narrative Book Database	Lexile Levels 0–100L Book Database
		Lexile Levels 100–150L Book Database
		Lexile Levels 250–320L Book Database
		Lexile Levels 320–380L Book Database
		Lexile Levels 380–450L Book Database
		Lexile Levels 450–480L Book Database
		Lexile Levels 500–700L Book Database

Main Folder	Sub Folder	File Name
	Guided Reading Prompting Guides	Informational Guided Reading Prompting Guide
		Narrative Guided Reading Prompting Guide
	Book Study Guide	*Great Habits, Great Readers* Discussion Guide
Part 1: Set the Habits of Learning	Chapter 1: Habits of the Classroom	Comprehensive Guide to Classroom Systems
		Keys to Effective Habits of the Classroom
		Sample Classroom Layout
		Lesson Plan Template
		Sample Lesson Plan on Teaching a Small Group-to-Group Transition
	Chapter 2: Habits of Discussion	Habits of Discussion Scope and Sequence: Teacher Training and Prompting Guide
		Sample Implementation Calendar: Habits of Discussion
Part 2: Teach the Skills of Reading	Chapter 3: What to Teach	Sample Kindergarten Curriculum Up to 150L
		One Week Sample Curriculum: Lexile Levels 250–480L
	Chapter 4: Read-Aloud	Read-Aloud: Key Guidelines to Remember
		Sample Read-Aloud Lesson Plan
	Chapter 5: Comprehension Skills	Comprehension Skills Framework
	Chapter 6: Phonics Instruction	Phonics Instruction Framework
		Phonics Prompting Guide
		Pronunciation Guide
		Word Attack Strategies: Multiple Resources
Part 3: Build the Habits of Reading	Chapter 7: Analysis and Action	Early Literacy Analysis Template
		Early Literacy Results Sample: STEP Analysis
		Effective Action: Sample Schedule for Guided Reading
		Effective Action: Sample Plan for Level 450–480L Group
		Effective Analysis: Sample for Level 450–480L Group
		Early Literacy Analysis Spreadsheet Template: STEP Analysis, Steps 8–12

Main Folder	Sub Folder	File Name
	Chapters 8, 9: Guided Reading	Anchor Chart Deep Retell: A Good Response
		Basic Structure of a Guided Reading Lesson
		Guided Reading Lesson Plan Sample for Levels 450–480L
		Guided Reading Lesson Plan Template: Reading Comprehension
		Guided Reading Lesson Planning
		Guided Reading Note-Taking Template
	Chapter 10: Independent Reading	Accountability for Independent Reading–Informational
		Accountability for Independent Reading–Narrative
		Independent Reading: Guidelines to Remember
Part 4: Lead by Habit	Chapter 12: Coaching Teachers	Top 12 Action Steps for Guided Reading
Part 5: Professional Development	Habits of the Classroom	Keys to Effective Habits of the Classroom
		Habits of the Classroom Handout: Systems and Routines
		Habits of the Classroom Reflection Template: Reading Routines and Organizational Systems
		Habits of the Classroom Workshop Session Plan
		Lesson Plan Template
		Habits of the Classroom PPT
	Habits of Discussion	Habits of Discussion Scope and Sequence: Teacher Training and Prompting Guide
		Habits of Discussion Reflection Template
		Habits of Discussion Workshop Session Plan
		Habits of Discussion Handout
		Monthly Map Template
		Habits of Discussion PPT
	Read-Aloud	Lesson Plan Template
		Read-Aloud: Key Guidelines to Remember
		Read-Aloud Handout: Before, During, and After Reading
		Read-Aloud Reflection Template: Before, During, and After Reading
		Read-Aloud Workshop Session Plan
		Read-Aloud PPT

Main Folder	Sub Folder	File Name
	Comprehension Skills	Comprehension Skills Framework
		Comprehension Skills Handout
		Comprehension Skills Reflection Template: I Do, We Do, You Do
		Comprehension Skills Workshop Session Plan
		Reading Comprehension Skills PPT
	Guided Reading Planning	Guided Reading Framework Handout
		Guided Reading Lesson Planning
		Guided Reading Planning Part II Handout
		Guided Reading Planning Reflection Template
		Guided Reading Planning Workshop Session Plan
		Guided Reading Text Selection
		Guided Reading Planning PPT
	Guided Reading Prompting	Guided Reading Narrative Prompting Guide
		Guided Reading Prompting Convo Role Play Cards
		Guided Reading Prompting Handout
		Guided Reading Prompting Reflection Template
		Guided Reading Prompting Workshop Session Plan
		Guided Reading Prompting PPT

DVD Video Contents

Here is an overview of the video clips for your quick reference.

Introduction

Clip	Technique	Description	Page
1	Comprehension—730L	**". . . Juvenile Delinquents!"** Erin Michels effectively prompts her students to use the knowledge from the informational texts to build meaning in the narrative.	1

Habits of the Classroom (Chapter 1)

Clip	Technique	Description	Page
2	Large-Group Transition	**"A nonfiction text, teaches us about . . ."** Meredith Pannia transitions from the desk to the rug to the start read-aloud, all while singing a song about informational texts.	30
3	Independent Reading Transition—Training	**"Group A and Group B"** Nikki Bowen trains her guided reading group to transition to independent reading.	37
4	Independent Reading Transition— One Month Later	**"Stand up . . . switch"** One month later, Nikki Bowen's students have mastered the independent reading transition.	39
5	Midlesson Transition	**"S-T-O-R-Y . . . story, story!"** In just eighteen seconds, Laura Fern has transitioned from Word Review to Reading a Story, all while keeping 100 percent of her students engaged.	40

Habits of Discussion (Chapter 2)

Clip	Technique	Description	Page
6	Master Clip	**". . . but that wasn't the big idea!"** Aja Settles guides her students to guide each other to the big idea of the text using *nine* of the habits of discussion.	48
7	Complete Sentences	**"Stretch it out"** Shadell Purefoy uses nonverbal cues and verbal prompting to ensure that students use complete sentences when answering the question.	56
8	Peer-to-Peer	**"I have evidence that he wasn't brave"** Yasmin Vargas prompts her students to direct their answers to one another.	56
9	Build Off Others' Answers	**"I can add off of that . . ."** Yasmin Vargas's students use a hand gesture that indicates they are ready to build off each other's answers.	59
10	Evaluate Others' Responses	**". . . we need to know what happened before . . ."** Erin Michels's students evaluate their peers' responses by prompting each other to use evidence from the text.	60
11	Prompt Peers with Universal Prompts	**"You have to use the text evidence too, like good readers"** Yasmin Vargas has trained her students to prompt each other with a set of universal prompts—in this case, "Where is your evidence?"	61
12	Hint, Don't Tell	**"Tyler . . . so who wants to solve the problem?"** Yasmin Vargas's students push one another to get to the right answer without telling their peer the correct answer.	62

Read-Aloud Lessons (Chapter 4)

Clip	Technique	Description	Page
13	We Do	**"Why are the boy and the dad probably smiling?"** Lauren Moyle reads aloud *Owl Moon* and guides her students to practice identifying characters' feelings at just the right moment.	106, 120

Read-Aloud Lessons (Chapter 4) (Continued)

Clip	Technique	Description	Page
14	Lesson Introduction	**"A character's thoughts, actions, and feelings . . ."** Lauren Moyle begins her read-aloud with a tight transition and a concise introduction of the skill the class is focusing on.	115
15	I Do	**"I'm going to get in his head"** Lauren Moyle picks a precise stopping point in the story to use a think-aloud to model how to use the skill effectively.	118
16	Check for Understanding	**"Give me some words . . . more"** In the final segment of her read-aloud, Lauren Moyle checks to make sure that her students have used the skill correctly and can describe how they used it.	121

Teaching Comprehension Skills (Chapter 5)

Clip	Technique	Description	Page
17	I Do	**"How to get to know a character"** Lauren Moyle's Comprehension Skills lesson is seamlessly aligned to the read-aloud, so she simply reviews the skill with her students.	136
18	We Do	**"What were the effects of the atomic bomb?"** Juliana Worrell scaffolds questions to build her students' ability to use knowledge from an informational text to guide their understanding of *Sadako*.	138
19	We Do	**"You have all new questions . . ."** Lauren Moyle gives her students a chance to practice preparing for a written response with her guidance.	138
20	You Do	**"What will you need to do first?"** In this clip, Lauren Moyle is no longer providing her students with scaffolding, but she still gives them an opportunity to practice a skill in a structured way.	139

Teaching Phonics (Chapter 6)

Clip	Technique	Description	Page
21	More Practice	**"Why is this word *mope* not *mop*?"** Laura Fern's students practice word solving at a brisk clip while Laura still makes sure that every answer is correct.	149, 150, 156
22	More Practice	**"How many sounds in the word *go*? . . . Prove it"** Jessica Lisovicz helps her students master sight words with a large number of "at bats."	151, 156
23	More Effective Practice	**"How many sounds in the word *make*?"** Jessica Lisovicz doesn't just ensure more practice: she makes sure the practice is effective by monitoring for and ensuring correct answers at each point in the lesson.	158
24	Make Phonics Fun	**"The more I read, the more I know"** Jessica Lisovicz brings an infectious joy to the work of phonics.	158
25	Make Phonics Fun	**"Yes a-a-a-a . . . good job!"** Andrea Palmer praises each of her students' correct answers and culminates with a cheer to celebrate their good work.	158

Part 3 Introduction

Clip	Technique	Description	Page
1	Comprehension—730L	**". . . Juvenile Delinquents!"** Erin Michels effectively prompts her students to use the knowledge from the informational texts to build meaning in the narrative.	167

Guided Reading Planning (Chapter 8)

Clip	Technique	Description	Page
26	Comprehension—600L	This comprehension conversation in Aja Settles's classroom is remarkably student driven. At the same time, it's entirely within Aja's control. Even as she turns the tough cognitive work almost entirely over to the students, she keeps them on the right path with the right prompts at the right times.	191

Guided Reading Execution (Chapter 9)

Guided Reading Execution (Chapter 9) (Continued)

Clip	Technique	Description	Page
36	Comprehension—480L	**". . . so the wind was crying."** Emily Hoefling-Crouch guides her student to reread the text to correctly determine the meaning of the figurative language in the text.	239
37	Comprehension—970L	**". . . so why does Momma keep her pictures locked in a trunk?"** Erin Michels asks key questions to help her students bring meaning to the symbolism in the story.	240

Coaching Teachers (Chapter 12)

Clip	Technique	Description	Page
38	Leading PD	Aja Settles uses videos in *Great Habits, Great Readers* to train teachers in using effective reading transitions.	292
39	Effective Feedback	Aja Settles uses Guided Reading videos from *Great Habits, Great Readers* to help Kristi Costanzo hone her own practice.	303
40	Effective Feedback—Practice	Role playing allows Juliana Worrell and Julia Thompson to practice phonics teaching techniques.	304
41	Planning	Aja Settles and Kristi Costanzo script out the questions for her upcoming Guided Reading lesson based on the assessment data.	304

For Ade'Shyah and every student like her:

that we may build your habits to read for life.

Foreword

Once there was a kingdom taller than the clouds, sadly out of reach for too many young people who might have entered. Only a few very lucky children were able to navigate their way through the labyrinthine forest, leap across the alligator-snapping moat, and unlock the hulking portal with magic passwords right out of *Arabian Nights*. Once inside, these children spent their lives exploring fertile lands and traveling a vital network of rivers and streams on an endless journey to greater wisdom.

Those of us who learned to read, and who love reading, are blessed to live in this amazing kingdom of knowledge. How grateful we should be to our earliest reading teachers who devoted their careers to the excruciatingly hard work of guiding us there! Unfortunately, even though these teachers have brought along multitudes of students, the vast majority of children are still shut out.

Today, with the publication of *Great Habits, Great Readers*, the book you now hold in your hands, Paul Bambrick-Santoyo, Aja Settles, and Juliana Worrell have given the next generation of earnest, hard-working reading teachers a detailed map for guiding their students through the forest, have fashioned the precise tools for building a durable bridge across the moat, and have written down for eternity the phrases that push open the doors for all children to read their way into, and happily across, the kingdom of knowledge.

I've seen Aja and Juliana perform these fests, initially as founding teachers at North Star Academy's first elementary school in Newark, New Jersey, under the tutelage of the legendary leader Julie Jackson, and then as principals of their own North Star campuses. In their classrooms, Aja and Juliana model what good readers think about as they read, transfer the cognitive load to their students, and facilitate conversations where seven-year-olds speak in complete sentences, elaborate on the ideas of their classmates, and point to specific pieces of text as evidence. These students were not born readers, but after four and five years of artful instruction, they came to love reading and do it all the time. It's no surprise that as third- and fourth-graders they were the first and second highest performing in the entire state.

Paul, who has already rocked the education world with *Driven by Data* and *Leverage Leadership*, took much of what was in the brains and classrooms of these champion reading teachers and translated it into training systems representing the best of Uncommon Schools's practices. These systems, in turn, have won a huge following among educators in a wide variety of school settings. Now, just in the nick of time, as the new Common Core standards raise the bar across the land, the three of them have assembled their "reading taxonomy" as a manual that all elementary-school reading teachers can use to lead their students to master difficult texts with deeper comprehension. More important, this is the book we all need to ensure that all children develop the great habits of great readers and go forth, in love with books, across the kingdom of knowledge.

Norman Atkins

Norman Atkins is the founder of Uncommon Schools
and the co-founder and president of Relay Graduate School of Education

Acknowledgments

It takes a village to raise a child. The same can be said for writing a book, especially one of this scope. *Great Habits, Great Readers* was born on-site in the direct work with teachers and students: the ideas stem from observing countless hours of the highest-achieving teachers. None of these ideas could have been captured without a tremendous support team.

First and foremost, Alyssa White, Steve Chiger, Dan Rauch, Angelica Pastoriza, and Jessica Ehmke served as an outstanding writing team—gathering ideas, shaping the drafts, and putting a touch of imagination into each round of edits. Without them, this project could never have been completed, and the writing would not have been nearly as effective.

This writing was informed by the input of some of the finest minds in K–4 reading from across the country. First and foremost, we are indebted to our colleagues at the University of Chicago Urban Education Institute (UEI), none more so than Molly Branson Thayer. She has been a key partner with us in this work, alongside Maggie Walsh and director Tim Knowles. As noted throughout this book, the STEP early literacy assessment and support provided by UEI's remarkable literacy team has been an important lever as we deepen student learning and accelerate achievement. We hope that this book allows other schools to benefit from the type of support we received from UEI.

Our inspiration to write this book saw its inception as we collaborated with the K–4 Reading Working Group, comprising the best teachers and leaders across our network of schools. It was in this group that the ideas started to flow: the initial frameworks, the PD lesson plans, and the thousands of hours of video of reading instruction that showed us what was making the difference in our most successful classrooms. Special thanks go to all the members of that working group: Nikki Bridges, Erin Michels, Katie Yezzi, Erica Woolway, Annie Hoffman, Julie Jackson, Emily Hoefling-Crouch, Annie Ferrell, Stacey Shells, Rob de Leon, and Jocelyn Goodwin. They were supported by a team of video analysts and project managers led by Jared McCauley, Melinda Evans, Jessica Ochoa Hendrix, and Laura Maestas. Their support was made possible and strengthened by the senior leadership at Uncommon Schools: Brett Peiser and Carolyn Hack.

But the feedback didn't stop there! It also came from Maryland and Delaware via the likes of Melody Deemer and Erika Murphy, two lifelong reading teachers and coaches who brought additional insight to the book.

The real heroes of this book, however, are the leaders, teachers, and students who do the work every day. In addition to those already mentioned, we thank Nikki Bowen, Yasmin Vargas, Lauren Moyle, Jessica Lisovicz, Valerie Samples, Meredith Pannia, Laura Fern, Shadell Purefoy, Erin Michels, Andrea Palmer, and so many more who have each served as an example to us of what high-quality reading instruction can look like.

In the end, the countless extra hours of work were supported at home: our spouses, children, and extended family, the rocks on top of which everything is built.

Thank you to each and every one of you. This book is a tribute to you all.

About the Authors

Paul Bambrick-Santoyo is the managing director of North Star Academies, nine schools that are a part of the Uncommon Schools network. During Bambrick-Santoyo's ten years at North Star, the schools have seen dramatic gains in student achievement, making them the highest-achieving urban schools in New Jersey and winners of multiple recognitions, including the U.S. Department of Education's National Blue Ribbon Award. Author of *Driven by Data: A Practical Guide to Improve Instruction* and *Leverage Leadership: A Practical Guide to Building Exceptional Schools*, Bambrick-Santoyo has trained more than seven thousand school leaders worldwide in instructional leadership. Prior to joining North Star, Bambrick-Santoyo worked for six years in a bilingual school in Mexico City, where he founded the International Baccalaureate program at the middle school level. He earned a BA in social justice from Duke University and his MEd in school administration via New Leaders for New Schools.

Aja Settles is the founding principal of North Star Academy's West Side Park Elementary School, part of Uncommon Schools. Settles joined North Star Academy in 2007 after teaching for three years as a Teach For America corps member in Camden, New Jersey. She has served many roles at North Star, including founding lead teacher, curriculum writer, instructional leader, and consultant. She is a graduate of Temple University, with a BA in sociology. Settles is also certified as a literacy coordinator through the Literacy Collaborative at Lesley University. Settles is currently working on her MA in education leadership from Teachers College, Columbia University.

Juliana Worrell is the founding principal of North Star Academy's Fairmount Elementary School, part of Uncommon Schools. Prior to becoming principal, Worrell did extensive work as an instructional leader and literacy curriculum developer at North Star Academy's flagship elementary school, Vailsburg Elementary. She also trains teachers and school leaders both internally, at Uncommon Schools, and nationally. She was a 2004 Teach For America corps member and has taught grades kindergarten through fourth grade. Worrell holds a BA in political science from Rutgers University and is currently pursuing her MA in education leadership from Teachers College, Columbia University.

About Uncommon Schools

At Uncommon Schools, our goal is to run exceptional public schools for low-income scholars so that every one of them can reach their fullest potential and enter, succeed in, and graduate from college. We know that the best way to consistently run such exceptional schools is by hiring, developing, and retaining great teachers and leaders, by investing heavily in their training, and by building systems that help leaders to lead, teachers to teach, and students to learn. We are passionate about finding new ways for our scholars to learn a little more today than they did yesterday. Every minute matters—for our scholars and for our staffs. Fortunately, we have had the opportunity to observe and learn from outstanding educators—both within and beyond our schools—who enable students from low-income families to achieve at dramatically higher levels. Watching these educators at work has allowed us to derive a series of concrete and practical findings about what enables great instruction, findings that we have been excited to share in books such as *Teach Like a Champion, Driven by Data, Leverage Leadership*, and *Practice Perfect.*

Great Habits, Great Readers shares a legacy with these prior publications—it is the product of many of our best teachers and leaders studying outstanding classrooms across Uncommon to identify the tangible best practices they have in common. By codifying this knowledge and sharing it within Uncommon, we are able to ensure all of our elementary school teachers—new and veteran alike—are approaching reading instruction as effectively and consistently as possible. Whether you visit an elementary Reading classroom in Brooklyn, Newark, Rochester, or Troy, these are the reading strategies you'll see in action!

Given the strong response to our approach of finding "what works," and turning this into practical text- and video-based trainings, we know that many educators, schools, and school systems are interested in what we are interested in — classroom strategies and tactical actions that work, at scale, that anyone can use to alter the trajectory of students' reading skills.

We hope our efforts to share what we have learned will be of some help to you, your scholars, and our collective communities.

Brett Peiser
Chief Executive Officer
Uncommon Schools

Uncommon Schools is a non-profit network of 32 public charter schools that close the achievement gap and prepare low-income students in New York, New Jersey, and Massachusetts to graduate from college. By 2017, Uncommon will manage 46 schools, serving over 16,000 K–12 scholars. This expansion plan, coupled with the organization's outstanding academic results, makes Uncommon Schools one of the fastest-growing and highest-performing charter networks in the country. To learn more about Uncommon Schools, please visit our website at http://uncommonschools.org and be sure to follow us on Facebook at www.facebook.com/uncommonschools and Twitter at @uncommonschools.

GREAT HABITS, GREAT READERS

Introduction

One morning in Erin Michels's third-grade classroom, four students are gathered around a crescent-shaped table, talking about a book. Although scenes like this unfold daily in elementary classrooms across the nation, this particular discussion will have a singular impact on these students' development as readers. Here's what we heard when we listened in.

 WATCH Clip 1: Erin Michels's Comprehension—730L

Excerpt from Erin's Video

Nasiyr:	These kids are troublemakers . . . these kids are troublemakers because they also . . .
Ms. Michels:	So I'm going to challenge you, so I'm hearing you say troublemakers, but I think we have another way to talk about them. *(Silence; then Ade'Shyah's hand shoots in the air)*
Ade'Shyah:	They are juvenile delinquents!
Ms. Michels:	Good—
Small Group:	Ooh!
Ms. Michels:	Good, what did you just do?
Ade'Shyah:	I thought about how they were trying to . . . when I read about it they were trying to steal the radio too, and in the text it says about they always . . . they take cars.
Ms. Michels:	Mhmm.
Ade'Shyah:	And then I think about that: if a person was a juvenile delinquent, they would do something like that.
Ms. Michels:	So as a reader, what did you just do? So yes, you pulled evidence from the text and then what else did you do?
Ade'Shyah:	Then I went back to what I had read about . . .
Ms. Michels:	In the what?
Ade'Shyah:	In the story, in the article *(looks to title and reads source name)*.
Ms. Michels:	In the informational article, excellent. So you used that background knowledge that you built. Nice job, Ade'Shyah.

These four students leave the table with a far deeper understanding of both texts they were reading—and with the crucial new reading skill of drawing connections among multiple genres. But how did they get there? Think of everything Ade'Shyah had to do in order to draw her conclusion: read a work of fiction, read an informational article, participate intently in a comprehension conversation, and apply a brand-new vocabulary term. It's unusual for third graders to accomplish such feats, and still rarer for them to do it with as little teacher aid as Erin provides in this clip. What, then, makes these third graders extraordinary?

It might be tempting to assume that Erin teaches a highly selective gifted-and-talented class and that her students' skills are the product of natural-born reading talent. Yet this is not the case. In fact, when the four students we just met entered kindergarten, each was in the 10th percentile of peer-group readers, and even by the third grade they were all considered around average within Erin's class. The idea that some students are simply "born readers" is a popular one, but it definitely doesn't apply here.

Instead, these four students have reached extraordinary heights because they have all developed extraordinary *habits*: a deeply learned database of skills and strategies that they can access automatically when they read. These habits, in turn, are the product of the choices their teachers have made. By making reading lessons about learning the right habits, teachers like Erin prove that great reading isn't something a few students are born with, but something every student can be taught.

Habit is a force to be reckoned with. As humans, we possess the remarkable ability to take even staggeringly complex behaviors and make them second nature.[1] If we needed to think carefully and decide intentionally about everything we do during the day (unscrew the toothpaste cap, hold the brush near the tube, squeeze the tube, . . .), we would be too overwhelmed to act. So we form habits, and they keep us moving. Each time we act in a certain way, we deepen a mental connection that makes it easier to act the same way in the future—without even pausing to think about it. Our repeated actions build our habits, and our habits build our skills.

Core Idea

Aristotle had it right: we are what we repeatedly do.

On a day-to-day level, the automaticity that comes with habit is the reason why we can type a sentence without looking at the keyboard or tie our shoes while talking to a friend. Yet when habit is intentionally harnessed, it's also what allows people to achieve the feats that most provoke our awe. Picture a concert pianist, hitting hundreds of keys precisely each minute. Or imagine a professional skateboarder, jumping up and performing four dazzling tricks before returning to the ground. Without great habits, these actions would not be merely difficult — they would be impossible.

The best coaches and trainers in a host of fields have long recognized the power of habit. The coach who has his team shoot three hundred free throws or the music teacher who has students practice a simple scale one hundred times is intentionally working toward automation, laying the groundwork for what seems superhuman. Indeed, as K. Anders Ericsson noted in a now famous study, the key determinant of success in any number of fields, from science to art to gymnastics, is the number of practice opportunities participants have.[2] The more habitual we make our skills, the more extraordinary our abilities will become.

If you begin asking yourself how the power of habit could change a child's life, the importance of reading instruction quickly becomes hard to ignore. For one thing, fluent reading is the currency of academic and professional success in our society. Reading proficiency in third grade has been linked to higher rates of graduation and college enrollment. Adults with lower levels of literacy and education, in contrast, are more likely to be unemployed, living in poverty, or even incarcerated than their peers with higher levels of education.[3] Furthermore, and just as important, reading is the key to the rich array of fiction, nonfiction, and poetry that lends depth and breadth to one's understanding of the world.

THE COMMON CORE STATE STANDARDS: WHERE DO WE GO FROM HERE?

The Common Core State Standards (CCSS) for English Language Arts are a veritable tribute to all these reasons why reading matters. By any account, the CCSS raise the bar for reading. They require students to read more difficult texts, and to demonstrate deeper comprehension of those texts, than ever before. And given that they've been adopted by forty-five states as of this writing, they have the opportunity to make this ambitious vision a reality.

Yet precisely because the CCSS reflect such high expectations for young readers, getting students to actually meet them poses an immense challenge to elementary educators nationwide. As the CCSS themselves declare, "By emphasizing required achievements, the Standards leave room for teachers, curriculum developers, and states to determine how those goals should be reached."[4] Although the beauty of giving teachers this level of freedom is clear, such freedom comes at a price: teachers and school leaders are now left to figure out for themselves how to run classrooms that will give students what they need to meet the CCSS. The CCSS have redefined what it means to read "on grade level"; we need to redefine *teaching* on grade level. Although the road ahead will be especially difficult for the multitudes of U.S. students who already struggle in reading—the full two-thirds of fourth graders, for example, who tested below proficient in reading on the 2011 National Assessment of Educational Progress[5]—it won't be easy for anyone.

Where, then, do we go from here? Certainly, it's helpful to lay out curricular scope and sequence of the CCSS in the earlier grades. But even once we know what we need to teach to align with the CCSS, the question remains: *How* will we teach it? What are the concrete, practical classroom strategies that will guide us from higher standards on paper to better results for our students?

If there are answers to be found, they lie with the highest-achieving classrooms in the country—classrooms where teachers, students, and school leaders are already proving that the CCSS are by no means out of reach. Over the past five years, we have worked closely with a select set of such classrooms. The teaching we witnessed there has demonstrated not only that great reading grows from great habits, but moreover that habit can empower students to meet even the very highest reading standards.

By way of illustration, let's go back to Erin's students. Since beginning kindergarten, each of these children has been immersed in an environment tailor-made to foster the habits of great reading. Their classrooms were organized to radically reduce the amount of time spent on transitioning between places, searching for pencils, or resolving student disputes, and to radically increase the amount of time spent on practicing key skills. More time for reading, however, was just the beginning: what happened during that time was also designed to optimize student success. In small-group guided reading sessions, for example, students had the chance not only to read but also to engage in a rigorous comprehension conversation with their teacher and peers, each moment of the lesson cementing a great reading habit more deeply. In the very moment that students made errors, their teachers were able to correct them, ensuring that every practice opportunity was a perfect practice opportunity. And by constantly focusing on what each student struggled with, teachers also ensured that students were always working on the skills they most urgently needed to master.

For the four students in the opening clip from Erin's classroom, the results of this constant habit building speak for themselves. And those four students aren't alone. Of the classrooms that we studied for this book (all in low-income urban neighborhoods), the kindergarten, first, and second graders together had a median Terra Nova score in the 97th percentile for their grades. Translation: the *average* student is reading at a higher level than 97 percent of his or her peers nationwide.[6] This sort of success isn't just happening in one classroom or one school; it's being replicated across multiple schools with diverse teachers and leaders. Take a look at the results, illustrated in Figure I.1.

We saw a similar story in these schools' upper grades. In third and fourth grades, the schools we investigated earned mean ELA scores on New Jersey's state test that put them second in the state out of thirteen hundred schools, regardless of income level. What's probably even more important, given the impending increase in rigor of tests to align to Common Core (PARCC and SBAC), is that the percentage of third- and fourth-grade students who scored Advanced Proficient on those state assessments ranked first and second in the state, respectively.[7]

Test scores aren't the only measure of this reading program's success, though. What matters much more is its long-term impact. By the end of their elementary school years, these students will read so well as to seem—like the students from the opening video—as if they were born knowing how to decode words, make inferences, and identify character motivation. In truth, they will have become great readers by learning great habits.

This book is about the choices we as literacy instructors can make to teach every one of our students the habits of skillful reading. It is for all teachers who set out to disprove the myth that reading is an innate talent for some students and a perpetual stumbling block for others. It is an instruction manual for giving each student the tools he or she needs for a lifetime of reading with skill, pleasure, and confidence.

We have faith in this outcome because, over and over, we have seen it happen. The experiences that we have garnered over three careers spent in teaching and instructional leadership have shaped this book at every stage of its writing. Although we will usually speak in one voice throughout this book, we felt that sharing our individual stories would be valuable to give some sense of where each of us has come from and why we have undertaken this project.

Figure I.1 Terra Nova Median National Percentile Ratings for 2011– 2012

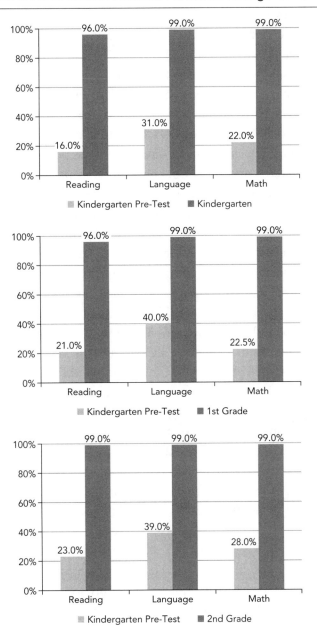

Aja's Story

Like many new teachers, when I began my career in a public school in Camden, New Jersey, I felt a mixture of excitement, enthusiasm, and nervousness. I knew very little about how to teach reading—or anything else—to my first graders, but I did know that I wanted to do what it took for each of my twenty-two students to learn to read. In my third week on the job, I found myself making late-night trips to the local Barnes and Noble to purchase everything I could on reading instruction: Fountas and Pinnell, Nancy Boyles, Lucy Calkins, and stacks of others. Over the next hectic months, I spent the (little) free time I had poring over these books, looking for the "secret sauce" that would lead my students to reading.

Each book offered important ideas, and a few offered brilliant teaching strategies. Yet although the individual pieces made sense, I was frustrated to realize that I had no sense of how they fit together. What made a "reading group" effective? How would phonics instruction connect with and support literacy skills? The books had no answers. Indeed, the more I read, the more I questioned what a truly great elementary reading lesson, start to finish, would look like. I was even less certain as to what a month of such lessons would look like, let alone a year. Without this understanding, the individual pieces I had drawn from each author felt deeply limited, and did not seem to offer the solutions my students needed.

Over the next several years, as I began to find my feet and adjust to teaching, I continued to look for ways to improve literacy instruction in my classroom. I attended professional development workshops on read-aloud, reading comprehension, and "morning meetings," and I worked to apply what I learned in my class. Through trial and error, things started getting better. Yet even after five years in the classroom, there were often more questions than answers: How does instruction need to change from grade to grade? What makes independent reading effective? Even after years in the classroom, I too often found myself feeling lost.

Fortunately, the answer I was looking for began to take shape in 2007, when I joined the staff of the newly formed North Star Academy Elementary School. It was here that I had the tremendous opportunity to work with teachers and leaders equally focused on the challenge of early elementary reading instruction. Together, we spent hours after school, on weekends, and over summers trying to take the puzzle pieces our esteemed predecessors had given us and turn them into a single, comprehensive whole. The results, over the past six years and counting, have been that I have finally built the reading classroom I wanted to create from the beginning.

My transition from the classroom to my current role as school leader required me to think beyond any one classroom—to consider elementary reading as a schoolwide, and even a district-wide, phenomenon. Yet as I worked on this book, I constantly remembered those hectic trips to the bookstore, and realized that what I wanted more than anything else is to create the book I would have wanted to read back then. It is my hope that this book fulfills that aspiration and, if nothing else, that it provides guidance to those teachers who want deeply to do the right thing but are not sure where to start.

Juliana's Story

When I think about the need for high-quality reading instruction, I think about my two sons. One of them has already proven an exceptional reader. Reading seems to come naturally to him, and from a very early age, he has demonstrated a love for reading that has propelled his creativity, vocabulary acquisition, and knowledge of the world around him. Meanwhile, some of the same skills for reading have come less easily to my other son. He has struggled with phonics, and simple questions about what is happening in a story don't always seem so simple to him. So is one destined to succeed in reading while the other is not? My response to this, of course, is a resounding no! Both of my sons will be great readers, because my husband and I will do everything possible to ensure their success.

What strikes me most about the differing early reading experiences of my two sons is how closely they parallel those of my students during my first year of teaching. I had some students who seemed to learn through osmosis; despite my novice teaching and sometimes convoluted language, they could still absorb important content and pick up key reading skills. But I also had students who struggled to gain the same knowledge that came so easily to others. At the time, I felt as though I was just saying the same thing over and over again, and still these students were struggling—and as fiercely as I wanted to do more for them, I didn't know what that "more" could possibly be.

My outlook changed dramatically when I began working for Uncommon Schools. Here I joined a team of teachers and leaders who, besides being committed in theory to teaching every student to read, were developing tools and techniques which proved that our goal was achievable. As a teacher, I've had the chance to put those tools into action in my own classroom, and as a school leader, I've helped other teachers to do the same. This book is about how to reach your most struggling students while still challenging your most exceptional. All children, like my two sons, deserve the assurance that one day they will be great readers; and all adults who care for them deserve access to the strategies that will make that happen.

Paul's Story

As the superintendent of the North Star Academy school network, I have sometimes been asked which classrooms have most impressed me, or which teachers have the "hardest" challenges. Of course, this is an impossible question: there is no way to say that a brilliant AP Calculus class is any "harder" to teach than a superb middle school theatre lesson. Yet as North Star has grown as a school network, I have consistently found myself in awe of our early elementary reading instructors. The ability to take students from knowing nothing of the alphabet to fluently reading chapter books in the space of ten months is on par with any other achievement in instruction. Even with years of classroom experience, I still find myself walking into kindergarten classrooms and feeling amazed.

Yet the most magical thing about those classrooms is that they are not magical at all. The work that Aja, Juliana, and our other elementary school leaders and teachers have done has convinced me that the keys to great reading instruction, to this awesome responsibility of introducing children to language, can work for any teacher in any school. By building the right habits for students, Aja, Juliana, and the dedicated educators like them are building better futures. We are writing this book because every day, our teachers and students show that children in America *can* have superb reading education, and because we know that with the tools we provide, many more children *will*.

THE READING-BY-HABIT CONCEPT

What makes reading growth happen for students? It's a question educators have been chipping away at for years, and in the era of the Common Core, it's one that we're seeing renewed effort to address. Where many of these efforts fall short—even those that are generally aligned with the Common Core—is that they focus on reforming curriculum without enhancing instruction. It is certainly important to choose rich texts and to increase the complexity of texts in each grade level. It's also important to increase the amount of instruction with informational texts and to require students to give responses that are grounded in textual evidence. But if the instructional shifts indicated by the Common Core are implemented in a way that is disconnected with students' real-time challenges, they will inevitably fail. We'll wind up back where we started, with curricula that still aren't delivering the results we want so badly for our kids. Failure means missing what may be the greatest opportunity for whole-school change in a generation.

This cannot happen, and it doesn't have to. Great teaching isn't a mystery. We have known for some time what makes the best teachers successful: they carefully and routinely tailor their instruction to the skills their students need the most. They differentiate. They adapt. And what works for these teachers will also work for anyone implementing the Common Core.

To meet the challenge of the CCSS, we must think very carefully about the types of mistakes our students will make on their journey to becoming great readers. Because ultimately, what matters most for them is what we do when those mistakes occur. It is in those moments that we'll be faced with the question: So, now what? This book, and the Reading-by-Habit model it proposes, are designed to provide concrete answers. *Great Habits, Great Readers* is not just about finding the right texts (though we'll cover that); it's not just about making discussions more text-dependent (though we'll address that, too). The Reading-by-Habit model is about addressing that seminal moment when a child gets something wrong, and knowing how to leverage that instant to begin forming the habits that will help him or her get it right. After all, when students are reading well, they are demonstrating that they already have the right habits. The key to teaching reading is knowing what to do when things go awry, as that is a powerful opportunity to build the habits students need.

Core Idea

Habits are started at the moment of error, not at the moment of success.

Ultimately, this is how we get our students over the text-complexity bar set by the Common Core—not simply by raising the difficulty of the texts they read, but by sharpening our instruction to match that complexity. Along with the quantitative measure of what level of texts students should be reading, we need the qualitative expertise of what skills students need to master at every step of the way. What's more, we need to know where to go when they struggle with those skills.

The lesson types we're about to describe—when used together in response to student achievement data—represent the best way we've found to bridge the rigor of the Common Core with the real-life needs of your class. Our model will allow you to address both the quantitative and the qualitative dimensions of text complexity, and it will shorten the time for students between learning a skill and putting it into authentic use. In short, it will give you the tools you need to address the Common Core across your language arts block in a sustained, meaningful way.

THE MOST DANGEROUS MYTHS ABOUT THE COMMON CORE

As we've engaged with colleagues about what implementing the Common Core will mean for our schools, we've encountered a few dangerous myths that need to be debunked before we can begin the work of this book. If your approach to the standards falls into these traps, you'll find your efforts to teach reading stymied from day one. Let's take this moment to set the record straight.

Myth: The Common Core requires that K–4 literacy classes spend 50 percent of their time on informational texts.

Reality: The NAEP distribution of literary versus informational texts, which has been endorsed by the CCSS, asks that fourth-grade students split their time equally between both. But as the standards point out, this does not mean that we need to remove literature from our classrooms. Rather, they argue that we must support literacy in other content-area classes as well: that we should teach science and social studies via authentic informational texts.[8] If you do that, then the reading block in your class doesn't have to be 50 percent informational, because you're already using informational texts elsewhere! In this book, we work from the assumption that in grades K–2, you are devoting substantial time to content-area instruction, so that 70 to 80 percent of your literacy block time can be spent on narrative text. (In third and fourth grades, the weight can shift further toward informational text. We detail how this works in Chapter Eleven.) To be sure, you'll still work with informational texts in your literacy block, but the majority of the work on them will happen outside those lessons. In fact, if you use the model we're about to outline, you'll in many cases exceed the expectation of 50 percent informational text use—and you'll do it without sacrificing student learning.

Myth: Vocabulary development and content knowledge are only built in the literacy block.

Reality: The fastest path to vocabulary acquisition and literacy skill development must include strengthening students' knowledge about whatever topic they are reading about. That is, the more students know about a topic, the faster they'll be able to apply the literacy skills they are learning to even the most difficult texts about it. Research suggests that this is one of the keys to supercharging students' vocabulary development and skill growth.[9] In fact, as students develop knowledge about a specific subject area, they can read beyond their level because they now have a mental model for thinking about the material. The more students learn about birds, the more challenging texts on birds they'll be able to try! Recognizing the need to increase text complexity between grades,[10] the Common Core framework recommends that students study topics for an extended period of time both within and between grade levels. It offers the exemplar shown in Figure I.2.

The knowledge base students bring to any text has a tremendous effect on how much learning they will derive from it—in terms of both content and skill development. Ultimately, your content-area instruction doesn't supplement what happens in your literacy block: it's *vital* to it. A good academic program simply cannot sacrifice science or social studies instruction, or it will sabotage both content knowledge and literacy development.

Figure I.2 Common Core Exemplar Texts on a Topic Across Grades

Exemplar Texts on a Topic Across Grades	K	1	2–3	4–5
The Human Body Students can begin learning about the human body starting in kindergarten and then review and extend their learning during each subsequent grade.	**The five senses and associated body parts** • *My Five Senses* by Aliki (1989) • *Hearing* by Maria Rius (1985) • *Sight* by Maria Rius (1985) • *Smell* by Maria Rius (1985) • *Taste* by Maria Rius (1985) • *Touch* by Maria Rius (1985) **Taking care of your body: Overview (hygiene, diet, exercise, rest)** • *My Amazing Body: A First Look at Health & Fitness* by Pat Thomas (2001) • *Get Up and Go!* by Nancy Carlson (2008) • *Go Wash Up* by Doering Tourville (2008) • *Sleep* by Paul Showers (1997) • *Fuel the Body* by Doering Tourville (2008)	**Introduction to the systems of the human body and associated body parts** • *Under Your Skin: Your Amazing Body* by Mick Manning (2007) • *Me and My Amazing Body* by Joan Sweeney (1999) • *The Human Body* by Gallimard Jeunesse (2007) • *The Busy Body Book* by Lizzy Rockwell (2008) • *First Encyclopedia of the Human Body* by Fiona Chandler (2004) **Taking care of your body: Germs, diseases, and preventing illness** • *Germs Make Me Sick* by Marilyn Berger (1995) • *Tiny Life on Your Body* by Christine Taylor-Butler (2005) • *Germ Stories* by Arthur Kornberg (2007) • *All About Scabs* by GenichiroYagu (1998)	**Digestive and excretory systems** • *What Happens to a Hamburger* by Paul Showers (1985) • *The Digestive System* by Christine Taylor-Butler (2008) • *The Digestive System* by Rebecca L. Johnson (2006) • *The Digestive System* by Kristin Petrie (2007) **Taking care of your body: Healthy eating and nutrition** • *Good Enough to Eat* by Lizzy Rockwell (1999) • *Showdown at the Food Pyramid* by Rex Barron (2004) **Muscular, skeletal, and nervous systems** • *The Mighty Muscular and Skeletal Systems*, Crabtree Publishing (2009) • *Muscles* by Seymour Simon (1998) • *Bones* by Seymour Simon (1998) • *The Astounding Nervous System*, Crabtree Publishing (2009) • *The Nervous System* by Joelle Riley (2004)	**Circulatory system** • *The Heart* by Seymour Simon (2006) • *The Heart and Circulation* by Carol Ballard (2005) • *The Circulatory System* by Kristin Petrie (2007) • *The Amazing Circulatory System* by John Burstein (2009) **Respiratory system** • *The Lungs* by Seymour Simon (2007) • *The Respiratory System* by Susan Glass (2004) • *The Respiratory System* by Kristin Petrie (2007) • *The Remarkable Respiratory System* by John Burstein (2009) **Endocrine system** • *The Endocrine System* by Rebecca Olien (2006) • *The Exciting Endocrine System* by John Burstein (2009)

Source: Content provided by corestandards.org © Copyright 2010. National Governors Association Center for Best Practices and Council of Chief State School Officers. All rights reserved.

A Word on . . . Content-Area Instruction

Content-area instruction—which, in most elementary classrooms, primarily translates to science and social studies instruction—is a huge topic, worthy of another book of its own! In the meantime, there are a few key moves we'd recommend to make sure that your whole classroom supports the work you do in the literacy block.

The first step is to embrace the CCSS's "ladder of text complexity." Begin by reading a simple passage on whatever topic your class is studying so as to learn the first set of key words your students will need in order to understand a simple passage. If your students are studying space, for example, they might need to know *planet, comet, moon,* and *star.* Then, pick a more complex passage that assumes that same content knowledge but introduces new language. For example, the next passage might involve meteors, asteroids, black holes, or supernovas. You'll find that students will be able to leverage their existing knowledge base to tackle texts that are increasingly complex, one after the other.

Where our students stagnate when they get older is in their ability to comprehend complex texts. The CCSS respond to that problem, encouraging a move away from person-to-text connections and toward text-based analysis of increasingly complex informational texts. Your content-area lessons are the ideal place to make that happen.

Myth: Reading complex texts eliminates the need for skill instruction.

Reality: Although it's true that the Common Core asks us to teach complex texts, if we treat them in the absence of a robust, multifaceted reading program, we will fail in our goal. Here is where implementation of the Common Core is likely to miss the mark, as reading cannot be boiled down to increasing complexity or changing the types of books we read. The Common Core does not ask us to sacrifice skill instruction in favor of rich, complex texts; it asks us to incorporate rich, complex texts into strong skill instruction. That is a critical distinction. On paper, it's all too easy to develop a curriculum that superficially meets the new standards but doesn't get its hands dirty in the actual work of improving instruction. But our students don't exist on paper. They're alive and eager, waiting in our classrooms for instruction that will allow them to soar academically. And in this book, we'll map out exactly how to design your lessons to make that happen.

THE READING-BY-HABIT MODEL

Now that we've debunked some of the myths about the Common Core, we're ready to explore the landscape of the Reading-by-Habit model. *Great Habits, Great Readers* is about how to build habits of successful readers in your students. It's designed to outline those strategies, systems, and lesson types that bring the habits of reading to life, creating countless high-quality opportunities for students to practice one of the most complex skills humans can learn. We have organized the book as shown in Figure I.3.

In Part One, we explain how to teach two types of habits that can revolutionize student learning in any discipline: habits of the classroom and habits of discussion. At first glance, it may seem bizarre to begin a book specifically about reading instruction with two chapters about optimal classroom setup and the process of getting students to speak in complete sentences. Yet as we'll explain in detail in these chapters, the right classroom systems can increase how long students

Figure I.3   The Reading-by-Habit Model

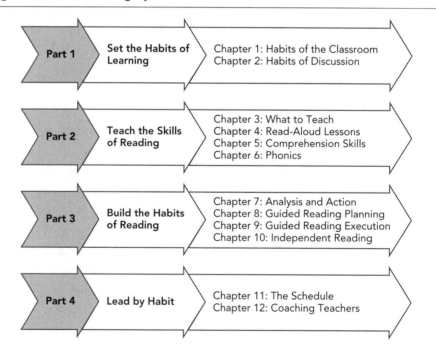

actually spend on reading by full *weeks* of instructional time, and teaching students to share an academic conversation makes an awe-inspiring impact on their reading comprehension capabilities. So, while the practical applications of these sets of habits are virtually limitless, they are also such extraordinary drivers of student literacy development that we would be doing you a disservice if we did not include them in this book.

In Parts Two and Three, we'll detail the five types of lessons that make up the heart of our reading program: read-aloud, comprehension skills, phonics, guided reading, and independent reading. As you look over Figure I.3, you'll see that we also cover the topic of assessment in a discussion split between Part Two and Part Three. Chapter Three, the first assessment chapter, will focus on using the CCSS to identify the right assessments and curricula for your students; Chapter Seven will demonstrate how to analyze assessment results so as to identify what each individual student needs most urgently.

If we imagine learning to read as learning to play the piano, we can picture the types of lessons covered in Part Two—read-aloud, comprehension skills, and phonics—as the types of exercises that would be covered in a piano technique book. They give students a chance to focus primarily on one specific reading skill at a time—the equivalent of learning to play specific scales or chords. Guided reading, which we'll explore in great detail in Part Three, is the equivalent of giving students a piano piece to learn—one that gives them opportunities to practice the skill they most need to work on, but that also gives them a chance to put all the skills they've learned so far into action at once. Then we'll examine strategies for facilitating an effective independent reading lesson—which is a student's time to sit solo at the piano bench, unfold a sheet of music, and play.

You can see the types of lessons in the Reading-by-Habit model summarized in Table I.1.

Any one of these components of the Reading-by-Habit model will help your students learn to read. If, however, you're in a position to implement every piece of it throughout your school, using them in tandem will make the biggest impact of all. Part Four will show you how to do this: first, in Chapter Eleven, by demonstrating how to put all this material together into a feasible schedule; and then, in Chapter Twelve, by explaining how to coach other teachers in the Reading-by-Habit model, so that each of them will be in the optimal position to help each student succeed.

Table I.1 Lesson Types in the Reading-by-Habit Model

Lesson Type	Group Size	What to Teach?	Definition	Structure
Read-Aloud (Chapter 4)	Whole class	Skills from yearlong syllabus	**Read-aloud lessons** offer deep modeling and extended group practice with a text. Use these to introduce and demonstrate a skill that students will apply independently later on.	I Do, We Do, check for under-standing
Compre-hension Skills (Chapter 5)	Small-group by reading level or whole class if necessary	Skills from yearlong syllabus	**Comprehension Skills lessons** teach a skill through the traditional I Do, We Do, You Do instructional design. Use these lessons to give your students practice with a new reading skill or to reinforce a previously taught one.	I Do, We Do, You Do
Phonics (Chapter 6)	Small group or whole class if necessary	Skills from premade program	**Phonics lessons** teach children to understand the relationship between written letters and spoken sounds. Teach this skill separately to give it the necessary attention.	Scripted, prefabri-cated lesson
Guided Reading (Chapters 8–9)	Small group by reading level	Skills determined by assessment analysis (Chapter 7)	**Guided Reading lessons** are flexible, small-group sessions that allow you to target the aspect of reading your students need support with most—even while they employ all the skills needed to make sense of a text. Use them to address specific student needs while providing greater (but not total) reading independence.	Before Reading, During Reading, After Reading
Indepen-dent Reading (Chapter 10)	Individual	Skills for all students	**Independent reading** time is a carefully designed, accountable moment for students to read a book without your support. Use this time to allow your students to use the skills you've already taught and to help them fall in love with reading.	You Do

WHERE THE COMMON CORE IS EMBEDDED IN THE READING-BY-HABIT MODEL

As you read about each aspect of our model, it's important to keep in mind that the Common Core is deeply embedded in its design. Many have begun dividing the language standards into six instructional shifts, five of which have direct implications for reading instruction during the literacy block. Let's consider how our model addresses each of these:

- *Balance informational and literary texts.* All of the lesson types in the Reading-by-Habit model are designed to allow ample time for informational and literary texts. In Chapter Eleven, we'll break down exactly how to apportion your time to meet this demand. Because we work from the assumption that you are including robust nonfiction work in your content-area classes, you will likely wind up with even more than 50 percent of your reading instruction focusing on informational texts.

- *Create a staircase of text complexity.* In Chapter Eight, we'll get in-depth about how to select texts for complexity. What's more, we'll show you how to go beyond simple quantitative measures to include qualitative ones that address the precise skills that your students should develop next. Text complexity can't be reduced to just a number, and we'll show you why.

- *Require text-based answers.* The Common Core requires students to use evidence to drive their conversations about texts. You'll notice that text-based answers are expected throughout the Reading-by-Habit model lessons. What's more, in Chapter Two, you'll learn how to make student conversations optimally productive and focused so that evidence use can shine. But what is most valuable to you is knowing what to actually do with those answers when you get them. In Chapter Nine, we'll show you how to ask the right questions and what to do when students get them wrong — as this is the moment you can help them build the skills they need most.

- *Write from sources.* Early in their reading development, most K–1 students will not have developed enough writing skills to write for meaning. However, as they develop, and as you'll see particularly in Chapters Five, Nine, and Ten, writing becomes the critical first step to grasping meaning from a text — and to giving the teacher insight into students' struggles. Writing, then, drives comprehension conversations, rather than the reverse—which is a significant shift for many elementary reading classrooms.

- *Use academic vocabulary.* In Chapter Four, we'll describe a model for read-aloud, a key place to introduce new vocabulary in the context of reading comprehension. The text-rich environment that the Reading-by-Habit model creates will also open the door to substantial indirect instruction as well. When students receive direct and indirect vocabulary instruction, and when you've supplemented that instruction by building their knowledge base in content-area subjects, they will be set up for success.

HOW TO USE THIS BOOK

As Aja's story related, our hope is that this book will serve as a guide to those who strive to teach the skills of great reading but find themselves frustrated by the results they're getting—and the tools that are available to help them. The unfortunate fact of the matter is that for most elementary school teachers, it's not easy to develop content expertise in literacy instruction. You may be able to find a curriculum or a procedure to follow without too much trouble, but what are you to do when these tools don't produce the results they promise? Many teachers have shared with us their exasperation at not being sure how to piece multitudinous elements of reading instruction together into one system, or how to vary their teaching methods based on the particular needs of their specific students. As long as the answers to these very important questions remain evasive, books—not teachers—will own content expertise.

So, as deeply as we believe in the power of this book, we are also extremely conscious of the need to deliver a text that will break that cycle, rather than repeat it. Part of our solution is to provide you not only with a text but also with a wide variety of other resources—from videos to workshop scripts—to be used in combination with it. We hope that these materials will help you move beyond simply studying the strategies expert literacy teachers use, and onward to knowing just how and when to put them into practice yourself. Here's an overview of the resources that come with this book.

See Habits in Action

Reading about an effective teaching strategy is useful, but seeing it in action is far more inspiring—and gives you a far better sense of how to wield it. Thus, for almost every key strategy we discuss in this book, we have included a video clip of a master teacher putting the strategy into action. If you choose to read this book without watching the accompanying DVD, we believe, of course, that you will still be able to implement what you read in your classroom and that your students will benefit. However, we strongly recommend that you take the time to watch the videos: they give a clearer image of what truly game-changing reading instruction looks like than our words will ever be able to.

Apply Your Habits

Throughout the text, we have included activities and questions that give you opportunities to determine what specific steps you will need to bring a habit-driven classroom to life. These activities, always under the heading "Apply Your Habits," are not meant to quiz you on the information in this book; they are meant as springboards to help you first to envision how the methods we describe would look in your own classroom, and then exactly how and when you could implement them. They also include lists of tools you might use to aid implementation.

Share Your Habits

The teaching methods we describe in this book are, above all else, replicable. We have witnessed teachers of all levels of experience using them to great effect. As a result, a number of the materials we've included will be useful to educators who hope to train others in the Reading-by-Habit model. A great place to begin is Part Four of the book, which shows how to build schedules that make the best of reading time and how to coach teachers in the area of literacy instruction. Part Five introduces you to the professional development workshops we've used to train our colleagues in the use of the material in nearly every chapter in this book, and the DVD Appendix includes full-length scripts of those workshops. Finally, we've included a discussion guide to allow you to facilitate discussions on each chapter within the professional learning communities at your school. With these tools at your disposal, you have the ability to meet the challenge set forth by the CCSS, not only in individual classrooms but across schools or school districts, too.

LET'S START HERE

The CCSS pose a great challenge to young students of reading, to their teachers, and to their school leaders. Yet those of us who have pursued careers in education are all here because we are deeply invested in giving students the knowledge they need to pursue their dreams—and we all know that when it comes to pursuing one's dreams, the ability to read well carries an importance that's hard to overstate. Thus, by insisting that we raise the bar for reading, the CCSS are as much an opportunity as a challenge. We can make them our chance to give students the quality reading instruction we've always wanted to provide: we just need to know where to begin. Let's start here.

Part

Set the Habits of Learning

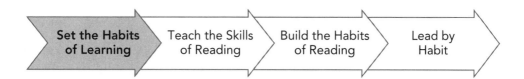

Part 1

Introduction: The Fundamental Habits

This book is about giving elementary students everything they need in order to be outstanding readers. Teaching phonics lessons, reading aloud to students, and developing a great curriculum—all of which we'll cover—fall squarely into this category, but there's another necessary element that may initially seem much less obvious: setting up effective habits of learning. The habits of learning are the most fundamental of the "great habits" to which the title of this book refers: if students lack them, they cannot develop exemplary reading habits. Accordingly, we've chosen to address them in the first two chapters of this book.

Here's an overview of the habits Part One will cover:

- **Chapter One: Habits of the Classroom.** Why talk about the setup of a classroom and the way students move through it when we've set out to talk about reading? Because a well-organized classroom and airtight student transitions can save you full days of teaching time. Chapter One shows how this works—and how to make it happen.

- **Chapter Two: Habits of Discussion.** Change how students talk about reading, and you will change how they think about reading. In Chapter Two, we'll present the habits of discussion that have enabled the most effective reading teachers we've observed to facilitate meaningful comprehension conversations among even their youngest readers.

As you may notice when you read through Chapters One and Two, many of the teaching techniques we describe in Part One can drive instruction in any subject — not just reading — further and faster than you could push it without them. However, they are such great enablers of game-changing literacy instruction in particular that this book simply would not be complete without them.

Chapter 1

Habits of the Classroom

Multiply Your Minutes

At the start of each college basketball season, legendary UCLA coach John Wooden gave new players the same speech. "You know," Wooden would begin, "basketball is a game that's played on a hardwood floor, and to be good, you have to change your direction, change your pace." Hearing this, the UCLA team could not have been surprised. Footwork and direction changes, after all, are practiced by almost every basketball team. But to the players' surprise, Wooden did not begin with a footwork drill. Instead, he started to pull on a sock. As the players looked on, Wooden explained the sock procedure: "Pull it up in the back ... run your hand around the little toe area ... make sure there are no wrinkles ... check the heel area." Why start from socks? "The wrinkle will be sure you get blisters, and those blisters are going to make you lose playing time, and if you're good enough, your loss of playing time might get the coach fired."[1]

As avid basketball fans, we have always been drawn to the career of John Wooden. In choosing to begin our exploration of literacy instruction with routines and procedures, we have been deeply influenced by leaders like Wooden. There is no doubt that Wooden's "sock talk" helped UCLA to victory over the course of his decades-long career. The talk suggests an invaluable mind-set: every habit we build in our students allows them to shoot higher. By the time Wooden's players were seniors, they had internalized a host of such habits: passing with perfect form, remaining respectful at practices, shifting one's feet for the precise block-out on a rebound. These habits existed because Wooden took the time to think about them and had the patience to teach them. The result was that it was far easier for the players to learn and apply the game's most complex ideas. Wooden's approach created a powerful advantage for his team, both on and off the court.

In teaching as in basketball, it would be tempting to start with the equivalent of a complex play—identifying the root cause of a comprehension error, for example. Yet just as the most subtle jump-shot technique is useless to a player injured by blisters, the most crucial reading skill won't help students if there is not time to teach it. Efficient classroom routines and procedures keep students from losing playing time, and more playing time allows them to build stronger reading skills. When you practice for only five minutes per day, there is simply no way to build the habits of great reading as thoroughly as you would if you practiced for twenty.

Core Idea

You can't add more hours to the week, but you can add more hours of instruction: just build tighter routines.

It may sound absurd to suggest that the difference between smooth classroom systems and dragging ones could be so significant. But pause and consider: in your classroom, how many times have you lost teaching time to the task of making sure all students have the right materials? How often have you glanced at the clock in frustration as students transitioned between activities? Because delays like these happen again and again in most classrooms, the lost time adds up. An invaluable rule of thumb for building the right classroom habits is to give high priority to efficiency in the systems that happen most frequently over the course of the school day. It is in these areas that small time deficits grow large the most quickly.

Core Idea

Time lost to systems is time lost for learning.

We'll illustrate this concept with one example: students making the transition from their desks to a carpet reading area. In an early elementary classroom, this transition may happen four or five times a day. Imagine a teacher, Ms. Stark, leading her students in such a transition.

Case Study

Ms. Stark's Transition

Ms. Stark is an experienced teacher whose classroom management practices are strong overall, but she feels less in control of transitions than of other moments during the school day. She'd like to change that, starting with desk-to-carpet transitions.

Ms. Stark has already established a basic routine for her students to follow as they transition from their desks to the reading carpet. The moment she says, "Let's go to the carpet," students begin to cross the room. Some students jostle each other slightly as they find themselves getting clogged between desk rows. Others talk to each other, drifting off task. One hasn't moved from his desk—he's still working on the writing assignment with which Ms. Stark opened class. "Lewis," Ms. Stark says sternly. The student begrudgingly sets down his pencil and scrapes his chair backwards away from his desk.

After two or three minutes, all Ms. Stark's students have finally reached the carpet. Once she joins them, however, she realizes that she has left her materials at her desk and must rush back for them. When she returns, two students are squabbling over the last spot in the "front row" of the carpet, requiring another admonishment. "I need *everyone* sitting quietly," Ms. Stark adds, glancing pointedly at a few students who are still talking. With that, the lesson can begin.

Stop and Jot

What advice would you give Ms. Stark to help her tighten up her desk-to-carpet transition? Take a moment to jot down some ideas.

_____

_____

_____

_____

_____

_____

_____

This transition is, at first glance, pretty effective. Note that Ms. Stark's classroom is, by and large, well behaved and compliant. Students are happy and want to learn, so the transition moves reasonably quickly and ends with everyone ready to go. But is there any way to get to that end point sooner?

Let's take a look at a very different transition, led by Meredith Pannia.

 WATCH Clip 2: Meredith Pannia's Large-Group Transition

Meredith's transition makes it all too clear what you can gain from exemplary transitions — even if, like Ms. Stark, you already lead fairly good ones. With only a single cue from their teacher, Meredith's students chant their way straight from one lesson to the next, demonstrating not only excitement about learning but also the discipline to dive straight into it. Total transition time? Thirty seconds. As you might imagine, the impact of such a system multiplies dramatically over the course of the school year:

• Number of times per day a teacher transitions from desks to carpet	5 times per day
• Amount of time this would take if the teacher spent 4 1/2 minutes on each transition	22 1/2 minutes per day
• Amount of time this would take if teacher spent 30 seconds on each transition	2 1/2 minutes per day
• Amount of time saved per day	20 minutes per day
• Amount of time saved per week	100 minutes per week
• Amount of time saved per school year (180 days)	60 hours
• Amount of time saved if the teacher teaches 6 hours per day . . .	**10 school days**

Incredibly, the simple fact of a thoughtful and intentional transition has saved *ten days* of instruction time. What's more, this is only one type of transition. What is the result when every transition, behavioral expectation, and classroom procedure has the same sort of efficiency? The answer is a classroom with far more students getting far more "game time," making transformational instruction truly possible. Excellent classroom routines and procedures give students more time to practice reading, and practicing reading builds great reading habits.

In the pages that follow, this chapter will focus on the two sets of routines and procedures that are put into use most frequently in a classroom and that therefore pave the way for the greatest—and most immediate—gains in student learning. These areas are

1. **Setting up the room:** how to structure a classroom to maximize student engagement

2. **Habits of effective transitions:** how to get students to move seamlessly from place to place within the room

That said, this chapter is *not* a comprehensive list of every procedure that could help your classroom reach its full reading potential. Instead, we have chosen to detail a few high-impact examples that show how transformational teachers of reading can intentionally create more time for instruction. For a far more extensive list of possible procedures for each of these categories, we have included a complete guide to habits of the classroom with details on every classroom system. You will find this guide on the DVD (if you own the print book) and also online here: www.wiley.com/go/GreatHabitsGreatReaders.

SETTING UP THE ROOM

Steve Jobs, Apple's former CEO, is famous as the developer of the iMac, iPhone, iPad, and a host of other sleek gadgets. His architectural exploits, by contrast, are less well known. Yet perhaps one of the signature moves of his career was the creation of a new office campus for his employees at Pixar Films. Rather than accept a standard office design — with separate buildings for animators, computer scientists, and executives — Jobs took personal control of the project. He set down a plan that seemed equal parts simple and crazy: convert the three-facility plan to one building with one atrium, one cafeteria, one set of meeting rooms, and one bank of bathrooms — all in the center of the facility. When asked why he would fight so fervently for the plan, Jobs revealed a crucial insight: the way our work spaces are set up can define how well we learn. Jobs had a surefire way of creating a system that would make it much easier for workers in different departments to see each other, to exchange information, and to develop new ideas. In fact, he considered the merging of the cultures of his designers and programmers one of his greatest achievements at Pixar.[2]

Just as the way an office campus is created shapes how successful a company can be, the way a classroom is set up can greatly influence how much students will be able to learn. And although we certainly don't recommend changing the architecture of your school's bathrooms, the larger point is an incredibly valuable one: the way you choose to set up your classroom can greatly accelerate learning.

Core Idea

The best classrooms don't just encourage student learning; they're designed for it.

We have found that the best literacy instructors set up their space and resources intentionally to maximize time whenever possible. To demonstrate the power of such an approach, we're going to lead you on a tour of second-grade teacher Ema Land's classroom.

As you enter Ema's classroom, you can immediately see that the room has been clearly divided into four spaces. The first is the students' desks, the second is a carpet for read-aloud. The last two are smaller group workstations: each consists of a kidney-shaped table with extra chairs arranged around it and elaborate signage on the wall behind it. Each kidney table is positioned in a corner of the room away from distractions, with students unable to touch or lean on a wall at any time. Why a kidney-shaped table instead of a standard rectangle? Because when students sit around it, they are automatically positioned to make eye contact with one another—and with Ema, too. Glance along the walls of the room, and you'll see that Ema has also developed a highly organized class library, with books arranged by genre, author, and difficulty level. Figure 1.1 shows the bird's-eye view.

Figure 1.1   Ema Land's Classroom

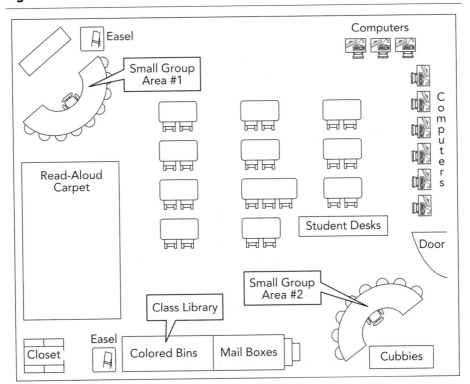

The signs around each small-group area quickly reveal that the two small-group workstations are for two distinctly different purposes. One set of signage focuses on phonics issues: the sounds different vowels make, for example. The other is clearly reading comprehension oriented, including posters that show the different parts of a story and lists of common character traits. Ema makes sure that all her students know, right from the beginning of the year, that the first workstation is for phonics lessons and the second for comprehension skills and guided reading lessons. How does this help students learn to read? "It sets the tone for what you do in that area," Ema says with conviction. "My students know they go to the phonics area to build their fluency and be better readers. They always know that."

Walk closer to either workstation and even more details emerge. The visual aids that will drive the day's lesson are already set up behind the single adult-size chair, and a binder is ready with the note-taking template Ema uses to track her students' progress during the lesson. In one neat compartment, Ema has dozens of extra pens and pencils to ensure that students will be able to stay on task. In another, extra copies of the texts students will be studying (and the comprehension questions that go with it) are stored, along with "sound cards" for students who have decoding difficulties. Each supply is stored in a clearly labeled plastic container. Though there are only eight students in each group, the table has ten chairs. The extra chairs prevent a vast range of sudden disruptions or accidents from halting the lesson—the off-task student simply joins the table.

Top Seven Materials to Have on Hand

1. Extra pencils—sharpened, please!
2. Copies of the text students are reading: one for each student, plus a few extra
3. Copies of comprehension questions students will be working on
4. Sound cards (these aren't necessary for extended readers)
5. An extra chair or two
6. All visual aids needed for the lesson
7. Note-taking template for recording student errors during instruction

---

How many times have you been right in the middle of a lesson, only to be interrupted when a student's pencil breaks? Ema's setup dodges that bullet well in advance by keeping her prepared for the unexpected. None of these details by themselves is noteworthy. But together they prevent the vast majority of standard lesson-killing distractions. The attention Ema pays to materials before the lesson allows her to ignore them during the lesson.

Core Idea

Pay attention to materials before the lesson … so you can ignore them during it.

A Word on … Carpet Squares

Many schools have opted for read-aloud carpets with premeasured, colored squares. These squares are the perfect size for little bodies (and yes, for taller students, too!) and can be a great aid to management of carpet behaviors. A typical carpet-square rug might have five columns and five rows, with each column a different color: red, orange, green, blue, and purple. When you've set up the carpet and appropriate classroom systems to go with it, you can move students smoothly from one spot to another, quickly attend to a student who is not in his or her correct spot, or address a specific group of students: "I see that the purple column is ready …"

Setting up your classroom involves a lot of personal choices. Although Ema's classroom is exemplary, there's no reason yours needs to be an exact replica of hers. We do strongly recommend, however, that you adopt a few of the specific features we described earlier:

- Separate areas for whole-group and small-group instruction
- Clear pathways for students to follow
- A class library
- A standard location for all materials (and for backups)

Now that we've considered the design of a well-set-up classroom, let's turn to ways to get students to move efficiently through it.

HABITS OF EFFECTIVE TRANSITIONS

Just as passing is the fundamental skill that holds a basketball team together throughout any game, transitions are the core systems that keep classroom instruction running smoothly throughout each school day. As we've already discussed — and as the video of Meredith Pannia showed — great transitions can enormously increase the amount of time students have for reading. In reading classrooms that make truly incredible gains, transitions are planned and executed with extraordinary meticulousness; they remind us that small differences matter.

Yet transitions like Meredith's don't become perfect overnight. Think of all the steps students needed to execute to make the transition work: leaving their chairs appropriately, pushing their chairs back in, walking to the appropriate line and standing an appropriate distance from each other, learning and singing a chant, and then finding their assigned seats. It is a complex choreography, and one that is made possible only by training the right habits and practicing them. We don't learn to dance in complex routines by hearing them read aloud to us; we learn through concentrated and focused practice, until our feet and bodies can move without our thinking about it. Great transitions are learned the same way: to make them work, you must first take the time to practice them.

Core Idea

To make great transitions work, you must first take the time to practice them.

So how do you accomplish this? How can you teach students to execute transitions flawlessly? First, you establish a tightly scripted procedure for each of the following common transitions:

- Large-group transitions

- Group-to-group transitions (that is, when students move from one small-group activity to another)

- Independent reading transitions
- Midlesson transitions

Then you need to introduce that procedure to your students, and the key is to practice, practice, practice. We already saw a large-group transition with Meredith. Let's look at an independent reading transition (when students transition from independent reading to their guided reading group and vice versa) and see how this is introduced.

How to Train a Transition—Case Study on Independent Reading Transition

We are going to watch Nikki Bowen's kindergarten class. We were able to capture her teaching this transition to independent reading in the first weeks of school.

 WATCH Clip 3: Nikki Bowen's Independent Reading Transition— Training

For a more precise look at the language and actions that go into teaching a great transition, let's walk through Nikki's lesson again (outlined in Table 1.1), taking a closer look at how her words and actions make the teaching of the transition work so well.

In watching the video, you can't help but notice how much fun Nikki's students are having learning the transition. After all, whereas John Wooden's point guards know that their hours of shooting drills will lead to winning games, our youngest students may not immediately comprehend the payoff of efficient classroom systems. In classrooms where students are excited about learning, excellent management and a high level of joy go hand in hand. And just as we saw with the video of Nikki teaching her transition, both of these are teachable.

In training this transition, Nikki took the time to both introduce the procedure and give students ample opportunity for practice. This is exactly what the best coaches and trainers in any field do: they give trainees a chance to try a new skill, and correct them whenever they fall short. The teaching process that works for teaching transitions works just as powerfully for any aspect of student behavior:

- **Introduce the behavior,** setting clear, high expectations for what you want students to do.
- Give students **plenty of opportunities to practice** the action.
- **Redirect students _every time_** they fail to implement the action correctly.
- Throughout the process, **use a positive tone,** give precise praise, and create a friendly sense of challenge.

By leveraging all of these components, Nikki has built a routine that will save hours of instructional time over the course of the year, a tremendously worthwhile investment. And this brings us to what's most impressive of all about Nikki's transitions: they take only a few lessons to teach and only a few weeks to master, following a process that _any teacher can emulate._ Generally, a teacher like Nikki will follow up her initial teaching of the transition with a next-day

Table 1.1 Nikki's Lesson Plan to Train Transitions

Teaching Strategy	Nikki Says . . .
Create a positive tone	"Now that we know what groups we're in, I'm going to show you other magic words you're going to hear."
Give specific instructions	"When I say 'stand up,' that means stand up behind your chair without your materials. Then you will hear the magic word 'transition.'"
Check for understanding	"What will I say?" _Students, in chorus: "Transition!"_
Model	"So let's pretend I'm Bianca and these are my materials. Watch. I'm in group A because I'm Bianca. Without my materials I stand up, I tuck in my chair a little bit, I put my hands on my chair."
Give time to practice	"So Ariel, grab your stuff. Ariel will walk along the right, and she's going to stop right here. Then Bianca is going to grab her stuff. She's going to stand right behind Ariel."
Challenge the team	"Group A, are you ready? All right, you earn a cheer if you get this perfect. Kamora, you're going to tell me if they do it good, great, or spectacular."
Give precise praise	"I love how Kristen is tracking because she wants Group B to do an even better job."
Correct as needed	"Thanks for being speedy, but don't forget your folder!"

review in which she'll spend a little less time modeling the transition and a little more time letting her students practice it without reminding them what to do. The class will keep at it until they get it just right. By the end of that second day, students will have mastered the transition. If teachers plan and teach their procedures intentionally, students will be remarkably quick to adopt any new system. (See the box "How to Teach Routines—Best Practices.") And before long, that system will become habit.

How to Teach Routines—Best Practices

- **Teach the routine with guided practice:**
  - **I Do:** 10% (3–4 min)
  - **We Do:** 60% (first time: 15–20 min)
  - **You Do:** 30% (first time: 10–15 min)
- **Rinse and repeat:** Perfect the routine with each successive practice.
- **Use positive framing:** Narrate what goes well, not what goes wrong.
  - **Assume the best:** Narrate the best effort of the students; assume they're trying to comply.
- **Challenge:** Make even the most dry transition something that is exciting: use cheers, team challenges, the tone of your voice, and so on.

So where did all this great planning and teaching get Nikki and her students? Let's find out. Here's a video of what Nikki's transition looked like a few months after she initially taught it to her students.

 WATCH Clip 4: Nikki Bowen's Independent Reading Transition— a Few Months Later

---

What began as a lesson has grown into a textbook example of a superb classroom habit—a complex behavior that has become fully automatic, allowing no instructional time to be wasted.

Keys to Effective Transitions—Case Study with a Midlesson Transition

The lessons learned from Nikki Bowen easily translate to other moments in the classroom. Let's look at how Laura Fern transitions within her phonics class from word work to story reading.

 WATCH Clip 5: Laura Fern's Midlesson Transition

What makes this particular transition, like Nikki Bowen's, so outstanding? The most important factors are as follows:

- **Teacher location.** Laura is seated precisely where she can see every student, just as Nikki was already positioned where students were headed, a position that allowed her to monitor her students easily and, if necessary, correct any off-task behavior.

- **Instructional materials.** Because all supplies were already in just the right position (with books underneath students' seats), neither Laura nor her students had to think twice about what they needed to bring to the next activity.

- **Designated pathways.** As you watch Laura's midlesson transition, you can see that every student action has been predesignated. Each student knew exactly what to do at each moment of the transition, and each followed through accordingly. Furthermore, if you look closely at the books the students are opening, you might notice that the page was already tabbed so that the class would immediately open to the correct page. This may seem like a minor detail, but think of the difference it makes: students never have the chance to get off task or slow down the lesson. The combination of predesignating student actions and setting up effective reminders ensures that students perform the right actions all year long.

- **Economy of language.** Did you notice how many words Laura used in this video at the point of the transition? Not one. That's even fewer than Nikki, who used only three: "stand up" and "transition." The less the teacher has to say in giving directions, the better the transition is. Originally, we had thought that the key to a great transition would be the use of very clear language. Yet although clarity does matter, when we asked the most successful teachers we work with about what makes a transition great, we heard again and again that the best transitions don't just use *clear* language: they use little to none. When the transition itself is clear and simple enough, teachers can manage it predominantly (or exclusively!) through nonverbal signals. This is yet another sign that the transition has truly become habit.

- **Immediate start.** As soon as students opened their books, Laura immediately began teaching. This removed any opportunity for students to get sidetracked and took full advantage of the learning time the transition created.

- **Chanting.** Chanting is an optional feature of a great transition. Nikki didn't choose to use it for her transition, but Laura uses the "Story" chant to bring energy and joy to hers. Chanting can be a great way to pique student enthusiasm and reinforce content or classroom values. It can also be an invaluable classroom management aid. When students have their voices busy singing and their hands busy clapping, it's much more difficult for them to spiral out of focus as they transition!

These six areas are the key to success for every transition, with only slight adjustments for the context of the transition.

Key Tips for Effective Transitions

- **Teacher location:** Teacher faces the class, ideally in a corner of that room (able to see everyone).
- **Instructional materials:** Materials are ready to go; they may be tabbed and under seats.
- **Designated pathways:** Actions are predesignated—each student knows just what to do throughout the transition.
- **Economy of language:** Teacher uses minimal narration and precise signals.
- **Immediate start:** Lesson starts immediately after transition.
- **Chants (optional):** Students can be engaged in a quick, upbeat transition chant related to content.

The moral of the story: building the right habits for transitions requires careful commitment and forethought. However, once the right habits are in place, you've built a set of automatic actions that require little further teacher or student effort and give back full days for teaching.

CONCLUSION: FROM SOCKS TO SUCCESS

In general, the most successful teachers we've observed made sure to set clear expectations for behavior that maximizes learning, both for each student and for those around him or her. The end result is that students know how to stay on task—even when working alone. When you foster a student's ability to put such behaviors on "autopilot," you guide him or her a long way toward success.

We began this chapter with a story about socks. Coach Wooden taught his players that there was one best way to put on socks, and his intentionality generated an important benefit. Socks, by themselves, probably did not make an enormous contribution. But they weren't the only detail Wooden took the time to address, either. With each small habit Wooden enforced—trimming messy, vision-blocking haircuts; arriving at practice on time; maintaining a clean locker room—Wooden's team gained more quality time to practice what really mattered, becoming a great basketball team. The results? Wooden's UCLA Bruins went on to become the most successful team in college basketball history, winning an unprecedented ten NCAA championships, seven of them consecutive.[3] Starting from socks, Wooden led players to greatness.

> ### Core Idea
>
> Repeatedly teach your students to be the class you want. Excellence is not an act but a habit.

As goes basketball, so goes reading instruction. When great classroom habits are implemented right from the beginning of the year, instruction—like coaching—can meet with dramatic new successes. By making intentional choices about seemingly small details, from how you arrange desks to where you'll stand during a transition, you will avoid large detractors from learning. Throughout this book, we'll show how to deliver the best possible reading instruction during the time these decisions gain you. Meanwhile, though, it's important to acknowledge that training students in excellent classroom behavior also grants them a much more immediate advantage: the habit of automatically behaving efficiently and working independently. In our next chapter, we'll explore a second set of habits—the habits of discussion—that give students similarly powerful tools for success.

Keys to Effective Habits of the Classroom

Room Setup

Top Materials to Have at Hand

- **Extra pencils**—sharpened, please!
- **Copies of the text students are reading:** one for each student, plus a few extra
- **Copies of comprehension questions** students will be working on
- **Sound cards** (these aren't necessary for extended readers)
- **An extra chair or two**
- **All visual aids needed for the lesson**
- **Note-taking template** for recording student errors during instruction

Transitions

Keys to Effective Transitions

- **Teacher location:** The teacher is in a place where he or she can see and access all students.
- **Instructional materials:** Materials are on seats or tables, underneath seats, or with students.
- **Designated pathways:** Students know where to walk during transition.
- **Economy of language:** The teacher uses minimal narration and precise signals.
- **Immediate start:** The lesson begins *immediately* after the transition is complete.
- **Chants (optional):** Students can be engaged in a quick, upbeat transition chant.

How to Teach Routines

Best Practices for Training Classroom Habits

- **Teach the routine with guided practice:**
  - **I Do:** 10% (3–4 min)
  - **We Do:** 60% (first time: 15–20 min)
  - **You Do:** 30% (first time: 10–15 min)
- **Rinse and repeat:** Perfect the routine with each successive practice.
- **Use positive framing:** Narrate what goes well, not what goes wrong.
  - **Assume the best:** Narrate the best effort of the students; assume they're trying to comply.
- **Challenge:** Make even the driest transition something that is exciting: use cheers, team challenges, the tone of your voice, and so on.

Apply Your Habits: Setting Up Your Room

Self-Assessment

1. What aspects of your classroom layout might you want to target to enhance student learning?

_____

_____

_____

_____

2. What are the "pain points" in your classroom routines? Which aspects of your classroom setup make it difficult to transition or to manage materials?

_____

_____

_____

_____

Tools to Use

- Keys to Effective Habits of the Classroom (also included in the Appendix and on the DVD)
- Sample Lesson Plan on Teaching a Small Group-to-Group Transition (sample lesson plan; included in the Appendix and on the DVD)
- Comprehensive Guide to Classroom Systems (included on the DVD)
- Professional development materials

Your Next Steps

_____

_____

_____

_____

Chapter 2

Habits of Discussion

Change Student Talk, Change Student Thinking

The habits we discussed in Chapter One focused mostly on teaching students how to conduct their bodies—when to stand up for a transition, where to walk, which materials to carry from desk to table. In this chapter, we'll begin focusing more on habits of the mind, starting with those that facilitate great conversation. We call these the habits of discussion.

The CCSS place a particular emphasis on habits of discussion by including a separate Speaking & Listening section. As they note,

"To build a foundation for college and career readiness, students must have ample opportunities to take part in a variety of rich, structured conversations."[1]

Nearly every educator would agree on the value of this goal, but not all of us are equally confident about what it means for elementary education. Can we really get first and second graders to conduct "rich, structured conversations"? Will such young students even benefit from such exchanges? To answer these questions, let's begin by comparing two very different classroom discussions.

Imagine a classroom where a teacher is teaching guided reading to a group of four students. The students have just finished reading the following portion of *Teamwork*, by Dawn McMillan (Figure 2.1). Take a moment to read it to understand the subsequent conversation.

Figure 2.1   Excerpt from *Teamwork,* by Dawn McMillan

When Karina came to her new school, she had thought that making friends would be easy. At her other school, she had known everybody. Now, in this big school, she was lonely.

"Don't worry, Karina. You'll soon settle in," said Mom gently.

At first, Karina joined in all the games at school. When they played baseball, she hit the ball high into the air, past the fielders, and scored a home run almost every time. When they played basketball, she raced past the other children to score, again and again. And when they played tag, no one could catch her—not even Lisa, who had always been the best runner in the class.

Soon, the children stopped asking Karina to play.

"We've got enough players on our baseball team today," said Lisa.

2

Karina was surprised that they didn't want her on the team.

3

Every lunchtime, Karina stayed in the library.

Mr. Walker, her teacher, was worried about her. "Take a break, Karina," he said. "Go out with the other children. Have some fun!"

"It's all right, thanks, Mr. Walker," replied Karina. "I like to get my homework done early." She turned back to her books. "No one wants me on their team anyway," she thought.

4

5

Source: Teamwork by Dawn McMillan, illustrations by Pat Reynolds. Text copyright © 2002 by Dawn McMillan. Illustrations copyright © 2002 by Pat Reynolds. All rights reserved. Reproduced with permission of Cengage Learning Australia.

Now imagine a small-group discussion that might take place as a result.

Case Study

Ms. Gordon's Class Discusses Teamwork

Ms. Gordon:	Did everyone get a chance to finish reading up to the Post-it note?
Students:	Yes.
Ms. Gordon:	What happened?
Elijah:	Well, Karina is upset because no one is playing with her. She's got a lot of homework too, so she wants to get it done, so she went to the library to get it done.
Ms. Gordon:	Why is that important in this story?
Elijah:	Well, she doesn't want to play with those other kids now. She, she has homework that she needs to do. She is new to the school.
Ms. Gordon:	Well, why don't the other kids want to play with her?
Elijah:	They are jealous.
Ms. Gordon:	Exactly! They are jealous. Does everyone else see what Elijah is saying?
Students:	Yes.
Elijah:	And look, it says right here *(pointing to the page)*. She wanted to get her homework done early.
Ms. Gordon:	Tell me more.
Elijah:	I know when I have a lot of homework I want to get it done. She just stopped worrying about those other kids.
Ms. Gordon:	I want you all to read this page. *(pointing to text)* Read where Mr. Walker is talking to Karina. What did you learn there?
Justice:	She was thinking. She was thinking about the other kids.
Ms. Gordon:	She was thinking about the other kids for what reason? Why was she thinking about them? Was it because of what Elijah said, that they were jealous?
Justice and Elijah:	Yes.
Ms. Gordon:	Exactly right! Let's keep reading to see what happens next.

On the surface, Ms. Gordon's lesson was perfectly satisfactory: she had students summarize what they had read and then guided them to focus in on the big idea of the text. Yet if you do a deeper analysis, you will note some subtle but significant flaws that undermine the quality of the critical comprehension for all students in the group. Elijah receives 90 percent of the attention in this interaction; moreover, although it initially appears that he understands the connections in the text, later he states that doing homework early is Karina's prime reason for staying in for lunch. Without an explicit statement of this connection by Ms. Gordon, Elijah is unable to connect the issue of jealousy to Karina's doing homework.

The remaining students only rarely engage in the conversation. They respond primarily to yes-or-no questions, with Ms. Gordon making strong hints as to which answer she expects.

If we were to map this lesson, it would look like Figure 2.2.

There is nothing inherently "wrong" with this sort of conversation, which exemplifies exactly what we've heard in most elementary reading classrooms that we have observed. Elijah probably benefited somewhat from the exchange, and his classmates may have made some progress as well. But what if we wanted to make sure that *every* student learned significantly more from the discussion? What would the lesson look like then? Consider the following discussion, led by Aja Settles after her students read that same passage.

 WATCH Clip 6: Aja Settles's Master Clip

Figure 2.2 Ms. Gordon's Lesson

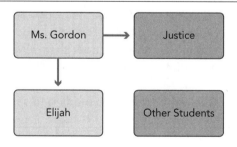

Great Habits, Great Readers

Here are some key lines from Aja's students' discussion.

Case Study, Take 2

Aja's Class Discusses Teamwork

Kurtis: So at lunch she went to the library because there weren't any friends there. It was only her teacher, Mr. Walker. And Mr. Walker said that she should have went outside with the kids, but when she got home she was crying because the other—

Ms. Settles: Can I stop you there? What do we think of Kurtis's retell? *(Julius shows a thumbs down while other students at the table flip through their books.)* Julius, good nonverbal. You completely disagree, or do you somewhat?

Julius: I somewhat disagree.

Ms. Settles: OK. What are you thinking?

Alejandra: I disagree, Kurtis, because I think—

Ms. Settles: What does Kurtis need to include in his retell?

Alejandra: He needs to include their feelings. Kurtis, you need to include their feelings and what they think.

Ms. Settles: OK, is there anything else that Kurtis needs to think about in his retell? What are you thinking, John?

John: He also, he—

Ms. Settles: "Kurtis," because you're addressing Kurtis.

John: Kurtis, you also need to add in that Karina was at the library—

Ms. Settles: And? You're not giving it to him; you want to prompt him.

John: Karina was at the library, and she was sad because—

Ms. Settles: Stop. You're giving it to him. We don't want to give it to Kurtis. We want him doing the what?

John: Work.

Ms. Settles: OK. What does Kurtis need to add, Julius?

Julius: Kurtis needs ... Kurtis, why did Karina go to the library?

Ms. Settles: Excellent. Excellent.

Kurtis: Karina went to the library because at the library no one was there but Mr. Walker and Karina. So there was no kids in there trying to tease her.

(continued)

Julius:	I disagree with you, Kurtis, because she wanted to go to the library because she wanted to finish her homework early.
Alejandra:	I agree with you, Julius, because when I read the text in Chapter Four, I even wrote it, and she said that, "No, they don't even want me on the team," and then she said that she wants to finish her homework early. So then what happened was that—
Kurtis:	But then—
Ms. Settles:	Do you agree with that?
Kurtis:	That wasn't the big idea.
Ms. Settles:	Ooh, so Kurtis is getting at a big idea. Kurtis, tell them what you're thinking.
Kurtis:	I'm thinking that when she went to the library and did her homework, that wasn't a big idea because that wasn't a part of the problem.
Julius:	Yes, it was.
Kurtis:	It wasn't part of the problem because the problem was that the other kids didn't want her on the team and that she thought that when she got home she thought that she was a show-off.
Ms. Settles:	So you see their responses? Where can you show them where your thinking was shown?
Kurtis:	On page six.
Ms. Settles:	Well, you were talking about why she went to the library, right? So where's the thinking shown there?
Kurtis:	It wasn't the problem that she didn't get her homework done early. It was the problem that no one wants her on the team. And no one thought of her because all the other kids are just playing with their other friends instead of Karina.
Ms. Settles:	What are you thinking now, Alejandra?
Alejandra:	I changed my reaction. Now I agree because now that Kurtis, now the problem that … I figured out the problem, because when it said that, "They don't even want me on the team," then she, then that means that that was the problem because they don't even want her on the team, and she wants to be on the team. But they just don't let her. So that's why I agree.

How does this discussion compare with the one in Ms. Gordon's classroom? Figure 2.3 maps it.

Figure 2.3 Aja Settles's Lesson

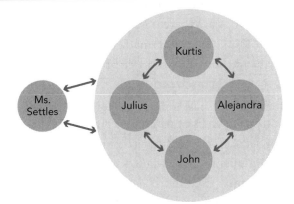

What we see here is a transformed discussion in which students successfully employ their best critical thinking skills and lead one another to a deeper understanding of the text. How did this shift occur?

Let's take a closer look at Aja's actions, which were strikingly different from Ms. Gordon's, even though both had the same starting point—students retelling the story. Here are just two comparative examples:

Ms. Gordon	Aja
[A student starts retelling the story.]	[A student starts retelling the story.]
"Exactly! They are jealous. Does everyone else see what Elijah is saying?"	"What do we think of Kurtis's retell?"
"She was thinking about the other kids for what reason? Why was she thinking about them? Was it because of what Elijah said, that they were jealous?"	"So you see their responses? Where can you show them where your thinking was shown?"

From the first teacher comments, we notice something different. In affirming a correct answer, Ms. Gordon has "tipped her hand": all other students now know that this is the correct answer and do not need to spend time evaluating their peer's response. Aja's prompt, in contrast—when delivered in the neutral style seen on the video—asks all the students to do the cognitive work. That is to say, even when students were on the right track, they couldn't figure out the right answer just by listening to Aja. Whereas Ms. Gordon's mode of questioning may have brought student thinking to a premature halt, Aja's pushed it further. As teacher, Aja wasn't the one looking for the right answer: she was focused getting students to do the analysis themselves.

As a result, Aja's students had to grapple with their misunderstandings and nimbly communicate with each other in order to unveil the "big idea" of the passage. When they went to the text for evidence, they did so authentically to support their own arguments. And when Kurtis and Alejandra reached their respective "aha" moments, they didn't get there by chance: those moments were created by a set of habits on which Aja intentionally insisted throughout the conversation. In essence, Aja changed the way her students thought about reading by changing the way they talked about it.

Core Idea

Change the way students talk about reading, and you'll change the way they think about it.

Changing the habits of discussion in your classroom is no cosmetic shift. It sets the stage for deeper discussion, peer-to-peer probing, and authentic conversations about reading. Want to shift your instruction to allow for more evidence-based discussion? Here's how you set the stage for that to happen.

THE POWER OF PROMPTING

At the heart of this transformation is the idea of prompting. Molly Branson is a longtime literacy coach and the director of literacy for the Urban Education Institute in Chicago. After years of observing literacy teachers, she comments, "Open-ended prompting is so unusual in schools that when a teacher does so, the students normally change their answers, because they're sure a teacher prompt can only mean they got the wrong answer." Think about the implications of this comment. Students receive an implicit message that they are simply looking for the answer that will get the teacher's approval. Moreover, the interactions become

Table 2.1 Universal Prompts—Use Them Anywhere

Prompt	When to Use
"Tell me more."	• Student gives a limited response.
"What in the story makes you think that?"	• Teacher wants a student to go back into the text to a place that shows his or her thinking. • Student uses too much personal experience in his or her response.
"Why do you think that?"	• Student gives a factual response, and teacher wants to understand *why* student has made that conclusion.
"Why is that important?"	• Student gives a fact but does not make an inference.
[Repeat original question]	• Student does not answer original question.

more about teachers *assessing* comprehension than about students having the chance to *learn* how to comprehend.[2]

In contrast, in Aja's classroom, the students know that they must grapple with the text themselves and push each other to get to a deeper level of comprehension. They are not surprised or alarmed when Aja prompts them—on the contrary, they expect to be prompted, both by their peers and by their teacher. So what prompts do Aja and other teachers like her use to push students to say more without telling them what to say? We'll discuss this in much more detail in Chapter Nine, but five basic prompts that can be used with any text and at any grade level are listed in Table 2.1.

This reenvisioning of prompting encourages students to provide longer, more thoughtful responses, and it also encourages deep listening among peers. You cannot cement critical thinking without conversation, especially at the earlier levels of reading before the students can write effectively. Teaching the habits of discussion, then, is at the heart of enhancing the comprehension of each student we teach. And it begins with the types of prompts you provide to students.

Core Idea

Change the way *you* talk about reading, and you'll change the way students do.

For the remainder of this chapter, we'll highlight the specific habits of discussion that brought Aja's students such success, and more of the teacher actions that make this type of success possible. In brief, the habits are tools to

- Maximize the amount of thinking students do when answering questions
- Maximize the amount of support students get from their peers
- Minimize the direct intervention of the teacher
- Train students to self-monitor and be metacognitive about their learning

Simply put, the habits of discussion maximize the number of opportunities for students to do as much thinking as possible. They come in two categories, the first paving the way for the second:

1. Learning to share
2. Learning to build

Let's take a look at the individual habits in each of these categories one by one.

LEARNING TO SHARE

In sports, the most basic fundamentals are also the most important. One of the foundational steps in soccer, for instance, is the ability to receive a pass and bring it into control. Mastering this skill will hugely increase any team's success, because the majority of any soccer game will be spent utilizing it. Sharing a conversation is to school what sharing the ball is to sports. Over the course of their lives, students will take part in thousands and thousands of academic discussions. When they become experts at sharing their thoughts—and at sharing the floor with others—they become exponentially stronger learners.

By way of example, let's think back to the clip we saw of Aja's classroom. What we saw students do during that clip was extraordinary, but just as critical is what they did *not* do—no talking out of turn, no breaking eye contact with the speaker, no mumbled responses. Aja's students have nailed the most basic habits of discussion—the habits of sharing—so completely that we may need to stop and think about it to realize how dramatically those habits are impacting the conversation. But impact it they do: at every second, knowing how to share is what makes these students' discussion possible.

> ## Core Idea
>
> A conversation is like a soccer game: it's hard to move up the field if your team doesn't know how to pass the ball.

Ultimately, students have made half the journey toward a great academic discussion when they've learned the most basic habits of sharing. Those basic habits are as follows. As you'll note, each aligns to the CCSS for Speaking & Listening.[3]

Listen and Talk Only in Turn

Common Core State Standard for Speaking & Listening: K.1.A, 1.1.A

Listening is probably one of the most underrated skills in our society. Beyond just encouraging students to listen, teachers can model that behavior and train the physical habits that accompany listening (looking at the person speaking, keeping one's hand down to focus on listening rather than sharing next, giving a person time to think about his or her response, and so on). We saw evidence of this in Aja's opening video: she used a series of verbal cues and nonverbal hand signals to remind students not to interrupt the speaker. And we'll see this habit in all the subsequent videos in this chapter. When done consistently, these cues work—every time. When it comes to teaching the habits of listening, tiny actions go a long way.

Speak Audibly

Common Core State Standard for Speaking & Listening: K.6

As adults, we rarely have to think twice about the appropriate volume at which to speak during a discussion—speaking audibly is one of our best-learned habits! But our youngest students, especially those who have not yet reached second grade, often vary widely in how loudly they speak. By setting an expectation that students will speak loudly enough to be heard by their peers, teachers help students build a habit that is essential for engaging in discussion. As important, they save a great deal of time and reduce distraction, because in the long run, they will need to interrupt far less frequently to ask students to speak up.

Speak in Complete Sentences

Common Core State Standard for Speaking & Listening: 1.6, 2.6

Having students speak in complete sentences instead of fragments from as early an age as possible will build invaluable habits of thinking in deeper and more precise ways. For younger children, who may not understand the concept of a sentence, teachers can use corrections like "stretch it out." Watch as Shadell Purefoy uses that tactic in this video, also introducing a nonverbal to encourage this behavior.

 WATCH Clip 7: Shadell Purefoy's Complete Sentences

The simple gesture Shadell uses, and the encouragement in doing so, make a significant difference. Over the course of a single year, students whose teachers maintain this expectation will be able to form literally thousands of more complete sentences than they otherwise would have, a tremendous practice opportunity that sets the groundwork for making deeper thinking "second nature."

Interact Peer to Peer

Common Core State Standard for Speaking & Listening: 3.1.A

Creating a "collaborative" discussion begins in a simple way: having students face the peers to whom they are speaking. When students learn the bad habit of always directing their responses to the teacher, it makes it tougher for them to begin truly engaging with one another's responses. Ensuring that students are in fact making eye contact with one another is a key way to ensure that they meaningfully stay on task. Watch how Yasmin Vargas subtly cues her students to look straight at one another while speaking.

 WATCH Clip 8: Yasmin Vargas's Peer-to-Peer

As adults, we sometimes take for granted the essential habits of sharing a conversation. But by teaching our students those same habits and by constantly insisting that students use them, we lay the groundwork for classroom discussions that consistently amaze us with their depth and professionalism. The habits of sharing are summarized in Table 2.2.

Table 2.2 Part One of the Habits of Discussion: Learning to Share

Learning to Share	Ideal Student Actions
Listen and Talk Only in Turn	• Track the speaker. • Keep hands down when someone is speaking. • Do not interrupt.
Speak Audibly	• Use a voice others can hear.
Speak in Complete Sentences	• Restate the question in the response; use no incomplete sentences.
Interact Peer to Peer	• Look at every group member, not just the teacher, when giving an answer.

LEARNING TO BUILD

Once students have learned the basics of sharing a conversation, the next step is learning to build that conversation up to the next level. This is the point at which students begin taking charge of the discussion themselves: expanding it based on what others have said and doing the work of leading it with considerably less hand-holding from their teacher. When the habits of learning to build are implemented properly, they also give students key opportunities to learn and practice critical thinking.

Think back to the case study of Ms. Gordon's class discussion of *Teamwork* from the beginning of this chapter. Part of what made it so much less rigorous than Aja's students' discussion was that the action was "Ping-Pong": every interaction was teacher-student, teacher-student. Moreover, it was teacher thinking—not student thinking—that dominated the conversation. As Doug Lemov, author of *Teach Like a Champion*, might put it, Ms. Gordon's discussion exemplified a "low-ratio" situation: a low proportion of students were doing the cognitive work of analyzing the text.[4]

The top teachers we interact with know that critical thinking is a habit, not a gift, and that to build this habit, each student needs as much practice as possible. To this end, teachers use a set of actions which ensure that *all* students practice critical thinking throughout the discussion. Let's think back to this moment from the video of Aja's class that we provided earlier:

Excerpt from Aja's *Teamwork* Discussion

Kurtis: Karina went to the library because at the library no one was there but Mr. Walker and Karina. So there was no kids in there trying to tease her.

Julius: I disagree with you, Kurtis, because she wanted to go to the library because she wanted to finish her homework early.

Alejandra: I agree with you, Julius, because when I read the text in Chapter Four, I even wrote it, and she said that, "No, they don't even want me on the team," and then she said that she wants to finish her homework early. So then what happened was that—

Kurtis: But then—

Ms. Settles: Do you agree with that?

Kurtis: That wasn't the big idea.

What happened here? In just a few seconds, three students contributed to a literary discussion, demonstrating an ability not only to grasp the nuances of the text but also to build off their peers' interpretations of what they had read. Moreover, by allowing Alejandra time to build off Julius's answer, Aja could gather information on precisely where comprehension was breaking down. This, then, is a "high-ratio" interaction. It is the students who do the work of analysis, giving each other multiple chances to think critically about the text. If the conversation in Ms. Gordon's class looked like a game of Ping-Pong, this one looked like volleyball.

Just like the habits of sharing, the habits of building can be taught with some attention to a few key techniques. What are these?

Elaborate on Your Answer

Common Core State Standard for Speaking & Listening: 3.1.D, 4.1.D, 5.1.D

Students should know how to elaborate on their responses when prompted to do so.[5] Adding detail allows a student to practice thinking clearly and comprehensively about a text, and it gives the teacher the chance to assess any comprehension errors a student is making. The most basic prompt a teacher can use in this case is "Tell me more," or a simple gesture to continue speaking. However, if a student doesn't elaborate when first asked, there are a number of other strategies the teacher can use, such as saying,

- "You said you were elaborating, but you didn't elaborate."
- "Remember, to elaborate means to add more detail, or explain more thoroughly."
- "Can you remind us what the definition of elaboration is?"

Teachers can also prompt students to elaborate by modeling elaboration themselves.

Build Off Others' Answers

Common Core State Standard for Speaking & Listening: K.1.B, 1.1.B, 2.1.B

After learning to elaborate on one's own answer, the complementary skill is to build off another student's answer.[6] If students haven't mastered this skill, you can get them to talk, but they won't have a real dialogue. Integrating others' answers into your own response sharpens your thinking and lets everyone know you're listening. Watch how Yasmin Vargas's students accomplish this. You'll notice that they have a special hand gesture (palms down and hands touching) to indicate that they're ready to build off a peer's answer.

 WATCH Clip 9: Yasmin Vargas's Build Off Others' Answers

The students in this clip arrive at a great conclusion about a character trait, but they don't jump to it: they climb there together by building directly off one another's responses. This is all the more valuable because the students show they realize what they're doing, via their hand gestures and their comments: "I can add onto that because . . . " The class, then, is a team working together to get to the answer. And they know exactly how that's happening.

Evaluate Others' Responses

Common Core State Standard for Speaking & Listening: 4.1.D, 5.1.D

From a very early age, students should be held accountable for not merely listening to their peers passively but also for actively evaluating the answers they hear.[7] Early on, this can be done by asking all students to give a thumbs-up if they agree or a thumbs-down if they disagree. As time passes, this evaluation can become more and more complex. For example, in the following clip, Erin Michels's student Nasir begins to retell the story, but he leaves out some important information. Rather than telling the students what is missing, Erin simply repeats back what Nasir said. One of the students doesn't sense the error, but the other two do. Watch as Erin allows the students to find the error and redirect their peer simultaneously.

 WATCH Clip 10: Erin Michels's Evaluate Others' Responses

Here we see how the students have taken up the comprehension conversation even more completely: when prompted, they can find the flaw in a peer's sharing and fill the gap.

Praise Your Peers

The ability to praise peers is not explicitly addressed in the CCSS, but we believe it should be: it is an absolutely fundamental skill for conversation. In the classroom, praise is a powerful tool when used well, and students value praise from their peers as much as praise from their teachers. By prompting students to praise each other's work or thinking, we narrate the positive actions we want to see and increase student engagement during a discussion.

Prompt Peers with Universal Prompts

Common Core State Standard for Speaking & Listening: 4.1.C, 5.1.C

The next few habits take the learning up even another notch.[8] Instead of just grappling to determine the answer themselves, here students start aiding their peers' learning as well. Universal prompts are general questions that students can ask each other that could apply to any text. Let's return to the scene of Yasmin Vargas's class. Now that they're already building off each other's answers, watch as the students push one of their peers to give a more complete answer.

▶ WATCH Clip 11: Yasmin Vargas's Prompt Peers with Universal Prompts

---

How can students learn these prompts? By hearing their teachers use them regularly. When it comes to prompting, student talk will mirror teacher talk. When you prompt often in your classroom, so will the students! That makes it possible for other students to change the way they speak and think about reading. The most effective prompts that we have observed in early literacy classrooms are

- "Tell me more."
- "What in the story makes you think that?" or "Where is your evidence in the text?"
- "Why is that important?"
- "Why do you think that?"
- [Repeat the original question.]

Moreover, when students take ownership of prompting their peers in a conversation, they practice comprehension at an even deeper, metacognitive level: they know not only the conclusion to draw from the text but also the strategies they used to do so and how to teach those to others. The result is a powerful learning environment.

Hint, Don't Tell

Common Core State Standard for Speaking & Listening: 5.1.C

Hint, Don't Tell is a natural continuation of the previous habit.[9] Rather than using universal prompts, students learn how to offer cues that are directly related to the text they are reading.

In the following clip, Yasmin Vargas's student Tyler has incorrectly identified the character who wants to solve the problem. Watch how his peers guide him to the correct answer.

 WATCH Clip 12: Yasmin Vargas's Hint, Don't Tell

Yasmin could have prompted the student herself. Or she could have tipped her hand with her nonverbal expressions to suggest that Tyler's answer was wrong. She did neither. Instead, she allowed the students to take over. Students then gave a prompt, not the answer. When a teacher has modeled prompting and gives enough opportunity, students start to prompt their peers naturally. When students can provide specific hints from the text to their peers, they and the peer both continue doing the work of critical thinking about that particular text throughout the discussion.

No Hands

Common Core State Standard for Speaking & Listening: 4.1.B, 5.1.B
To facilitate a naturally paced discussion, students should begin to understand wait time — the practice of delaying a few seconds before expecting an answer — and know when to share and when to prompt a peer in the conversation.[10] A teacher's correct implementation of nonverbal prompts aids the students' ability to conduct a conversation without raising their hands.

Lead

Common Core State Standard for Speaking & Listening: 4.1.B, 5.1.B
When students have mastered all of these habits of discussion, they can learn to lead a conversation from start to finish without help from the teacher.[11] A critical component of leading the discussion is that students are required to stay focused on the core question, independently identifying when the sharing strays from the core question so that they can redirect the conversation. By setting the expectation that students will take turns speaking without relying on raised hands, teachers set the stage for student ownership of the discussion. Then, when the students drift off topic, the teacher can prompt them just enough to get them back on track without taking the lead in the discussion.

Come Prepared in Writing

Common Core State Standard for Speaking & Listening: 3.1.A, 4.1.A, 5.1.A

Often, "coming prepared" can be confused with simply having read the text. Getting students to put their thoughts down in writing, however, does much more. It solidifies the comprehension process by pushing students to crystallize and synthesize their ideas; moreover, it ensures that each student does his or her own thinking before hearing from other students. It can also encourage close reading by focusing a student's attention on key learning tasks. And, just as valuable, it allows a teacher to check for understanding of each student immediately, even before the comprehension conversation begins. Later in this book, we'll discuss the written responses students might be asked to provide during independent reading. For this chapter, suffice it to say that incorporating written work students have done into reading discussions can be an extremely powerful learning tool. As the teacher, you can prompt students to do this by saying something like, "At your seats, you were all writing about how the characters in stories changed from the beginning of the story to the end. What evidence did you choose for how the character changed, and why is your evidence the strongest?"

The habits of discussion we've outlined will be instrumental in raising the quality and rigor of your students' discussions about what they read. Together, they highlight another key point: when it comes to learning how to read, there is power in the group.

Core Idea

Learning to read can be a team sport; your students don't have to be out on the field alone.

Think of how much more learning occurs when three students evaluate an answer than when a teacher simply does it. Now imagine this gain being realized not just once but thousands of times over the course of the year. The result is a class that has built a fundamentally new culture, one that is constantly driving student thinking forward. Table 2.3 summarizes the habits of learning to build.

Table 2.3 Part Two of the Habits of Discussion: Learning to Build

Learning to Build	Ideal Student Actions
Elaborate on Your Answer	• When prompted, add relevant detail to an answer.
Build Off Others' Answers	• Build off what the previous student said; comments are not in isolation.
Evaluate Others' Responses	• Use thumbs up, to the side, or down: agree, slightly agree or disagree, disagree. • Say, "I agree with what you said because . . ." or "I somewhat agree with what you said, but . . ."
Praise Your Peers	• Praise each other's work or thinking.
Prompt Peers with Universal Prompts	• Say, "Tell me more." • Ask, 　"What in the story makes you think that?" 　"Why do you think that?" 　"Why is that important?" • Repeat the original question.
Hint, Don't Tell	• Give a hint to another student to find the answer without telling him or her.
No Hands	• Understand wait time, and know when to prompt a peer in the conversation.
Lead	• Stay focused on the core question. • Identify when the sharing strays and redirect conversation.
Come Prepared in Writing	• Use written responses done during independent reading to guide the discussion.

MAKING THE HABITS HAPPEN

Like every set of habits we'll present in this book, the habits of discussion can be incorporated by *any* teacher in *any* classroom. Here's how to train your students in great habits of discussion and then provide the guidance that will keep students practicing those habits all year round.

Training the Habits

Introducing the habits of discussion to your students is no different from training them in a classroom routine: the most critical actions are simple ones. Think back to Nikki Bowen, whom you watched teach a transition in Chapter One. She made her expectations for the transition clear, modeled them, and gave her students opportunities to practice. A few months later, her class was performing the transition spotlessly at the cue of just one word: "transition." The habits of discussion work similarly.

Table 2.4 is a complete list of the habits of discussion with the training topics and prompts that can help you build consistent habits.

The key to training a habit of discussion is to start with a verbal cue ("Complete sentence, please"), then move to a hand signal or nonverbal prompt (put hands together and pull apart as if pulling gum apart, suggesting "stretch it out" to a complete sentence). Once the students respond to a nonverbal, you have reached the point where you can start to work on the next habit of discussion.

Figure 2.4 shows how the process of bringing the habits of discussion to life in your classroom typically unfolds.

Of course, you can't teach all these habits at once. Instead, you can design an implementation calendar that meets your school's needs—beginning in kindergarten and moving from there. For example, Table 2.5 shows the scope and sequence that Aja's school follows.

Maintaining the Habits

Once you've trained the students in each habit of discussion, the real challenge is to maintain *consistency*, ensuring that these expectations are constantly reaffirmed and reviewed. Highly effective reading teachers concretize the habits of discussion

Figure 2.4   Training Students in the Habits of Discussion

First, train students in each of the habits of discussion, following the *How to Teach Routines* model presented in Chapter One.

Next, for two to three weeks after teaching each habit, verbally prompt students to use the habit. Accompany your verbal prompt with a nonverbal hand signal.

Then, for the rest of the school year, use just the nonverbal hand signal to hold students accountable for using the habit.

Table 2.4 Maintaining the Habits of Discussion: Teacher Training and Prompts

Core Habit of Discussion	Teacher Training or Prompting to Encourage These Actions
Listen and Talk Only in Turn SL.K.1.A, SL.1.1.A	• Teacher models "hands down": when one student has been called on, all other students must put their hands down. • Teacher uses eye contact, hand movement. • Teacher prompts students to give peers a chance to think and talk.
Speak Audibly SL.K.6	• Teacher prompts: "Loud and proud."
Speak in Complete Sentences SL.1.6, SL.2.6	• Teacher uses nonverbal prompt: fingers pursed together and then spread apart (like pulling gum apart).
Interact Peer to Peer: direct answers to the group SL.3.1.A	• Teacher uses nonverbal prompts: fingers pointing to eyes and then to the rest of the group. • Teacher prompts: "Tell *him*."
Elaborate on Your Answer SL.3.1.D, SL.4.1.D, SL.5.1.D	• Teacher prompts for a more developed answer: "Tell me more." • Teacher gestures for student to keep going.

Build Off Others' Answers
 	
SL.K.1.B, SL.1.1.B, SL.2.1.B
	• Teacher says,
	  "Build off that."
	  "Tell me more about what ___ said."
	  "Can you tell me more about what ___ is thinking?"

Evaluate Others' Responses (agree, disagree, somewhat agree or disagree) SL.4.1.D, SL.5.1.D	• Teach the stems of agree, disagree, and somewhat agree or disagree: "I agree with what you said because ..." and "I somewhat agree with what you said, but ..." • Teacher prompts the group: "What do you think about that?" "Do you agree?"

(*continued*)

Table 2.4 Maintaining the Habits of Discussion: Teacher Training and Prompts (*continued*)

Core Habit of Discussion	Teacher Training or Prompting to Encourage These Actions
Praise Your Peers	• Teacher prompts for praise: "What did you like about [student]'s answer?" "Could someone offer some praise for that answer?"
Prompt Peers with Universal Prompts SL.4.1.C, SL.5.1.C	• Teacher trains: "So now we're at a point where if you don't agree, you need to prompt that student with a universal prompt."
Hint, Don't Tell: cue peers to help them in their response SL.5.1.C	• Teacher could say, "I want you to help your neighbor" or "Instead of telling the answer, you could have prompted like this . . ." • Teacher could tie in another lesson: "Remember in read-aloud this morning what we did? How can you [tie that in, use that here]?"
No Hands: aid the conversation without raising your hand SL.4.1.B, SL.5.1.B	• Teacher uses a nonverbal prompt: he backs away in his chair and reaches out his hands to the students to encourage them to continue the conversation.
Lead: facilitate the conversation from start to finish SL.4.1.B, SL.5.1.B	• Teacher takes no action (but gives signs of watchful oversight). • Teacher demonstrates to redirect a literature circle that's off task. Once this has been demonstrated, teacher signals to students to redirect the conversation themselves. • Teacher intervenes: "What is our core question? Are you answering that question?"
Come Prepared in Writing: use written response to aid discussion SL.3.1.A, SL.4.1.A, SL.5.1.A	• Teacher prompts: "As you were writing, I noticed that many of you wrote _____. What were you thinking?"

ble 2.5   Sample Implementation Calendar: Habits of Discussion

abit	Timeline
Kindergarten	
• Listen and Talk Only in Turn • Speak Audibly	• First two weeks of school (Sept)
• Speak in Complete Sentences	• Third week of school (mid-Sept)
• Elaborate on Your Answer	• Start of Month 2 (Oct)
• Evaluate Others' Responses	• Middle of Month 2 (mid-Oct)
• Interact Peer to Peer	• Month 3 (Nov)
Grade 1	
• Reinforce K habits of discussion	• Month 1 (Sept)
• Praise Your Peers	• Middle of Month 1 (mid-Sept)
• Build Off Others' Answers	• Months 2–3 (Oct through Nov)
• Prompt Peers with Universal Prompts	• Months 4–5 (Dec through Jan)
Grade 2	
• Reinforce K–1 habits of discussion	• Month 1 (Sept)
• Hint, Don't Tell	• Months 2–3 (Oct through Nov)
• No Hands	• Months 4–5 (Dec through Jan)
Grade 3	
• Reinforce K–2 habits of discussion	• Month 1 (Sept)
• Come Prepared in Writing	• Month 1 (Sept)
• Lead	• Months 2–4 (Oct through Dec)

with many of the same strategies they would use in any other instance of strengthening a habit. Here are two of the most effective strategies:

1. **Narrate the positive.** As highlighted in Doug Lemov's *Teach Like a Champion*, if you want a student to repeat an action, narrate when he or she does it well, rather than only issuing corrections when you see the wrong behavior.[12]

2. **Stay poker-faced.** As teachers, we often inadvertently give away the right answers with our bodies as well as with our words — for example, by issuing

unintentional nonverbal cues (eyebrows raised, slight grin, and so on) or by changing the intonation of our voices. When we avoid doing this, we make it much easier for our students to master independent critical thinking and authentically evaluate each other's ideas. Note that in Aja's video, her face remained neutral whenever she prompted a student.

Most important, please remember: the key to developing students' habits of discussion is to make sure *they* are doing the talking! Remember, changing teacher talk is what leads to the changes in student talk and ultimately to the changes in student thinking.

CONCLUSION: FROM FUTSAL TO THE "BIG GAME"

In the game of futsal, a miniature version of soccer that is popular in Brazil, the small size of the field and walls surrounding it create a game during which you touch the ball far more frequently than in a typical soccer game. Many authors, such as Daniel Coyle, attribute Brazil's tremendous success in soccer to futsal, because the increased number of touches speeds up a player's development. A classroom conversation that utilizes the habits of discussion is like a game of futsal: it gives students the chance to develop their speaking, thinking, and reading skills with dramatically greater speed and accuracy. And in this analogy, teachers are like the walls of the futsal court: they use the habits of discussion to bounce the ball back to the players, to return the thinking to students as fast as they can.

Futsal, however, is never meant to be any athlete's "big game": on the contrary, it's a training device which ensures that when the walls are removed and you're playing real soccer, you're ready. In the same way, using the habits of discussion in a four-person reading group is not intended to be an end point for students, but a beginning. It guarantees that as they enter middle school, high school, college, and the professional world, they will be prepared for the "big games" of intellectual discussion that await them there. When the support of the walls—their elementary school teachers—is no longer there to remind them how to conduct themselves, they will remember on their own how to listen, share, and make the most of their turns to speak.

Habits of Discussion Training and Prompting Guide

Learning to Share (Start in Grades K–1)		
Core Habit of Discussion	**Ideal Student Actions**	**Teacher Training or Prompting to Encourage These Actions**
Listen & Talk Only in Turn SL.K.1.A, SL.1.1.A	• Track the speaker • Keep hands down when someone else is speaking. • Do not interrupt.	• Teacher models "hands down": when one student has been called on, all other students must put their hands down. • Teacher uses eye contact, hand movement. • Teacher prompts students to give peers a chance to think and talk.
Speak Audibly SL.K.6	• Use a voice others can hear.	• Teacher prompts: "Loud and proud."
Speak in Complete Sentences SL.1.6, SL.2.6	• Restate the question in the response; use no incomplete sentences.	• Teacher uses nonverbal prompt: fingers pursed together and then spread apart (like pulling gum apart).
Interact Peer-to-Peer: direct answers to the group SL.3.1.A	• Look at every group member, not just the teacher, when giving an answer.	• Teacher uses nonverbal prompts: fingers pointing to eyes and then to the rest of the group. • Teacher prompts: "Tell *him*."

Great Habits, Great Readers: A Practical Guide for K–4 Reading in the Light of Common Core, by Paul Bambrick-Santoyo, Aja Settles, and Juliana Worrell. Copyright © 2013 Uncommon Schools and/or Paul Bambrick-Santoyo. Reproduced by permission.

Learning to Build (Start in Grades 1–3)		
Core Habit of Discussion	Ideal Student Actions	Teacher Training or Prompting to Encourage These Actions
Elaborate on Your Answer SL.3.1.D, SL.4.1.D, SL.5.1.D	• When prompted, add relevant detail to an answer.	• Teacher prompts for a more developed answer: "Tell me more." • Teacher gestures for student to keep going.
Build Off Others' Answers SL.K.1.B, SL.1.1.B, SL.2.1.B	• Build off what the previous student said; comments are not in isolation.	• Teacher says, "Build off that." "Tell me more about what ___ said." "Can you tell me more about what ___ is thinking?"
Evaluate Others' Responses (agree, disagree, somewhat agree or disagree) SL.4.1.D, SL.5.1.D	• Use thumbs up, to the side, or down: agree, slightly agree or disagree, disagree. • Say, "I agree with what you said because …" or "I somewhat agree with what you said, but …"	• Teach the stems of agree, disagree, and somewhat agree or disagree: "I agree with what you said because …" and "I somewhat agree with what you said, but …" • Teacher prompts the group: "What do you think about that?" "Do you agree?"
Praise Your Peers	• Praise each other's work or thinking.	• Teacher prompts for praise: "What did you like about [student]'s answer?" "Could someone offer some praise for that answer?"

(continued)

(continued)

Learning to Build (Start in Grades 1–3)		
Core Habit of Discussion	Ideal Student Actions	Teacher Training or Prompting to Encourage These Actions

Prompt Peers with Universal Prompts
 	
SL.4.1.C, SL.5.1.C
	• Say, "Tell me more."
	• Ask,
	   "What in the story makes you think that?"
	   "Why do you think that?"
	   "Why is that important?"
	• Repeat the original question.
		• Teacher trains: "So now we're at a point where if you don't agree you need to prompt that student with a universal prompt."

Hint, Don't Tell: cue peers to help them in their response SL.5.1.C	• Give a hint to another student to find the answer without telling him or her.	• Teacher could say, "I want you to help your neighbor" or "Instead of telling the answer you could have prompted like this . . ." • Teacher could tie in another lesson: "Remember in read-aloud this morning what we did? How can you [tie that in, use that here]?"
No Hands: aid the conversation without raising your hand SL.4.1.B, SL5.1.B	• Understand wait time, and know when to prompt a peer in the conversation	• Teacher uses a nonverbal prompt: he backs away in his chair and reaches out his hands to the students to encourage them to continue the conversation.

Great Habits, Great Readers: A Practical Guide for K–4 Reading in the Light of Common Core, by Paul Bambrick-Santoyo, Aja Settles, and Juliana Worrell. Copyright © 2013 Uncommon Schools and/or Paul Bambrick-Santoyo. Reproduced by permission.

Learning to Build (Start in Grades 1–3)		
Core Habit of Discussion	**Ideal Student Actions**	**Teacher Training or Prompting to Encourage These Actions**
Lead: facilitate the conversation from start to finish SL.4.1.B, SL.5.1.B	• Stay focused on the core question. • Identify when the sharing strays and redirect the conversation.	• Teacher takes no action (but gives signs of watchful oversight). • Teacher demonstrates how to redirect a literature circle that's off task. Once this has been demonstrated, teacher signals to students to redirect the conversation themselves. • Teacher intervenes: "What is our core question? Are you answering that question?"
Come Prepared in Writing: use written response to aid discussion SL.3.1.A, SL.4.1.A, SL.5.1.A	• Use written responses done during independent reading to guide the discussion.	• Teacher prompts: "As you were writing, I noticed that many of you wrote ___. What were you thinking?"

Apply Your Habits: Habits of Discussion

Self-Assessment

Of the habits of discussion described in this chapter, which would you like to focus on to add the most value to your classroom discussion? Circle them.

- Listen and Talk Only in Turn
- Speak Audibly
- Speak in Complete Sentences
- Interact Peer to Peer
- Elaborate on Your Answer
- Build Off Others' Answers
- Elaborate on Others' Answers
- Evaluate Others' Responses
- Praise Your Peers
- Prompt Peers with Universal Prompts
- Hint, Don't Tell
- No Hands
- Lead
- Come Prepared in Writing

Tools to Use

- Habits of Discussion Scope and Sequence: Teacher Training and Prompting Guide (also included in the Appendix and on the DVD)
- Sample Implementation Calendar: Habits of Discussion (also included on the DVD)
- Professional development materials

Your Next Steps

_____

_____

_____

_____

Great Habits, Great Readers: A Practical Guide for K–4 Reading in the Light of Common Core, by Paul Bambrick-Santoyo, Aja Settles, and Juliana Worrell. Copyright © 2013 Uncommon Schools and/or Paul Bambrick-Santoyo. Reproduced by permission.

Part 2

Teach the Skills of Reading

| Set the Habits of Learning | **Teach the Skills of Reading** | Build the Habits of Reading | Lead by Habit |

Part 2

Introduction: The Art of Targeted Teaching

Just by implementing the habits of learning discussed in Part One, you will have dramatically increased the effectiveness of reading instruction regardless of how you teach. But what are the essential skills of reading that will take your students as far as possible? And how can you teach those skills most effectively?

At this point, you may be expecting us to offer the "silver bullet" of literacy instruction, a single approach that will work for all students. The recent history of literacy instruction reflects myriad shifting perspectives on the best way to teach children to read.[1] The list will only grow as groups move to respond to the CCSS. Yet as most of the literature on reading has already confirmed, and as we have also learned through hard experience, there is no one silver bullet for teaching great readers. Instead, the key to success for all students lies in a simple but powerful concept: overdetermination.

In *Influencer*, a team of management experts examined how leaders create seemingly magical transformations that radically improve lives.[2] What they found was that in any difficult transformation, the most successful leaders did not limit themselves to any one approach, whether interpersonal, social, or political. Instead, these leaders *overdetermined* their success by applying every path at their disposal and using them to reinforce one another. In an analogous way, the best elementary teachers realized that the solution was to use multiple approaches and to use them at the same time. In itself, there is nothing revolutionary about this way of teaching reading; it is well supported by decades of literacy research.

The more difficult question is how to put these all together in one consistent way. If you recall from Aja's personal experience, this was her key obstacle to becoming a good reading teacher. When we observed the most highly effective early literacy classrooms, especially those where a newer teacher was inserted and able to match the success of his or her peers, we saw an integrated system with two core areas:

1. Do targeted teaching of the skills of reading
2. Match the right skills, students, and texts at the right time

The next two parts of this book are going to deal with these areas. Part Two addresses how to teach the skills of reading. Part Three will address matching those skills to the right student and text at the right time. In Part Two, the following chapters will address the teaching of reading skills:

- **What to Teach (Chapter Three).** Before we discuss *how* to teach reading skills, we need to identify *what* to teach. Here we'll explore the integral connection between a scope and sequence of reading skills and the world of early literacy assessment.

- **Read-Aloud Lessons (Chapter Four).** The value of reading aloud to children is already widely acknowledged, but this chapter will show you how to make read-aloud even more powerful. The lessons we'll highlight here use read-aloud to introduce and illustrate a core skill for readers, such as understanding a character's motive as it influences the story. Students are able to see an excellent model of fluent reading and are free to focus entirely on the skill being taught.

- **Teaching Comprehension Skills (Chapter Five).** Comprehension skills lessons reinforce core skills for readers following a traditional guided practice model: provide an example of the strategy in action, practice in tandem with students, and finish with students having time to practice and apply the skill on their own.

- **Teaching Phonics (Chapter Six).** To be able to accomplish great feats of comprehension, students need to master phonics skills, too. In phonics lessons, the teacher works with students to develop skills for creating and decoding individual sounds, striving to create as many practice opportunities as possible for as many students as possible, and to identify the specific changes needed to drive phonetic skills.

What makes the implementation of these lessons effective is their tight connection to each other and their positioning as the first steps on a continuum. Moreover, these foundations prepare students for the heart of the matter in the lessons we describe in Part Three, during which they'll match these skills to the complex act of reading a book.

In so many ways, these chapters are not new lesson types. This sort of "balanced literacy" approach has been seen elsewhere, and each of the components can be found in schools across the country.[3] What sets the very best elementary literacy instructors apart is not which lesson types they use but how they use them: how they implement each lesson type so as to accelerate development of the right reading habits. In the chapters that follow, we will show you.

Chapter 3

What to Teach

Defining a Road Map for Rigor

At a recent high school commencement ceremony, the keynote speaker—a local councilperson—shared the unexpected tale of his brief brush with greatness on the Duke basketball team. Though not a recruited athlete, he spent his first year at Duke playing intramural basketball constantly, participating in internal competitions against other Duke students. And he was good. So good, in fact, that by the end of his first year he had mastered the intramural domain. When fall tryouts for Duke's official varsity team were announced, the speaker was encouraged by his friends and teammates to take a shot at joining one of the nation's best teams.

When the week of the tryouts came, the young athlete was at his best. Trained by years of practice, he effortlessly showed off the skills that had made him so successful as an intramural player: fast breaks down the court, elaborate behind-the-back passes, slick dribbling moves. He was so sure he'd made the team that he spent the next day explaining to his fraternity, extracurricular organizations, and even his girlfriend that he was about to have a much busier schedule, but that he would still find time for them. Then he sat down to wait for the call.

At this point in the speech, the soon-to-be high school graduates were expecting a traditional happily-ever-after: through hard work and grit, the speaker made it onto the team and achieved his goals. But that isn't what happened. Days passed, then weeks, then a month, but no call came. Finally, he managed to meet with one of the coaches who had watched the tryouts unfold. The coach pulled no punches. "You're a great athlete," he said, "but you've picked up all the wrong habits—intramural habits. It takes varsity habits to make this team."[1]

The very techniques, skills, and tactics that the athlete had built over years of ball were his undoing. His problem was not that he did not have talent but that his talent had not trained him for the real challenge ahead. Years later, his final message to the high school class of 2012: don't confuse developing mediocre habits with working toward success.

As a highly successful politician and lawyer, the keynote speaker was able to look back at this story and laugh as heartily as anyone in the audience. Yet the lesson of his Duke experience is an incredibly powerful one: forming habits is not enough—they need to be the *right* habits.

Core Idea

Forming habits is meaningless if they aren't the *right* habits.

Up to this point, we have focused a great deal on how great teachers can help students build the right habits of learning. We've seen how classroom expectations, management systems, and habits of discussion can strengthen the work on the complex skills of reading. Our next step before diving into topics of explicit reading instruction is to determine the bar that needs to be set. This is a crucial question. Just as it is possible for an intramural athlete to master the elaborate and flashy behind-the-back pass without learning the fierce basketball technique a varsity team needs, it is possible for us to teach our students a set of skills and understandings that simply do not add up to great reading. If we leave our students with only "junior varsity" skills, then no amount of practice or habits will be enough to make them varsity readers.

In recent years, there has been a great deal of effort to address this issue by building standards that ensure that students learn the reading habits they need. The CCSS are the latest attempt. These standards, combined with the work of generations of education experts, suggest that the bar needs to be elevated in a number of ways to become truly rigorous. What we need, they effectively argue, are varsity reading habits, the ones that a great reading curriculum must instruct if it is to be effective.

The Common Core provides a foundation for developing these habits, but saying that students must, for example, "recount stories . . . and determine their central message, lesson or moral" (CCSS for Reading: Literature: RL 2.2) will not be sufficient. As much as these standards have pushed for clarity, this description is still like a statement that basketball players need to focus on "passing" or "shooting." Although those needs are true and urgent, they are also broad, and naming them won't be enough. Instead, we will need to set a clear road map for precisely what rigorous mastery of finding the "central message, lesson or moral" should look like. Let's get started.

ASSESSMENT—CREATE THE ROAD MAP FOR RIGOR

Few teachers enjoy giving tests. Whether it's because tests remind us of anxiety from our childhoods or because we don't feel as though we're *teaching* during them, assessment often is the least favored part of a teacher's day. And although no one contests the need to evaluate our pupils, we've begun to see suggestions that, in the age of the Common Core, the tests we choose matter only marginally in the context of effective, standards-aligned teaching. If the readings continue to become increasingly complex, the argument goes, that should be enough.[2] We could not disagree more.

Consider the story used for an early kindergarten assessment (see the box "Four Early Literacy Assessments"). This assessment is for readers who are just beginning to follow patterns (Fountas & Pinnell [F&P] Level C). The text remains the same, but four different assessments check for comprehension in four distinct ways.

Four Early Literacy Assessments

The following is the story text; assume that every sentence is on a separate page and accompanied by a picture:

When I grow up, I want to put out fires. I want to play ball. I want to go to the moon. I want to teach school. I want to fix cars. But now, I am happy to be a kid.

Here's how four major early childhood assessments check for comprehension of this passage:

DRA (Diagnostic Reading Assessment)

Students need to

- Retell the story
- Make a personal connection

DIBELS (Dynamic Indicators of Basic Early Literacy Skills)

No test for comprehension is given; fluency in reading combined with proper decoding via "nonsense" words is considered an adequate predictor of comprehension.

Running Record

(This is one sample; different teachers use Running Records in different ways). Students need to

- Tell what happened in the story
- Answer "right there" basic comprehension questions

STEP (Strategic Teaching and Evaluation of Progress) Assessment

Students need to answer the following questions:

- What is the first job the girl thinks about doing?
- What job would make her leave Earth?
- Why does the girl say that for now she is happy being a kid?

As noted, each of these four assessments uses the same text. Yet students who can pass one of these assessments will not necessarily pass another one. How could that be possible? The DRA focuses primarily on basic recall, whereas the STEP assessment requires the reader to determine the main character's motivation in a critical thinking question. Indeed, each of these assessments has taken a different "stand" on what constitutes proficient reading, and that stance has serious implications for instruction.

This example reveals an invaluable truth: standards alone will not define the high expectations needed for success. Rather, the way we assess a standard—the level of rigor and complexity embedded into that assessment—provides the path to developing the varsity habits our kids need. Think back to our opening parable. The CCSS make sure we're all playing the same game, by the same rules. Our choice of assessments, however, determines who's intramural and who's playing varsity ball.

Core Idea

Standards are meaningless until you define how to assess them.

We assess what we value, and value what we assess. If we only assess basic comprehension, that will create the baseline for teaching. Yes, teachers will still try to teach critical thinking or "higher-order" skills, but they will have an inconsistent measure of whether those skills are being mastered. The consequence? Dramatically different levels of rigor between classrooms.

Let's bring this closer to home, using third-grade standards from the Common Core:

> Ask and answer questions to demonstrate understanding of a text, referring explicitly to the text as the basis for the answers. (RL.3.1)
>
> Determine the central message . . . and explain how it is conveyed through key details in the text. (RL.3.2)
>
> Determine the meaning of words and phrases as they are used in a text, distinguishing literal from nonliteral language. (RL.3.4)

On the surface, these standards appear to give a clear sense of what students should know. But do they really?

Imagine four different classrooms where teachers all developed curriculum units that included the teaching and application of these standards. Six weeks later, they each selected a different literacy assessment to see if their students are progressing proficiently in their reading (see the box "Four Assessments at Reading Level P"). All texts were at F&P Level P. That is where the similarities ended.

Four Assessments at Reading Level P

Classroom Assessment 1

Length: 400-word passage from chapter 3 of *Encyclopedia Brown Saves the Day* (first chapters were read together in class)
   Text difficulty: 570L
   Students need to answer orally:

- Retell the story, scoring 16 on a comprehension rubric that includes

  - Giving proper sequence of events

  - Including details from text

  - Referring to characters

  - Literal interpretation (inferential interpretation would be advanced)

Classroom Assessment 2

Length: 500-word story
   Text difficulty: 470L
   Students need to answer orally:

- What happened in the beginning of the story?
- What did John say to Mary?
- Why was John angry?
- How would you apply the lesson of this story to your own life?

Classroom Assessment 3

Length: 250-word passage
   Text difficulty: 520L
   Students need to answer orally:

- Tell what happened in the story.
- What is the theme of the story?
- What does "enraged" mean on pg. 2?

Classroom Assessment 4

Length: 750-word story, *Ella's Magic*
   Text difficulty: 590L

Students need to answer in writing:

- What is the central message of the story? Select three sentences that support your answer.

Students need to answer orally:

- What does the author mean when she says, "Ella saw a faint light. She blinked"? What is happening?
- Who says, "I am the fairy godmother"? What is happening in this passage?

A Word on . . . What's Up with the "L"?

You'll notice that we refer to Lexile scores throughout the text. Lexile scores (written as a number followed by the letter L) are one of the most cited measures of quantitative text complexity identified by the CCSS. Calculated based on word frequency and sentence length, they are a critical first step to determining the quantitative aspect of text complexity.

The CCSS mention that we also need to look at the qualitative measures of a text's complexity when we select it for instruction, but there's a solid body of research which suggests that if you don't have the right text complexity, these other factors won't matter. This is why you'll see us start with the Lexile measure as the common denominator for reading complexity. In other parts of the book, we'll discuss other measures you can use to evaluate and select texts for your class.

What do we notice? Each assessment is set at Level P, yet they all are setting a different bar for rigor. Here are some of the factors that reveal this variation:

- **Lexile scores.** The Lexile scores for these passages cover a dramatically wide range. This suggests that although each assessment uses a Level P text, the word difficulty and sentence length are very different between each passage, meaning that the complexity of the reading varies significantly.

- **Prior knowledge of the book.** In the first assessment, students can access their general knowledge of the book and its themes based on the classroom conversations around the first two chapters. This can make it difficult to ascertain their ability to read a passage cold.

- **Oral versus written comprehension.** The first three assessments test a child's comprehension through oral questioning; only the fourth assessment also requires students to answer in writing. There is a significant difference between the ability to articulate an answer orally and having to write it down coherently.

- **Retell versus cited detail.** Each assessment chooses a different means of testing the first two standards. The first assessment relies solely on a retell; the second one adds comprehension questions and a question asking you to apply the theme to your own life—extending beyond the scope of the story itself. The third one adds an explicit question about theme, but only the fourth one requires students explicitly to cite the evidence that supports their answers.

- **Vocabulary in context versus meaning of nonliteral phrases.** As for the third CCSS (meaning of words and phrases), the first two assessments assume that you understand words and phrases if you can retell the story or answer general questions. The third asks the student for the meaning of a word in context, but the fourth one requires the reader to understand the real meaning of a phrase that isn't literal.

What's the bottom line? These four different assessments will yield four very different senses of a child's comprehension. If you are truly trying to assess students' mastery of CCSS 3.1, 3.2, and 3.4, then you will be left in the dark by the first three assessments. Getting a student to retell a story is not enough to assess that student's comprehension. Nor is simply choosing a text at the appropriate F&P level. And not all comprehension questions are alike.

Given these differences, an assessment cannot be seen as just "a test." Rather, it sets up goalposts for which skills students need to master to demonstrate proficiency at a specific level of reading. Where we choose to put those goalposts has everything to do with the way we teach, as that choice tells us both what students need to be able to do and—once we've assessed them—whether or not they are able to do it. In short, our choice of assessment will reveal our expectations for students. If you don't know your final destination, you cannot draw a map to get there.

The differences you just saw underscore how crucial it is to select the right assessments for your students. The tests we choose or develop have much to say about the ultimate rigor of instruction and expectations for our students and ourselves.

So how do we pick or develop the right assessment? Let's go into detail about exactly how to choose.

SELECTING AN EARLY LITERACY ASSESSMENT

The ideal literacy assessment will allow you to do a few key things:

- Choose the right texts.
  - ○ Assess students over time, using texts of ever-increasing difficulty.
  - ○ Assess comprehension with both narrative and informational texts.
- Choose the right skills.
  - ○ Assess phonics, fluency, and accuracy in the early reading levels.
  - ○ Assess CCSS-aligned comprehension skills that have growing complexity to match the increasing rigor of the passages.

In short, text difficulty *and* skill difficulty matter. And contrary to some public perception, the CCSS agree.[3] Let's take a brief look at each of these more closely.

Text Choice

One of the biggest contributions of the research behind the Common Core is that text difficulty matters, and matters significantly. Moreover, the difficulty of the words in the passage combined with the sentence length is one of the most accurate predictors of students' ability to comprehend it.[4] Given these factors, Lexile measures have become one of the leading measures for determining text difficulty. The Common Core establishes a Lexile band into which texts should fall at each grade level, starting in first grade. The key to a quality assessment is to have each assessment take you progressively up the Lexile bands. We hope this will become common practice quickly. However, right now many commercial leveled assessment programs actually do not move up the Lexile bands in an orderly fashion—some even go down from one assessment to the next. This is likely due to giving higher priority to less objective measures of complexity (such as the themes or symbolism of the story). These factors do matter—and Common Core agrees—but there is no reason to sacrifice Lexile complexity in favor of other factors: they can go hand in hand. So as a starting point, check out the Lexile levels of the assessments you choose!

Skills Assessed

If you have texts that progress in difficulty, what does it look like for comprehension skills to move up in complexity alongside the texts you use? Consider the progression of inference questions from early kindergarten to grades 2–3 taken from the STEP assessment (see the box "Not All Inference Questions Are Equal").

Not All Inference Questions Are Equal

Moving Up the Band of Skill Complexity

- **Lexile 75L: "Which job [astronaut] would make her leave Earth?"**
  - Question focus: using pictures to support meaning; understanding character actions
  - Skills needed: relate background knowledge to text
- **Lexile 275L: "Why doesn't Ashley know what to answer when Margo says, 'I always know best'"?**
  - Question focus: character motivation, struggles, interactions
  - Skills needed: understand how the main character affects secondary characters, taking into account character personality; identify a problem; understand schema related to bossy characters; add up details over time

---

- **Lexile 450L: "Why does Jeffrey's mother trust him to mail the letters?"**
  - Question focus: connecting earlier and later parts—figuring out how everything works together
  - Skills needed: use details from the text; analyze multiple characters, multiple points of view, character motive, and theme
- **Lexile 650L: "Did Ella really turn into a squirrel and a pigeon? How do you know?"**
  - Question focus: figurative language, interpretation, genre
  - Skills needed: understand a genre (fantasy); work to comprehend texts that are removed from personal experience; connect different parts of the text; hold on to multiple plots

As the questions demonstrate, not all inference questions are equal. "Making inferences" is a broad skill that isn't well defined or even helpful until we create a ladder of increasing complexity. At each level of STEP reading proficiency, students are required to make inferences in a more complex or nuanced way. This level of granularity is absolutely invaluable for teaching students to read. Consider the difference between a teacher who can say "My students need to work on making inferences" and one who can say "My students struggle when they have to compare the characterization of a protagonist and antagonist." The first teacher has only a fuzzy sense of what students need in order to move forward. The second is ready to target the skills the students need. In Chapter Seven, we'll go into detail about how to translate assessment data into results in your classroom, but you can do that only if the assessment you've chosen provides that data in the first place. Increasing levels of text complexity won't be enough. The exam must also be able to provide you with clear data on where, specifically, student skills break down. If it can, you'll be able to analyze student work deeply, and that is the key to tailoring your instruction to meet your students' needs.

Core Idea

The quality of your assessment dictates the depth of your analysis.

By now you may have noticed that we've referred to the Strategic Teaching and Evaluation of Progress (STEP) assessment in a number of examples. The strength of this assessment is that it provides a level of detail that allows for the rich analysis you'll want to do with your students. STEP isn't perfect, though. There are plenty of areas where it's limited because it's not fully aligned with the CCSS. A STEP assessment won't, for example, tell you if second graders are able to "compare and contrast two or more versions of the same story" (CCSS for Reading: Literature: RL 2.9) or if third graders can "explain how specific aspects of a text's illustrations contribute to what is conveyed by the words in a story" (RL 3.7).

In fact, as we looked at all the current assessments on the market, we found that none of them were 100 percent aligned to the Common Core, rigorous in both text and skill complexity, and capable of providing the rich data needed to drive student growth on all of the CCSS. Certainly in the upcoming years we will see the leveled reading assessments evolve and improve to adapt to the Common Core landscape. What to do, then, in the meantime?

Given the incredible complexity involved in designing your own effective leveled assessments, the best answer for the moment is to choose one of the existing assessments that most moves up the Lexile bands and supplement it by tracking the skills that are not covered by that assessment. You can do the same exercise we did earlier: pull out all the assessments and compare the reading passages and questions side by side. Don't judge them by what their user guides say they measure; judge them for yourself: passage versus passage, question versus question. Then consider the additional questions or tasks you will design to bridge the gap to the Common Core. (As you can probably infer, we chose the STEP assessment for the classrooms with which we work.)

The key is to be aware of the deficiencies of whatever assessments you choose and be prepared to address them. Only then can you create the kind of curriculum that your students need.

ASSESSMENT MEETS CURRICULUM

Once you have an assessment that sets the right bar, you can begin to design a rigorous curriculum. In brief, this process is about knowing the bar that your assessment sets, then planning lessons accordingly. To illustrate this process, the remainder of this chapter focuses on the ways in which we have seen one kindergarten teacher and one second-grade teacher use the skills they identified through assessment to plan their curricula for the year.

Here's one example. Shadell Purefoy is a kindergarten teacher, and nearly all of her students arrive in the kindergarten not knowing their letters, let alone being able to read. So her curriculum meets students where they start and moves them to proficiency by the end of the year. The CCSS give her some guidelines, but how will she break down the anchor standards into discrete units over the course of the year? This sample curriculum starts from assessment: in addition to its increasing text and skill complexity, it includes "bottom lines" that state the specific skills a student must master in order to move from one level to the next. These bottom lines are the starting point for the curriculum (see the box "Building the Framework for Your Curriculum: Sample Kindergarten Bottom Lines").

Building the Framework for Your Curriculum

Sample Kindergarten Bottom Lines: Up to 150L

Comprehension	
Assessment Bottom Line	**Common Core**
FACT: Recall factual information and find it in the text.	RL.K.1
SEQUENCE: Retell parts of the story accurately in a proper sequence.	RL.K.2
CITING EVIDENCE I— DETAIL: Recall text details and use them to support meaning.	RL.K.2
STORY ELEMENTS I AND II: Respond to questions around setting and characters. Identify primary problem and solution in a story.	RL.K.3
CHARACTER FEELINGS: Draw conclusions about character feelings.	RL.K.3
COMPARE AND CONTRAST I—CONNECTIONS WITHIN A TEXT: Describe the connection between two individuals, events, ideas, or pieces of information in a text.	RL.K.9

With sets of skills like these planned out, you can begin moving toward transforming your classroom practice and building a truly rigorous curriculum to match the assessment.

Each bottom line becomes the focus of lessons and units that are spread out over the course of the year. Remember: what makes for great reading is ensuring that all of these bottom lines become habits that are integrated and used with any text. Thus, when we talk about building a scope and sequence, this is really just where the bottom lines are *introduced*; they will be used always thereafter. Of course, students' varying reading levels will necessitate differentiation of instruction within the curriculum; guided reading lessons (Chapters Eight and Nine) will directly address that need. A scope and sequence simply guarantees that every child has the opportunity to learn and master the skills he or she needs, even if some students move faster than others. Table 3.1 shows a sample unit of the scope and sequence based on the assessment and bottom lines we just looked at.

What are the characteristics of this scope and sequence that make it effective?

- **Scope and sequence is aligned to the assessment.** This scope and sequence guarantees that you are teaching what you will assess: your road map consistently links curriculum with assessment. That's what makes the curriculum so powerful.

- **Skills are bite-sized.** The CCSS have been broken down into smaller chunks that can be taught one step at a time for young children.

- **Informational and narrative texts are integrated.** Informational and narrative texts are integrated into the plan. Just as significant, texts are selected along with the skills to make sure that student comprehension is growing in both skill and text complexity.

So what does this look like further along in the reading continuum? Table 3.2 offers a sneak peek at a corresponding scope and sequence.

Table 3.1 Sample Kindergarten Curriculum Unit: Up to 150L

Focus, Books, and Vocabulary	Standards	Lesson Overview
Week 2, Part 1 **Compare and Contrast** **Books** *Click, Clack, Moo: Cows That Type*, by Doreen Cronin *See How They Grow: Calf* (DK Publishing) **Vocabulary** fiction, nonfiction	RL.K.1. Ask and answer questions about key details in a text. RL.K.9. Compare and contrast the adventures and experiences of characters in familiar stories. RL.1.5. Explain major differences between books that tell stories and books that give information. W.K.2. Compose informative/explanatory texts in which they name what they are writing about and supply some information about the topic.	• Model using the cover of the books to think about whether the pictures are real or make-believe and then do a picture walk. • Display a Venn diagram and enter in characteristics of both fiction and nonfiction. • Independent: complete a Venn diagram.
Week 2, Part 2 **Characterization** **Books** *Lost*, by David McPhail *Beatrice Doesn't Want To*, by Laura Numeroff **Vocabulary** attribute, character actions	RL.K.1. Ask and answer questions about key details in a text. RL.1.3. Describe characters, settings, and major events in a story, using key details. RL.1.5. Explain major differences between books that tell stories and books that give information. W.K.2. Compose informative/explanatory texts in which they name what they are writing about and supply some information about the topic.	• Define and review character: people, animals, or objects talking in the story. • Discuss different types of characters. • Read *Lost*, and chart about the boy and bear characters. • Independent: identify the characters in the story and write down their physical characteristics. • Model charting the actions of the main character. • Get students to identify the actions of the character.

(continued)

Table 3.1 Sample Kindergarten Curriculum Unit: Up to 150L *(continued)*

Focus, Books, and Vocabulary	Standards	Lesson Overview
Week 3 **Story Element: Characters (main vs. secondary)** **Books** *Sheila Rae*, by Kevin Henkes *Jamaica's Find*, by Juanita Hill **Vocabulary** main & secondary characters	RLK.1. Ask and answer questions about key details in a text. RLK.3. Identify characters, settings, and major events in a story (identify the main character in the story; distinguish between the main and secondary characters of a story).	• Review definition of *character*. • Define main character (on most pages). • Define secondary character (on a few pages). • Read and chart how many times the character is seen (Sheila Rae, Louis, Mother, Father, classmates, and so on; Jamaica, Mom, Dad, and so on).

Week 4
Drawing Conclusions: Character
 	
Books
Sheila Rae, by Kevin Henkes
David Goes to School, by David Shannon
 	
Vocabulary
character trait
	RLK.1. Ask and answer questions about key details in a text.
	
	RLK.3. Identify characters, settings, and major events in a story.
	
	  ○ Identify a character's actions in story.
	  ○ Identify how a character feels and the reasons why.
	  ○ Define character traits as a way to describe a character.
	  ○ Identify the character trait on the basis of the character's actions.
		• Review character actions.
		• Review that character's actions reveal what the character may be feeling. (This has been covered in read-aloud.)
		• Introduce feelings and traits and define.
		• Chart actions of character, and model thinking aloud how the character may be feeling.
		• Independent: review actions in stories and decide the feeling that best describes the character.

Week 5
Story Elements:
Characters and Setting
 	
Books
Gaspard at the Seashore, by Anne Gutman
A Weekend with Wendell, by Kevin Henkes
In the Small, Small Pond, by Denise Fleming
 	
Vocabulary
setting, evidence
	RL.K.1. Ask and answer questions about key details in a text.
	
	RL.K.3. Identify characters, settings, and major events in a story.
	
	  ○ Define setting.
	  ○ Identify the setting of a story.
	  ○ Provide evidence for determining the setting of a story.
	
	RL.K.6. Name the author and illustrator of a story and define the role of each in telling the story.
		• Review definition of setting.
		• Read story and point out "clue words" and picture clues to help identify the setting.
		• Independent: determine setting of page and provide written evidence from text and picture clues.
		• Reinforce that all stories have story elements.
		• Read story, focusing on setting and characters.
		• Independent: students will complete the first part of S-T of the S-T-O-R-Y worksheet (should be familiar from read-aloud).

Week 6
Sequence
 	
Books
Pancakes for Breakfast, by Tomie DePaola
Good Dog, Carl, by Alexandra Day
 	
Vocabulary
sequence, order of events, first, next, then, last, finally
	RL.K.1. Ask and answer questions about key details in a text.
	
	RL.K.2. Retell familiar stories, including key details.
	
	RL.K.3. Identify characters, settings, and major events in a story.
	
	  ○ Define sequence.
	  ○ Use sequence words to tell story.
	  ○ Identify the beginning and the ending of a story.
		• Review sequence and sequence words.
		• Introduce picture book, and tell students they will practice using sequence words as they tell the story of the book.
		• After reading, chart the events of the story with students.
		• Independent: draw a picture and write about what happened at the beginning of the story and the end of the story.

Table 3.2 Sample Curriculum: 250–480L

Focus, Texts, and Vocabulary	Standards	Lesson Overview
UNIT 6, Days 1–3 **Informational: text features and main topic** **Texts** "I Have a Dream" by Martin Luther King Jr. *The World Made New*, by Marc Aronson, John W. Glenn *Oil: A Messy Resource*, by Ned Jensen **Vocabulary** informational text, text features, headings, table of contents	• Identify some text features of an informational text (table of contents, headings, and subheadings). • Predict whether a text is fiction or nonfiction using the front cover, back cover, the title, and the author's note. • Identify facts in an informational text. RL.2.12, RI.5	Main Topic: • Read "I Have a Dream" speech. • I Do: teacher think aloud about using the table of contents and heading. • GP: T and S stop and discuss MLK's life. • IP: SW write key parts of MLK's "dream," citing evidence. Table of contents and heading: • Review table of contents and heading. • I Do: TW model answering a question using table of contents and heading. • GP: T and S use table of contents and headings to answer questions about the text. • IP: SW use table of contents and headings to answer questions about the text.

| **UNIT 6, Days 4–7**
Informational: Glossary,
Captions, and Index

Texts:
Mighty Glaciers, by Ned Jensen
The World Made New, by Marc Aronson, John W. Glenn
Endangered Birds, by Rachel Lawson
Flying Machines, by John Meyer
Introducing the Penny, by Jane Sellman

Vocabulary
caption, glossary, bold text, index | • Identify some text features of an informational text (bold text and glossary).
• Use text features to find information in a text.
• Use textual evidence to draw conclusions from informational texts.
• Use background knowledge (schema) to draw conclusions from informational texts.

RL.2.1, 2.RI.4, 2.RI.5, 2.RI.7 | • Intro: review definition of the glossary.
• I Do: TW model answering a question using the glossary.
• GP: T and S use glossary to answer questions about the text.
• IP: SW use glossary to answer questions about the text.

• Intro: review definition of pictures, captions.
• I Do: TW model answering a question using the pictures and captions.
• GP: T and S use pictures and captions to answer questions about the text.
• IP: SW use pictures and captions to answer questions about the text.
• IP: SW complete written responses about a nonfiction text. |

(continued)

Table 3.2 Sample Curriculum: 250–480L *(continued)*

Focus, Texts, and Vocabulary	Standards	Lesson Overview
UNIT 6, Day 8 **Compare and Contrast** **Texts** *Crocs and Gators*, by Kira Freed (Reading A–Z) **Vocabulary** compare and contrast	• Use information in a text to compare and contrast using a Venn diagram. • Use nonfiction text features (photo, illustrations, captions, labels) to support understanding of concepts. • Use text features to find information. • Use textual evidence to draw conclusions from informational texts. RL.2.1, 2.RI.5, 2.RI.9	• Intro: introduce how to compare and contrast using a nonfiction text. • I Do: identify what causes crocodiles and alligators to be similar; chart in Venn diagram. • GP: T and S identify what causes crocodiles and alligators to be similar; chart in Venn diagram. • IP: SW complete written responses about the similarities and differences between crocodiles and alligators.
UNIT 6, Days 9–11 **Articles: Main Idea** **Texts** *Layers of the Rain Forest*, Bessie Coleman, Jackie Robinson **Vocabulary** article	• Determine the point of view in a nonfiction text. • Compare the difference between two opposing points of view on the same topic in a nonfiction text. • Determine the argument they agree with based on the evidence in the nonfiction text. RL.2.1, 2.RI.5, 2.RI.9	• Intro: review how to ID main idea of a text. • I Do: TW identify the main idea of a paragraph and record details. • GP: T and S determine the main idea of each paragraph and record details. • IP: SW identify main idea and complete written responses about the text.

Here's an example of how bottom lines might look in a first-grade teacher's curriculum.

Building the Framework for Your Curriculum

Sample Bottom Lines: 250L–500L

Comprehension	
Assessment Bottom Lines	**Common Core**
DEFINITIONS I—GLOSSARY: Use a glossary to understand definition of key or bolded words in the text.	RI.1.4
CITING EVIDENCE III: Use details and events in a story to support answers to inferential and critical thinking questions.	RL.2.1
TEXT FEATURES II—SUBSECTIONS: Use headings and table of contents to find the right subsection to answer a specific question.	RI.2.5
TEXT FEATURES III—CAPTIONS: Use captions and their corresponding images to understand a core detail or concept from the text.	RI.2.5
COMPARE AND CONTRAST III—IMPORTANT DETAILS: Compare and contrast the most important points presented by two texts on the same topic.	RI.2.9

CONCLUSION: TIME TO BEGIN THE JOURNEY

Our first major task is now complete: we have defined the "what" that we want to teach our students. Through the use of a curriculum aligned to a series of rigorous assessments, students and teachers alike know how far they've come and where they need to go. Once you have created that alignment, you will have completed your road map. What comes next is the "how": How do we follow our road map to maximal success? Now you are ready to embark on the journey!

Apply Your Habits: Assess Your Assessment

Self-Assessment

Conduct an assessment audit: What expectations in the Common Core State Standards might be unaddressed by your assessment?

_____

_____

_____

_____

Tools to Use

- Common Core State Standards, available at http://www.corestandards.org/
- Sample Kindergarten Curriculum Guide: Up to 150L (included on the DVD)
- One-Week Sample Curriculum Guide: 250L– 480L (included on the DVD)

Your Next Steps

_____

_____

_____

_____

_____

_____

_____

Great Habits, Great Readers: A Practical Guide for K–4 Reading in the Light of Common Core, by Paul Bambrick-Santoyo, Aja Settles, and Juliana Worrell. Copyright © 2013 Uncommon Schools and/or Paul Bambrick-Santoyo. Reproduced by permission.

Chapter 4

Read-Aloud Lessons

Teachers Model for Success

Lesson Type	Group Size	What to Teach?
Read-Aloud	**Whole class**	**Skills from yearlong syllabus**
Comprehension Skills	Small group by reading level or whole class if necessary	Skills from yearlong syllabus
Phonics	Small group or whole class if necessary	Skills from premade program
Guided Reading	Small group by reading level	Skills determined by assessment analysis (Chapter Seven)
Independent Reading	Individual	Skills for all students

Ask the next nonteacher you see what he or she remembers about early elementary school, and you're likely to hear about "story time": a teacher reading to an excited group of students. Ask where the teacher sat, and the answer is probably going to be a rocking chair. The image of the early elementary teacher in a "reading rocker" is certainly a familiar one. In fact, it's such a powerful ideal that a 2003 kerfuffle erupted between New York City and its teachers' union after educators got the impression that rocking chairs were going to become a mandatory reading accessory. If there had really been an explicit "rocker rule," it could have been a great boon to the furniture industry; but even as a rumor, it proved a real gift to the city papers' headline writers. (The *New York Daily News* went with "Off Their Rockers."[1])

To give credit where credit is due, the rocker rule did get one thing right: top literacy teachers know that the way their classroom reading area is set up will go a long way toward making read-aloud a success. As we highlighted in Chapter One, setting up a clear area for read-aloud and designing smooth procedures to transition students there is a powerful tool for effective reading instruction. But let's think more carefully about what teaching read-aloud from a rocking chair actually suggests. In our culture, rocking chairs are passive places: places for lazy rocking on a back porch, places of rest for elderly relatives and tiny babies. By association, a policy like the "rocker rule" implies a passive approach to reading to students: read in a relaxed and calm way, letting the words wash over students, and meaningful enrichment will surely follow.

There is no doubt that reading to students has considerable benefits: hearing someone read texts fluently is of key importance for young readers and can prepare them to tackle more and more complex skills. From the "habit" perspective, read-aloud is a key opportunity to learn the right way to practice and to gain more opportunities to practice. And this can certainly be accomplished while seated in a rocking chair. Yet the very best elementary teachers have realized that for these benefits to work, the rocking chair "mentality" must be left behind.

Core Idea

To get the most from read-aloud, leave the rocking chair mentality behind.

To get a sense of what truly effective read-aloud lessons might look like, let's peek into the classrooms of two different teachers: Ms. Indra and Lauren Moyle. We'll start by taking a look at Ms. Indra's class.

Case Study

Ms. Indra's Class Reads Big Smelly Bear

Ms. Indra has been teaching second grade for five years. She's well loved by both her students and her colleagues and achieves good reading results on the whole. However, she's been concerned lately about a few of her students who don't seem to be developing the same proficiency in reading as their peers. She's wondering if there are changes she could make to her read-aloud lessons that would help them progress.

Read-aloud seems to Ms. Indra like a logical place to begin, because it's a favorite part of the day for eager and hesitant readers alike. On this particular day, all her students sit up straight with anticipation at their designated spots on the carpet, their full attention on their teacher. Ms. Indra smiles warmly at them and takes a seat at the front of the carpet, book in hand.

"Okay, class," she announces, "we're going to read a really wonderful book today. It's called *Big Smelly Bear*, and I think you're all really going to like it. As you listen, you'll hear that no one likes Big Smelly Bear because he is so dirty. Will he ever take a bath? Be sure to listen carefully so you can predict what will happen. Let's begin now!"

Ms. Indra reads *Big Smelly Bear* with great expression. The students listen raptly, laughing at all the funny parts of the story. After reading most of the book out loud, Ms. Indra stops reading and asks her class a question: "What do you think will happen next in the story?"

A number of hands pop up. "He still won't take a bath!" one student predicts gleefully. "He's going to get in a fight with the other bear," another suggests. "And maybe he's mad that the fluffy bear won't help him," offers a third.

"Hmm," says Ms. Indra, nodding. "I'm hearing some really interesting predictions. Let's finish reading."

They read on to discover what happens at the end of the story. "Wow!" exclaims Ms. Indra. "Some of our predictions were correct! Wasn't that a great story, everyone?"

"Yes!" the class choruses.

"Excellent," says Ms. Indra. "Good job today, class. Let's transition back to our desks."

Ms. Indra's read-aloud lesson reflected a number of great strengths. She's clearly skilled at classroom management and at bringing joy to her classroom. There's no doubt that reading *Big Smelly Bear* fueled her students' enthusiasm for reading and gave them a better sense of what fluent reading sounds like. Yet you might have also noticed what was missing: students were passive listeners; their participation was limited to making one prediction near the end of the story. So let's help out Ms. Indra: How could she enhance read-aloud lessons to leverage more learning from the same twenty minutes?

Stop and Jot

Having read this summary of Ms. Indra's read-aloud lesson, how do you think she could make read-aloud a richer learning opportunity for more of her students? Jot down the advice you'd give her.

_____

_____

_____

_____

Let's begin a journey with another teacher, Lauren Moyle, who has a lot in common with Ms. Indra. She, too, teaches second grade and is committed to giving each of her students the instruction he or she needs to become a great reader. Here's how one of Lauren's read-aloud lessons unfolds. She is reading the story *Owl Moon*, and her class is focusing in on character motivation as the story evolves. In this clip, Lauren has just finished reading the most important part in the story, where the boy and his father—who have been owl watching without success—finally see an owl. Let's watch how Lauren leverages this critical juncture to help students use their understanding of a character's motivation to understand the boy's feelings in that moment.

 WATCH Clip 13: Lauren Moyle's We Do

Lauren's students were deeply engaged in this lesson, and thanks to her dramatic reading, they got an extremely strong model of how words on a page sound when translated into spoken sentences. Lauren, however, demanded even more of her students. She also used this read-aloud lesson to teach them a specific reading skill—identifying character motivation—both by demonstrating how to use the skill and, in this clip, by inviting the class to try it with her and then with a peer. For Lauren, read-aloud doesn't just mean modeling the decoding of words: it also means modeling what good readers think about as they read.

This increase in rigor brings Lauren's students the richer learning opportunities that Ms. Indra hopes to offer her class. Teaching read-aloud this way gives early readers the opportunity to glean as much wisdom as possible from an expert reader, so that when the time comes for them to do all the work of reading on their own, they'll know what to do. We'll spend the remainder of this chapter showing how to plan and teach a read-aloud lesson like Lauren's. The box "Read-Aloud Lessons" offers a quick overview of what such a lesson looks like.

Read-Aloud Lessons

Read-aloud lessons offer deep modeling and extended group practice with a text. Use these to introduce and demonstrate a skill that students will apply independently later on.

Lesson prework	Teacher plans read-aloud lesson focused on a precise objective.
Lesson introduction 5 minutes	Teacher gets students excited and introduces them to the reading skill they will learn.
I Do 5 minutes	Teacher models how readers apply the reading skill.
We Do 7–12 minutes	Teacher and students practice the reading skill together.
Check for understanding 3 minutes	Students briefly practice using the skill and describe how readers apply this skill.

TOTAL LESSON TIME = 25–45 MINUTES

You may notice that this read-aloud lesson bears many similarities to a traditional guided practice lesson that follows an "I Do, We Do, You Do" structure: the teacher models the skill being taught, the teacher and students work together to practice the skill, and then the students practice the skill independently.

When it comes to read-aloud, however, an authentic You Do can't take place, because the teacher is doing most or all of the reading. Accordingly, we've labeled the final activity in read-aloud as "check for understanding" instead of You Do. As we continue through the other types of reading lessons in this book, you'll see that in other cases, students take on the work of independent reading practice more fully, making the term You Do a more appropriate one to use.

Let's take a closer look at each component of a read-aloud lesson.

LESSON PREWORK: PLANNING FOR READ-ALOUD

Remember how excited both Ms. Indra's and Lauren's students were about read-aloud? Both teachers picked texts that their students enjoyed, and that made their lessons fun and engaging. One crucial factor that brought Lauren's lesson up to a higher level of rigor, though, was that she didn't pick a book to read to her students only on the basis of whether they would like it; instead, she intentionally chose one that would help them learn to identify character motivation, which was the skill they most urgently needed to work on at that time. Teaching a great read-aloud lesson begins with this kind of planning: selecting a text that will teach students what they need to learn, and determining exactly how you'll use the text to teach the skill.

We'll break down the steps of this planning process as follows:

1. Pick the text to match the skill.

2. Pick stopping points to teach the skill.

3. Create an anchor chart.

Pick the Text to Match the Skill

Some have interpreted the Common Core to suggest that read-aloud is primarily a place to expose students to texts above their grade level and build content knowledge. Others have traditionally used this time to model comprehension skills. We feel you should do both. Building content knowledge while modeling skills students need leverages read-aloud to serve your students most effectively. You don't have to—and shouldn't—sacrifice skill instruction at the altar of text complexity, or vice versa. If you recall from our introduction, text complexity is only meaningful if we are developing student skills to match it. And skill instruction soars when students are challenged to approach increasingly complex material on a subject they are learning about. To plan the most effective read-alouds, we'll need a balanced approach.

The first step of planning your read-aloud lesson is to identify the single reading skill you most urgently need to teach your students—and to select a text that includes the richest opportunities possible for readers to use this skill. Identifying the right skill is fairly straightforward: if you've followed the assessment and curriculum design processes we detailed in Chapter Three, you've already done it. Once you have these tools in place to tell you what your students need to master next, you know what to teach during read-aloud.

Core Idea

You don't need to spend time considering which skill to target in read-aloud. A good assessment will have already told you.

As you proceed to pick out a text that will help you teach this skill, a good rule of thumb is to choose a text one to two grade levels higher than the level at which your students are reading. Because you're the one who will be doing the work of reading the text, read-aloud is more about "listening comprehension" than it is about reading comprehension. Most students are able to comprehend texts at a higher level during read-aloud than they would be able to while reading independently.

Once you've selected a text, it's important to read it all the way through as a reader in your own right. Why? To simulate the authentic experience your students will have when you read them the text. When something in a story makes you as a reader laugh, think, or feel a certain emotion, ask yourself how the author sparked that reaction in you. Knowing why you react to the text in a certain way will help you anticipate how your students will react to it—and determine whether that moment will be good for teaching the skill you want to teach.

For more details about selecting the right text for the lesson you need to teach, look to Chapter Eight.

A Word on... Read-Aloud and Content-Area Instruction: Climbing the Ladder of Text Complexity

Because 70 to 80 percent of your literacy block will focus on narrative texts, most of the time your read-aloud lessons will dive into those. When you're teaching content-area classes, however, you have a key opportunity to develop students' knowledge using informational texts. In fact, the educators we work with find read-aloud the perfect tool for teaching science or social studies. There's only one adjustment: in your literacy block, the skill you are modeling takes center stage; in content-area instruction, the content becomes primary, and the skill plays second fiddle.

Even outside the literacy block, read-aloud presents a key opportunity to supercharge your students' literacy development. A growing body of research suggests that students learn reading skills fastest when they are reading about material they already know something about. When students develop their knowledge base about a topic, their ability to make inferences about it or determine the meaning of new vocabulary words dramatically increases. If you've ever wondered how students can possibly pick up enough vocabulary words to be literate, here is your answer. Direct instruction and determining words from context are pathways to development, but building background knowledge acts as force multiplier for student growth.[a] Sometimes this is called a "Matthew effect," referring to the idea that in literacy, the rich get richer and the poor get poorer.

If we are looking to provide our students with multiple opportunities to broaden their content-area knowledge, read-aloud texts can be clustered around a content area that students are studying in the science, arts, or social studies portions of your curriculum. Doing this will not only allow you to model the skills you have targeted but also give you the chance to broaden students' knowledge area on a subject. David Coleman, one of the architects of the CCSS, notes that the standards are designed to encourage this sort of synergy, both within your grade levels and between them.[b] Not only will utilizing read-aloud in content lessons naturally bring more informational texts to your curriculum, but you'll be able to significantly increase these texts' complexity as students build an understanding of the topic. As it turns out, the more your class already knows about a specific subject, the faster they can use reading—even when it's of complex texts—to supplement that knowledge.

Assembling read-aloud books simultaneously by skill and content area is a herculean task, and may not be something that you'll have time for in the immediate future. Recognizing that gathering texts in this fashion will take time, some groups are already providing clustered read-aloud materials to help teachers quickly find materials linked around specific subject matter.[c] However, there is a danger to these lists—they may not include the right choices to develop the literacy skills your students most need. If you're just getting started, we recommend that you stick to clustering texts during your social studies and science blocks. Linking read-aloud lessons to content-area learning is an important goal, but it is secondary to mastering the selection of skill-appropriate texts.

[a]Adams, M. J. (2010). Advancing our students' language and literacy. *American Educator, 34*(4), 3–11.
[b]Coleman, D. (2011). *Bringing the Common Core to life.* Retrieved from http://usny.nysed.gov /rttt/docs/bringingthecommoncoretolife/part4transcript.pdf.
[c]EngageNY. (2012). Grades K-2 core knowledge language arts listening and learning files. Retrieved from http://engageny.org/resource/grades-k-2-core-knowledge-language-arts-listening -and-learning-files.

Pick Stopping Points to Teach the Skill

Once you've picked out the right text, you'll choose a few points within it to pause in your reading and use those opportunities to teach the key skill. These moments are critical for both the I Do and the We Do value of a read-aloud lesson, as the teacher uses them to instigate both modeling and practicing of the skill. To identify a great moment in the text to pause, simply ask yourself, "Is this point in the text the best opportunity for my students and me to put the skill we're working on into action?" If the answer is yes, then you've picked the right time for modeling and practice.

To keep your students' general understanding of the text you're reading where it needs to be, it is important that you not plan too many stopping points. Imagine if you were reading a novel or a newspaper and had to pause and answer a question after every few paragraphs—most of us would stop reading in disgust. Students, too, need to be able to listen to you read for more sustained periods of time before pausing to answer questions. Choosing just two or three strong stopping points, as opposed to a large number of mediocre ones, will both keep your students interested in the text and give them time to gather enough information about it to answer your questions well. The most successful reading teachers we observed found it helpful to use sticky notes to mark the pages of their intended stopping points in the book. That held them accountable for pausing only when they'd planned to do so.

Table 4.1 Sample Anchor Chart for Read-Aloud

What does the character do or say?	What does the author want us to know about the character?
Page 2—Sadie skips all the way to school.	[To be filled in during the lesson] Sadie likes going to school.
Page 6—Sadie interrupts her teacher without raising her hand.	[To be filled in during the lesson] Sadie is impatient.

Create an Anchor Chart

Another tool that serves many great literacy teachers well during read-aloud lessons is an anchor chart. Written on chart paper or easel paper, the anchor chart is a graphic depiction of how the reading strategy you're teaching works, and tracks how you implement it over the course of the lesson. To show how this works, Table 4.1 presents one example of an anchor chart on characterization: how characters' words or actions reveal their traits.

As you see noted in the chart, you only need to complete one column of the anchor chart in advance of the read-aloud lesson: the one that shows the text evidence you'll use to model or practice the skill you're teaching. Your students will help you fill in the second half of the chart as you teach the lesson.

Providing an anchor chart ensures that you reach the more visual learners in your class. Furthermore, it gives all your students a way to remember what they've learned as the lesson continues and after the lesson ends. Once the anchor chart has been filled out, you can post it on a classroom wall, and students will be able to refer to it again and again throughout the school year.

When you know which text to read to your students and how to use it to teach a skill, you're ready to teach a read-aloud lesson. Let's dive into read-aloud lesson delivery, beginning with the lesson introduction.

LESSON INTRODUCTION: MAKING IT CLEAR AND MAKING IT MATTER

A well-known psychological research study took place in a setting all too familiar to most teachers: a big line in front of a Xerox machine.[2] For research purposes, two different people asked others in the line if they could move to the front. The first person received a predictable answer—he was told to wait his turn, as the rest of the people there had been waiting long before his arrival. But the second person didn't just ask to cut in the line: he also explained why he felt that h urgently needed to get his copying done first. People let him. The lesson of the study is a simple one: when someone explains *why* doing something is important, we're more likely to do it.

The same principle applies to teaching reading. When you set out to teach a read-aloud lesson, you're setting out to model a certain reading strategy so that students will grow adept at using it themselves. And as the Xerox machine study suggests, students will get the most out of the lesson when they understand—right from the start—why that strategy matters.

There are three steps to a great introduction for a read-aloud:

1. Hook the reader.
2. Identify the skill.
3. Preview the text.

Hook the Reader

Let's take our story about the individual who successfully cut the line to the Xerox machine a step further. Would it have been enough if he had stated his reason for wanting to cut in a bland, dispassionate voice, as if it didn't *really* matter whether he got his copying done? We don't think so. His success wasn't just about giving information: it was about making it seem urgent and necessary. In order to convince his listeners, he had to hook them.

Teaching read-aloud is no different. Here are some types of hooks that the most successful reading teachers we've worked with have used to build a class's enthusiasm for a read-aloud lesson.

- **Create suspense.** The most common and effective way to hook early readers is to introduce the lesson in a way that makes them feel as though reading this story is one of the most exciting things they'll do all day. Build suspense, and students will be eager to dive into the story.

- **Make a real-world connection.** Unsurprisingly, connecting the day's read-aloud activities to the world with which your students are familiar can give them a much keener understanding of why those activities matter. Your real-world connection can be any anecdote or comparison your students will be able to relate to—it could come from your classroom or even from your own life.

- **Perform a skit.** We've seen a number of teachers create extremely effective read-aloud hooks by performing skits for their classes. For example, one teacher introduced a lesson on making inferences by miming eating a snack, and asking her students how they were able to tell that she was eating without being told explicitly. Note, however, that a skit must be *short*—just one to two minutes—keeping you safely within your total lesson introduction time of five to eight minutes. Otherwise, it may derail the rest of the lesson.

Note that none of these activities do any of the work of comprehending the text: they hook the students without giving anything away!

A Word on . . . Read-Aloud and Vocabulary Acquisition

Learning new vocabulary is a critical component of the development of literacy skills. A particularly sobering statistic confirming this importance is that the average low-income five-year-old enters kindergarten having been exposed to thirty million fewer words than his or her high-income peer.[a] The CCSS, the National Reading Panel,[b] and everyone in between have concurred on the need to increase vocabulary acquisition.

In *Bringing Words to Life*, Isabel Beck drives home that the most effective instruction involves immersing students in the words in multiple forms, both indirectly and through direct instruction.[c] Through this type of instruction, it is estimated that students can be explicitly taught approximately four hundred words per year in school. Not being able to teach all of the words necessary, vocabulary instruction must also include indirect instruction. Read-aloud can play a vital role, given that you are choosing texts that are above the students' reading level and thus are likely to include the perfect words to develop with the students.

It is easy to include vocabulary instruction as a part of the read-aloud structure, allotting time at the beginning of read-aloud to teach vocabulary from Text Talk (Isabel Beck) or—even better—from the read-aloud text itself. Teachers can provide specific word instruction prior to or after reading. This helps both vocabulary learning and reading comprehension. The instruction should be spiraled and repeated throughout the week so that students have multiple exposures to the words.

There are only six words presented in a Text Talk book, and the rule of thumb should be to introduce no more than eight words during any given read-aloud. When the lesson focuses on words that are critically important to the comprehension of the text and words whose meaning cannot easily be derived from context, students will be more likely to apply these words in their normal speech.

Even as you include this in your read-aloud, remember: even if you teach sixteen hundred words per year—quadruple the number Beck recommends—you still will never close the thirty-million-word gap. The best way to develop vocabulary, then, is to read voraciously and get to higher reading levels as quickly as possible, where vocabulary acquisition increases exponentially. That's why we'll spend most of this section devoted to accelerating students' reading development.

[a]Hart, B., & Risley, T. R. (2003). The early catastrophe: The 30 million word gap. *American Educator, 27*(1), 4–9.
[b]National Reading Panel. (2000). *Teaching children to read: An evidence-based assessment of the scientific research literature on reading and its implications for reading instruction.* Bethesda, MD: National Institute of Child Health and Human Development.
[c]Beck, I. L., McKeown, M. G., & Kucan, L. (2002). *Bringing words to life: Robust vocabulary instruction.* New York, NY: Guilford Press.

Identify the Skill

The hook gets students excited about what they're about to learn. The next step—identifying the reading skill to be taught—clarifies exactly what that is, focusing students on the lesson ahead. There are two steps to making sure you identify the skill effectively. First, it's vital to define it in precise, student-friendly language. A vague or convoluted definition won't prevent student confusion—on the contrary, it might create it.

Let's go back to Lauren's classroom to see how this works.

WATCH Clip 14: Lauren Moyle's Lesson Introduction

What Lauren has done is follow a very simple method for defining a skill, as shown in Table 4.2.

Table 4.2 Read-Aloud Introduction: How to Define a Skill

Skill Introduction	Teacher Might Say...
Name the skill.	"Readers, today we are going to look closely at character traits."
Define the skill.	"Character traits are ways we describe what a character is like based on what the character says or does."
Explain why readers use the skill.	"Good readers pay close attention to character actions so that they can determine character traits and understand what a character is like."
Model how to apply the skill. • K–1: cite evidence • 2–4: justify the evidence	"For example, in the book we read yesterday, *Mufaro's Beautiful Daughters*, I remember when Manyara said, 'I am certain that Father loves you best...but your silly kindness is only weakness.' What did that tell us about Manyara? Yes, it tells us that she's jealous of Nyasha and mean. That helps us understand what Manyara is like."
Have students state what they will do to help them understand the text as they read.	"What can we, as good readers, do if we want to understand what a character is like? That's right, we can pay close attention to the character's actions and use them to figure out character traits."

Then, before moving on to the next step of the introduction, Lauren double-checks that the students have understood her definition of the skill. She utilizes one of the most efficient ways of doing this: asking for a choral response. Every time Lauren asked her students for a choral response, 100 percent of her students gave the response right on time. This way, before she proceeded with the lesson, she knew that every student was ready for it.

Preview the Text

At this point in the read-aloud introduction, you've thoroughly introduced the skill you're going to teach, but you still haven't introduced the book you're going to read! Your next step, then, is to provide your students with a preview of the text, tying it back to the skill around which the lesson will focus.

Planning a text preview is a good time to put your authenticity goggles back on—that is, to think once again about yourself as a reader. How do you preview a book when you look at it in a bookstore? Typically, you pick it up, make some observations about the front and back cover, and perhaps look at the table of contents or the first few sentences. If you were holding a novel, you might try to figure out whether it was part of a series; for a biography, you'd want to identify which parts of the subject's life most interested the biographer. You can preview a text with students in a very similar manner: look at the front cover, look at the back cover, read text that appears on either, and state (or ask students to predict) basic information about what the day's reading will be about.

At this moment, we should take time to address the concept of previewing a text in light of the Common Core. In the trainings around implementing CCSS, Common Core author David Coleman and others have warned that previewing a text can lower the rigor of the comprehension work that a student needs to do. It is important to distinguish this commentary from what we're discussing here.

As we mentioned earlier in this chapter, the true You Do of reading—whereby students apply the skills of reading—occurs in guided reading and independent reading. Read-aloud is the first entry point on the continuum of learning to read, focusing much more on I Do and We Do. As such, it is the most scaffolded of all the lesson types presented in this book. How?

- The teacher holds the text and does most (if not all) the reading.

- The teacher models the strategy.

- Students apply a comprehension strategy while *listening*, not reading.

For this reason, a text preview for read-aloud includes far more scaffolding than an introduction for any of the other reading lesson types we will cover in this book. For comprehension skills lessons or guided reading lessons, you'll see us describe much more minimal introductions that leave more cognitive work for the students to do.

That said, you may choose to conduct more minimal text previews even for read-aloud as students advance to higher reading levels. Table 4.3 outlines how we'd recommend that you adjust your text previews to match students' progress.

One last note about previewing the text: if you've read part of it in a previous day's read-aloud, it will be important to review with students what they've already heard. The review should be fast paced so that you can move on quickly to the

Table 4.3 Previewing the Text: Adjusting to the Development of the Reader

Student Reading Level	Appropriate Way to Preview the Text
Up to 100L	Teacher previews text for students: focus on pictures, front and back covers.
100–300L	Teacher teaches students how to preview text themselves: include first pages.
300–500L	Students preview the text themselves.
500L+	Students preview the text themselves and identify possible themes.

heart of the current lesson. One extremely effective strategy is to ask students questions that review the story line, such as the following:

- Who can summarize what we read yesterday?

- What happened first in the story we read yesterday?

- Okay, now someone else tell me what happened next.

Now let's follow Lauren Moyle's class through the remaining components of a read-aloud lesson: I Do, We Do, and check for understanding.

I DO: MODELING THE SKILL

After you have introduced your read-aloud lesson, you can get right to the heart of it: reading the text and modeling use of the key reading skill.

As you read out loud, you should demonstrate excellent, phrased reading—exactly what you expect from students when they read. The key is to make the reading engaging, with an emphasis on great intonation and pacing. Then, as we've mentioned, you should stop at those passages that you have marked as effective opportunities for modeling the specific skill you're teaching that day. Let's look at this video of Lauren modeling a skill.

 WATCH Clip 15: Lauren Moyle's I Do

At first glance, it is striking that Lauren includes her students so much in the I Do part of her lesson. But if you look at the clip closely, you'll see that they're simply repeating the definitions of the reading strategies that they learned in the lesson introduction. Lauren, in contrast, is doing all the heavy lifting of comprehension, modeling it for them.

When you model, you're letting students inside your head as you use the skill they're learning. For this reason, we call this modeling during read-aloud the "think-aloud." Components of a successful think-aloud are

- **Precise, preplanned language that ties back to the skill.**

- **A cue in and out of the think-aloud.** You probably noticed that Lauren prefaced her think-aloud by reminding her students, "I'm in his [the character's] head." Saying something like "I'm thinking" or "I'm wondering" also works well, as these phrases alert students that you are inviting them into your thinking process. When, at the end of the think-aloud, you clearly state, "Now let's go back to the text," you let them know that you're going to continue reading.

- **Use of an anchor chart.** Here you get even more use out of your anchor chart (see the sample anchor chart in Table 4.1). After presenting your thinking to your class (but before saying "back to the text"), you'll add it into the chart, giving students a way to see, as well as hear, the thought process you're modeling.

WE DO: PRACTICING THE SKILL

When you pause in your reading of the text, it's time not only for the I Do (modeling the skill) but also for the We Do (practicing it).

The We Do will only be effective if you modeled effectively in the I Do and you plan to ask questions that target the precise skills you want students to learn with this text. To that end, the most effective reading teachers we observed came to class prepared not only with the questions they would ask of students but also with a list of student answers they predicted they might receive. For maximum preparation, after writing your questions, either copy them on the sticky notes you've used to prepare the text you're reading, or cut them out directly from the lesson plan and tape them inside the text. This ensures not only that you are stopping where you planned to stop but also that you are ready to jump in immediately when students are struggling.

Let's take another look at the clip from Lauren's class that we watched at the beginning of this chapter. How does Lauren use pre-scripted questions to get her students to practice a reading skill?

REWATCH Clip 13: Lauren Moyle's We Do

In this clip, Lauren avoided a common practice pitfall: for the teacher and one other student to end up being the only two people speaking. To ensure that all students learn to use the skill you're teaching, it's crucial to have 100 percent participation during practice. The tactic Lauren used to make that happen here is called Turn and Talk: the teacher asks a question and then, rather than calling on one student, has all students turn and talk with a predesignated partner about the answer. The best times to use Turn and Talk are

- When you're asking a question that is directly related to the objective.
- When all students have their hand up to respond to a question.
- When you're asking a critical thinking question.

A Turn and Talk serves not only as a guarantee that all students must think and discuss the text but also as a means of checking for understanding. While students confer with their partners, teachers like Lauren walk around the carpet and listen to the conversations they are having. This will provide you with a quick assessment of each student's comprehension and application of the skill. It will also clue you in to how well they're implementing the habits of discussion, which are integral to effective use of Turn and Talk.

What can you do if your students produce off-track responses during the We Do? Use the same universal prompts we presented at the beginning of Chapter Two on the habits of discussion. As we stated there, prompting without revealing what answer you're looking for is the optimal way to get students more comfortable with expanding and deepening their answers—and to get a better sense of what they're thinking.

CHECK FOR UNDERSTANDING: MAKE SURE YOUR PRACTICE WAS GOOD PRACTICE

Checking for understanding is integral not only when students go into Turn and Talk but throughout the rest of the time you spend on practice, too. Although practicing always lies at the foundation of forming great habits, it only works if it's *good* practicing—and it's only when you check for understanding that you discover whether practice has been good or poor in quality. In read-aloud, checking for understanding is how you learn whether you've successfully left the rocking chair mentality behind or not.

The typical way to check for understanding at the end of a read-aloud lesson is to ask one final critical thinking question that nails the reading skill that the lesson targeted, take responses from students, and then recap the strategy that the students learned in this lesson. Here's how Lauren completed her lesson.

 WATCH Clip 16: Lauren Moyle's Check for Understanding

Lauren's students are able not only to use their understanding of character motivation to deepen their comprehension of the story but also to do the metacognitive work of explaining what they have done. Think back to the very beginning of this chapter, when we first considered how teachers could do more with read-aloud than simply get students more excited about reading. Lauren has met that challenge full force, and by the end of her twenty-minute lesson, it's clear that her students are benefiting immensely from her success.

To make sure that you check all students for understanding, you must get each one of them to answer the final critical thinking question. As you saw, Laura uses Turn and Talk to this end. However, as students advance to higher reading levels, the final check for understanding in read-aloud can also be a great time to get them to practice writing. If you go this route, you'll want to send all students back to their desks to write out an answer to the critical thinking question. When do we recommend this? Table 4.5 will show the trajectory.

Meanwhile, now that we've worked through each component of a read-aloud lesson, let's see what those components look like when we put them all together in a lesson plan (see Table 4.4).

Table 4.4 Read-Aloud Lesson Plan

TITLE:	Horrible Harry Moves Up to Third Grade	AUTHOR:	Suzy Kline	GENRE:	Narrative Fiction

<table>
<tr>
<td rowspan="4" style="text-align:center">Lesson Prework</td>
<td colspan="2">OBJECTIVE(S)</td>
</tr>
<tr>
<td colspan="2">

• Students will be able to define cause and effect.
• Students will be able to identify the cause-and-effect relationship between characters in a story.

</td>
</tr>
<tr>
<td colspan="2">GRAPHIC ORGANIZER(S)</td>
</tr>
<tr>
<td colspan="2">

• Cause-and-effect anchor chart
• Cause-and-effect definitions
• Cause-and-effect graphic organizer

Cause	Effect

</td>
</tr>
</table>

Lesson Intro	• "Students, yesterday my mom and I were talking on the phone. She said that she was planning my dad's surprise party and that she didn't know how she would get everything done in time for the party on Saturday. What do you think I did when she told me that? Yes, I hopped in the car and headed over to her house to help with the planning!" • "Students, this is a perfect example of cause and effect. Cause is WHY something happens, and effect is WHAT happens." Teacher will repeat two more times and then have students chorally respond with "Cause is [choral response: WHY something happens], and effect is [choral response: WHAT happens]." • "Last night, the EFFECT or WHAT happened because my mom told me she didn't think she could get everything done is that I drove to her house to help." (Teacher will chart in the graphic organizer as an effect example.) "The CAUSE of my driving to my mom's house or WHY I drove to my mom's house is that she told me she didn't know how she would get everything done in time for the party on Saturday." (Teacher will chart this in the graphic organizer as a cause example.) • "Today, we are going to talk about cause and effect in a fictional story because cause and effect moves the plot of a story along, making events happen. To do this, we will read our first chapter book, and you will be reading about characters that all of you know well—the characters in *Horrible Harry*! As we read *Horrible Harry*, we are going to focus specifically on the cause-and-effect relationship between the characters in the text and how one character's actions impact another character's actions." • Teacher will preview text (front cover, back cover, and first page). ○ "After previewing, I already have a clue about the cause-and-effect relationship in this text. From the back cover, it is clear that Harry and Sydney are sworn enemies, and when Sydney kills Harry's spider, it causes Harry to want to get revenge. As we begin reading, we will have to figure out more about the relationship between Harry and Sydney."

Table 4.4 Read-Aloud Lesson Plan (*continued*)

TITLE:	*Horrible Harry Moves Up to Third Grade*	AUTHOR:	Suzy Kline	GENRE:	Narrative Fiction

	• "Remember, cause is WHY something happens, and effect is WHAT happens." Teacher will repeat two more times and then have students chorally respond: "Cause is [choral response: WHY something happens], and effect is [choral response: WHAT happens]."
I Do and We Do	**[Q-Question; TA-Think Aloud; F-Factual; I-Inferential; CT-Critical thinking]** • **p. 1 (TA)** The narrator, Doug, just gave a clue that there was a problem on the first day of school. Let's read to find out what is CAUSING this problem on the first day. • **p. 3 (Q, I) Why do they think Mr. Moulder is hiding Ms. Mackle?** Ms. Mackle used to teach in Room 2B, and that is where Doug and Harry expected their class to be. Now Mr. Moulder is teaching in her classroom, and they are confused about what happened to Ms. Mackle. • **p. 5 (Q, I) Why did they scream?** Instead of being greeted by Ms. Chan, they were greeted by Ms. Zaharek, who was not their old kindergarten teacher. This CAUSED them to scream. Now they are very confused with the changes at their school. *Teacher will think aloud:* The boys are confused because everything at school seems to have been changed—this is the cause. The effect is that they scream when they see the new kindergarten teacher. This is an example of cause and effect. *Teacher will chart cause and effect.* • **p. 7 (Q, I) Why didn't the boys know which classroom to go to?** The **effect** of the boys not reading the number on their report card was that they went to the wrong room. They should have gone to room 3B. *Teacher will think aloud:* The **effect** of forgetting to read their report card was that they thought there were in the wrong school and got confused. *Teacher will chart cause and effect.* • **p. 11 (Q, CT) Why is Doug worried?** Doug is worried because he thinks that everything is going to change in third grade. The first day has already been full of so many changes that he is worried that everything might be different in third grade, too. • **p. 15 (Q, I) What is the relationship between Harry and Sydney like?** Harry and Sydney do not get along very well. Sydney does something silly and then Harry gets mad and decides to get revenge. *Teacher will think aloud:* This is an example of a cause-and-effect relationship. Sydney does something silly, which is the effect. Then it starts a new cause, which is Harry getting revenge on Sydney. Harry gets revenge because he doesn't like what Sydney did. *Teacher will chart cause and effect.* STOP at p. 15.

(*continued*)

Table 4.4 Read-Aloud Lesson Plan (*continued*)

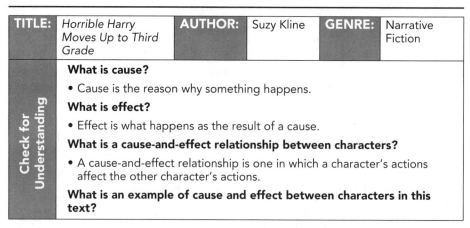

TITLE:	*Horrible Harry Moves Up to Third Grade*	AUTHOR:	Suzy Kline	GENRE:	Narrative Fiction
Check for Understanding	**What is cause?** • Cause is the reason why something happens. **What is effect?** • Effect is what happens as the result of a cause. **What is a cause-and-effect relationship between characters?** • A cause-and-effect relationship is one in which a character's actions affect the other character's actions. **What is an example of cause and effect between characters in this text?**				

Table 4.5 Check for Understanding: Match to Students' Reading Level

Students' Reading Level	To Check for Understanding...
Up to 300L	Have students do a Turn and Talk.
300–600L	Have students either do a Turn and Talk or produce a written response.
600L+	Have students produce a written response.

CONCLUSION: WHAT GREAT READING LOOKS LIKE

Humans learn largely by paying close attention to role models, and during read-aloud, great reading teachers leverage that way of learning to their students' advantage. By setting an example of what great reading looks like—in terms of both decoding and comprehension—teachers give students an exciting glimpse of what great readers can accomplish; and by approaching read-aloud from the habit-building perspective, those same teachers can give students a first taste of what great reading *feels* like, too. From there, students are in a prime position to practice their reading skills even more and to get a chance to try them independently. We'll cover this in Chapters Five and Six, where we look at comprehension skills and phonics lessons.

Read-Aloud: Key Guidelines to Remember

Preparation (Prework Before the Lesson Begins)

- Flag the text. (Premark book for stopping and thinking points.)
- Prepare anchor chart and post.

Lesson Introduction

Teacher explains exactly what the students will do
8 min (new skill); 6 min (review of skill)

- [Optional] Start with a vocabulary mini-lesson (Beck's Text Talk, or words from the text).
- Include a hook or catchy opening (skit, metaphor, real-world connection, choral review of previous skills and strategies).
- Introduce and define reading skill.
  - Precise and student-friendly
  - Check for understanding: choral response and student hand gestures
- Preview the text.
  - Adjusted to the reading level of the students (in other words, students do more of the previewing themselves as they progress in their reading levels)
  - Tied to the objective
- Summarize the previous day's reading (if a continuation of book).
  - Fast paced
  - Includes bridging from the teacher (if needed)
  - Includes questions that review plot

I Do
Teacher models exactly what the students will do
5 min

- Read the text while modeling fluency; remember to bring the drama!
- Conduct a think-aloud.
  - Use precise, scripted language on targeted skill.
  - Cue students in and out ("I'm realizing/thinking . . . " "Now back to the text").
  - Chart thinking (as needed).
  - Teach vocabulary (as it is encountered in the text).

(continued)

(continued)

We Do

Teacher continues to model; students begin to practice
12 min

- Continue to think aloud.
- Continue to teach vocabulary.
- Ask targeted questions that build to the objective. (Often the big question related to the skill might be the final question rather than repeated continuously, as would happen with "theme.")
  - Utilize Turn and Talk for inference and critical thinking questions.
  - Use strategic universal prompts to deepen understanding or address student confusion.

Check for Understanding

Teacher reviews and reinforces targeted skill
3 min

- Ask a critical thinking question that nails the targeted skill.
- Ensure that all students have an opportunity to answer.
  - Up to 300L: Turn and Talk
  - 300L–600L: Turn and Talk or written student response
  - 600L+: written student response
- All students answer, recapping how they applied the skill to the reading.

Great Habits, Great Readers: A Practical Guide for K–4 Reading in the Light of Common Core, by Paul Bambrick-Santoyo, Aja Settles, and Juliana Worrell. Copyright © 2013 Uncommon Schools and/or Paul Bambrick-Santoyo. Reproduced by permission.

Apply Your Habits: Improve Read-Aloud

Self-Assessment

Which of the read-aloud practices we described will have the biggest impact on student learning in your class?

_____

_____

_____

_____

Tools to Use

- Read-Aloud: Key Guidelines to Remember (also included in the Appendix and on the DVD)
- Sample Read-Aloud Lesson Plan (included on the DVD)
- Professional development materials

Your Next Steps

_____

_____

_____

_____

_____

_____

Chapter 5

Teaching Comprehension Skills

Stanza by Stanza

Lesson Type	Group Size	What to Teach?
Read-Aloud	Whole class	Skills from yearlong syllabus
Comprehension Skills	**Small group by reading level or whole class if necessary**	**Skills from yearlong syllabus**
Phonics	Small group or whole class if necessary	Skills from premade program
Guided Reading	Small group by reading level	Skills determined by assessment analysis (Chapter Seven)
Independent Reading	Individual	Skills for all students

Think of a violin prodigy, and chances are good you'll think of speed. The performances that seem most impressive to an outside audience are fast paced indeed: the fastest violinist in the world plays more than 14 notes per second, or close to 840 notes per minute. Given this astonishing rate, it would make sense that the best violin teaching and coaching occurs at such a speed, working to practice as fast as possible.

Dig a bit deeper, however, and a different picture emerges. Those musicians who have learned most effectively and fluently certainly have the capability to play quickly, but their actual learning occurred very differently. Nowhere is this principle more salient than at Meadowmount music school. Among elite musicians, Meadowmount has long been renowned for packing an incredible amount of growth into just a few months of time. In fact, the school advertises that it can fit a year's worth of growth into just seven weeks.[1] Walk into a practice room, however, and you're likely to meet a deeply unfamiliar—and deeply unsettling—cacophony: the sound of music being played at a radically decelerated speed. As one Meadowmount teacher noted, if you can recognize the song being played, practice is too fast.[2] Instead, the approach is to move one note at a time, ensure that every single stanza is mastered, and to move on only when mastery is reached.

This approach does not only apply to concert violinists. Imagine the novice piano player. Eventually when you play the piano, your fingers do the thinking for you: you're not concentrating on how your finger presses down on the black F-sharp key. But as you start learning to play D major chords, you have to slow down and watch your middle finger press down on the F-sharp key. Then you play the chord without looking at the keys, then with the other notes in one stanza, then in longer stretches, and finally embedded in an entire musical piece. You wouldn't be able to play the whole piece right away without all that preparation—but with it, your abilities develop at a surprisingly high rate.

Meadowmount is on to something. For those complex skills that require demanding and nuanced habits, the best learning occurs when skills are broken down and built back up systematically, one on top of the other. In few areas is this as clear as with the multitude of skills that make up reading: the teachers who see the best results design lessons that zoom in on one individual skill and teach it to mastery, then layer that skill into the greater body of reading work. This level of specificity and depth gives each reading skill plenty of room to grow, and it builds a comprehensive set of such skills, which can then—like the many notes in a symphony—be used correctly all at once.

Core Idea

Students master comprehension as a musician masters a symphony—one stanza at a time.

So what would Meadowmount-style reading instruction look like in action? Practicing one reading skill at a time, at each text difficulty level, and then integrating them into the act of reading. Comprehension skills lessons pick up where read-aloud lessons leave off. To use the analogy of the piano player, these two lesson types get students to focus on pressing each key in a D-major chord, which they'll later use to play full-length piano pieces in the key of D major during guided reading. Comprehension skills lessons teach similar skills to those taught in read-aloud lessons, but they diverge from them in one very significant way: comprehension skills lessons place their emphasis on a You Do, during which students practice a skill independently.

Let's translate this concept into concrete terms: the structural elements of a comprehension skills lesson (see the box "Comprehension Skills Lessons").

Comprehension Skills Lessons

Comprehension skills lessons teach skills through the traditional I Do, We Do, You Do instructional design. Use these lessons to give your students practice with a new reading skill or to reinforce a previously taught one.

Lesson Prework	Teacher plans the comprehension skills lesson, including anchor chart and key comprehension questions.
I Do 5–10 minutes	Teacher models the reading skill.
We Do 10–15 minutes	Teacher and students practice the reading skill together.
You Do 10–20 minutes	Students practice the reading skill independently.

TOTAL LESSON TIME = 25–45 MINUTES

Even a quick glance at any comprehension skills lesson plan reveals the critical importance of independent practice to this lesson type. Of course, that doesn't mean that the other components of the lesson aren't important, too. Let's walk through the details of executing each piece effectively.

LESSON PREWORK: "TEACH THE READER" MEETS "TEACH THE TEXT"

Eighty percent of the success of a comprehension skills lesson comes in the preparation. This preparation involves three key actions:

1. Prepare the text for the readers.

2. Design "Teach the Reader" and "Teach the Text" questions.

3. Chart your thinking.

Let's look at each action in detail.

Prepare the Text for the Readers

Effective reading instructors take time to ensure that their plans can be seamlessly put into action during the lesson. As with read-aloud, one of the easiest but most powerful steps is to "flag" the book you will be teaching at any critical points where the students will be able to apply the skill you are targeting. You can flag these areas with sticky notes or other means of note-taking. This way, you'll know exactly when to stop reading the book and work on the key skill you're teaching.

A Word on ... Text Selection for Comprehension Skills Lessons

Because students can comprehend text they read as a group at a higher level than text they only read independently, it's a good idea to choose texts for each group that are around half a grade level higher than the students' independent reading level. For more on how to assess these levels, see Chapter Seven.

Design "Teach the Reader" and "Teach the Text" Questions

With the onset of Common Core, a new debate has surfaced in the world of reading. One of the core principles of current literacy coaching has been "Teach the reader, not the text." At its essence, this idea focuses on building the skills students need to approach reading *in any context*—not just as applied to one text. Teach them how to analyze cause and effect, proponents would argue, and students will be able to do so with any reading passage. At face value, this principle probably sounds simple and logical enough.

In recent years, however, the trainings around Common Core have emphasized a close reading and teaching of content-rich texts. The skill of understanding cause and effect is not important; the mastery of the Gettysburg address is. Some have interpreted this to be saying "Teach the text, not the reader."

We would argue that this is a false dichotomy. Just watch the Common Core authors simulate a book conversation, and watch the most effective literacy teachers do the same. When you get to the concrete actions, the philosophical differences melt away. In reality, they are both critiquing the same thing: teachers are doing too much of the work for the students. A well-designed comprehension skills lesson can meet the standards of both groups.

Let's take a look at how this could come into play in a comprehension skills lesson. Imagine you are going to read Robert Kraus's *Leo the Late Bloomer* with your kindergarten students, who have not yet learned to read. You now must plan the questions you will ask them during the We Do and You Do components of comprehension skills lessons. (Remember that at this early age, "evidence" in the text will come from both words and pictures. Finding evidence in pictures is actually a perfect scaffolding for a nonreader to learn the importance of close reading as expected by the Common Core.) Let's look at how this might work with the following passage from the text (Figure 5.1).

Here are two standard questions a literacy teacher could generate:

1. What is Leo's father worried about?

2. Was Leo's father really watching television?

These questions are pointed and directly tied to this book. Yet both sides of the debate would argue that these questions are flawed. Why? They do too much of

Figure 5.1 Excerpt from *Leo the Late Bloomer*, by Robert Kraus

"Are you sure Leo's a bloomer?"
asked Leo's father.
"Patience." said Leo's mother.
"A watched bloomer doesn't bloom."

So Leo's father watched television
instead of Leo.

Source: Leo the Late Bloomer by Robert Kraus, pictures by Jose Aruego.
Text copyright ©1971 by Robert Kraus. Illustrations copyright © 1971 by
Jose Aruego. Used by permission of HarperCollins Publishers.

the work for the reader. You take away the cognitive task of actually determining
that Leo's father *is* worried, and you plant the seed that he's not really watching
television before the reader has to discern this for himself or herself. As a result, you
have weakened the task for the reader. The "teach the reader" proponents would
argue that you're "teaching the text"; the "teach the text" proponents would argue
that you're overscaffolding the comprehension.

In the end, they're both right. Effective literacy teachers bring those two worlds
together, such that "teach the reader" meets "teach the text." How? Take a look
at some alternative questions in Table 5.1.

What do we notice? Each successive level of questioning puts more of the
cognitive demand on the student. In the first set of questions, you have already
told the student that Leo's father is worried and that he's not really watching
television. In the second set of questions, you've removed *some* of the scaffolding,

Table 5.1 Generating Effective Questions: "Teach the Reader" Meets "Teach the Text"

Leo the Late Bloomer, by Robert Kraus		
Weak questions	What is Leo's father worried about?	Was Leo's father really watching television?
Better	What is Leo's father's problem in the story?	What do you notice about Leo's father on this page?
Teach the reader *and* **teach the text**	What are the characters feeling in the story?	What words and pictures struck you on this page? What is the author trying to tell you?

but you've still made it clear that Leo's father has a problem he's trying to solve and that his actions are the key things happening on this page. The final set of questions, however, meet the criteria of *both* "teach the reader" and "teach the text": the students have to determine the characters' feelings and have to read the words and look at the pictures closely to determine what the author is trying to say. No teacher is tipping his or her hand as to what is actually going on in the story.

The final two questions require the student to "read like a detective" (one of the most popular images of the CCSS) by requiring word-level analysis of meaning, which falls under the umbrella of "teach the text." Yet they also are couched in language that could be applied to any text, which fits right into the realm of "teach the reader." (That's the key way to assess whether a question is "teach the reader": just ask, "Can this question be applied to multiple texts?")

The power of asking the right questions cannot be overstated. (In fact, we will devote Chapter Nine, on guided reading, to determining the right questions to ask your students.) The right questions teach the reader *and* the text, driving students to unlock meaning across any number of texts and genres. By writing such questions into your lesson plan, you ensure that students will have to practice doing exactly that.

If you are relatively new to teaching reading, generating these sorts of questions will not always be easy. The best tip? Lean on a literacy coach or a master teacher, or grab a hold of existing lesson plans that include scripted questions. Just like your students, you can only improve with practice!

Chart Your Thinking

A final planning strategy that can be just as valuable in comprehension skills as in read-aloud is to have an anchor chart prepared and positioned when the lesson begins. By way of review, an anchor chart is a large piece of poster paper or easel paper on which teachers can record their thinking while they are teaching. This chart drives instruction in a number of ways: it not only helps draw in students who may learn better visually but also can be posted in the classroom later on as a reminder of the skill being developed. The result is that even something as casual as looking up at the wall in a classroom can aid students' development as readers (not just their understanding of individual texts). For an example of what an anchor chart looks like, turn back to Chapter Four (Table 4.1).

I DO: MODELING THE SKILL

As in read-aloud lessons, the I Do in a comprehension skills lesson consists of the teacher modeling the reading skill for the students. Here's where we see the power of linking your read-aloud lessons to your comprehension skills lessons. When you do so, the students experience the continuous development of a targeted skill. This also allows you to keep your I Do very concise because students have already seen it once: review the skill and do a quick model.

Core Idea

Don't double-model a skill. Your students' time is better spent practicing it.

Let's go back to Lauren Moyle's class and see how her comprehension skills lesson picks up from where her read-aloud ended.

 WATCH Clip 17: Lauren Moyle's I Do

As you can see, Lauren's read-aloud and comprehension skills lessons are utterly aligned, creating even greater leverage and longer-term mastery. She begins by referring to the read-aloud lesson from earlier in the morning. Then she makes a specific connection to the skill the students will work on now: how to write a high-quality response. Lauren's first goal in introducing the skill is to clearly identify the objective. Her explanation is brief yet purposeful, just what Lauren's students need to be ready for her modeling.

Note that Lauren's student-friendly language here is paramount. She carefully models and practices the strategy, first without the jargon and then with the correct label for the skill. This redundancy in skill practice allows her students to realize that comprehending is not just being able to say what you are doing but also actually applying it to the reading.

Once the objective for the day has been introduced, you can dive into modeling the skill you're teaching at a predesignated point in the text. In her lesson, Lauren does this with the help of a marker and a sheet of chart paper. She shows her students how to write responses to comprehension questions by filling out the answer to a sample question she's already written on the chart paper, all the while narrating exactly what she is doing.

As Lauren's lesson shows, there are many opportunities to engage student thinking during modeling. These can also serve as checks for understanding: for example, when you use call and response, when you break down steps as much as possible and then ask students to repeat what the steps are, or when you end the I Do by asking students, "What did I just model for you?" By holding all students accountable for their learning as you introduce new material, you can ensure that the lesson is as engaging as possible — and that students are ready when it comes time for the We Do.

WE DO: PRACTICING TOGETHER

Once you have modeled the objective of the lesson for students and have checked for understanding, you will lessen the scaffold by having students interact with the text and practice the skill that you have just modeled. It's during this We Do segment of the lesson that you'll ask the "teach the reader *and* the text" questions you've planned.

We Do is essentially a time to give heavy scaffolding to students' practice. For example, in this clip, Juliana Worrell is getting students to build the skill of using knowledge from an informational text to guide their understanding of a narrative text. They have just read an informational text on the effect of the atomic bomb in

World War II, and they are about to start reading Eleanor Coerr's *Sadako and the Thousand Paper Cranes*, a narrative account of one girl's life after the bomb fell. In this chapter, the main character mentions attending a Peace Day and looking for "lucky signs" in the sky. Without knowledge of the atomic bomb, the students would not be able to understand why Sadako is looking for "lucky signs." Let's look at how Juliana does a classic We Do: working with the students to use the knowledge they've gained from the informational text.

 WATCH Clip 18: Juliana Worrell's We Do

Note how even though Juliana is going to ask the students to answer the comprehension question, she gives them major clues as to how to do so, making the segue from her modeling to the students' working on the skill. It won't be a complete You Do until the teacher doesn't provide *any* hints (which is what we'll see in the next section).

Requiring students to practice the skill while you're still available to provide support enables you to identify student misconceptions or misunderstandings, clearing them up before students begin the You Do. Juliana did that in the previous clip by utilizing Turn and Talk. In the next clip, Lauren Moyle picks up her comprehension skills lesson on written responses by cold calling students to break down the next steps for writing their response.

 WATCH Clip 19: Lauren Moyle's We Do

Lauren's teaching is effective because she introduces the new questions about the character before her students begin to read the book. She then directs the students to read the new questions first, so that they can identify the key words in the question to guide their reading. Lauren's use of cold calling to identify key words to circle or underline is another source of her lesson's power: it gives her the ability to check each student for understanding. In addition, other students are able to disagree with their peers' responses and then come to a decision together under Lauren's guidance.

Our final word of advice about the We Do: keep it tightly timed! You need to be sure to leave room for the You Do so that students have all the time they need to practice independently.

YOU DO: MAKING INDEPENDENT PRACTICE SACRED

Independent practice, or You Do, is the heart of what comprehension skills lessons are about. It is what most distinguishes comprehension skills lessons from read-aloud lessons. During the You Do, students apply a new comprehension skill to a text and thus become prepared to apply it to reading as a whole.

Watch as Lauren Moyle gives her students an independent practice assignment.

 WATCH Clip 20: Lauren Moyle's You Do

Note that the students are practicing with a new writing prompt—not the one that Lauren already modeled how to answer. This is where comprehension skills lessons truly break away from read-aloud: they shift a text (or a section of a text) squarely from the hands of the teacher into the hands of the students. Lauren is no longer providing her students with scaffolding, but, because she's observing them as they work, she hasn't sent them out on a solo flight yet, either. In sum, the You Do piece of a comprehension skills lesson gives students an opportunity to practice a skill in a structured way before you ask them to perform that skill on their own.

> ### Core Idea
> Comprehension instruction is like driving school; it lets your students practice the basics before hitting the streets.

For students in the second through fourth grades (and even earlier), we recommend that the You Do task require them to write as well as to read. For those grade levels, it's also helpful to provide a new text (or excerpt of a text) for the You Do, rather than the one you've worked with for the I Do and We Do.

This ensures that students are doing as much cognitive work as they are able at every reading level.

CONCLUSION: A FIRST TASTE OF INDEPENDENCE

By the time students have worked on a reading skill from the beginning of read-aloud to the end of a comprehension skills lesson, they have had not only multiple opportunities to observe expert modeling and engage in guided practice but also between fifteen and twenty minutes to perfect the skill independently. The I Do and We Do of these lessons are instrumental, to be sure; but this You Do is students' first taste of reading independently—and that's what everything in the reading program we present is working toward. Teaching one reading skill at a time may occasionally feel excruciatingly slow, just as playing symphonies slowly must frustrate the artists at Meadowmount from time to time. But the fact is that when you build a comprehension skills lesson on the foundation of "teach the reader meets teach the text," you give students knowledge and practice that takes them closer—one step at a time—to truly being readers in their own right.

Comprehension Skills Framework

Preparation (Prework Before the Lesson Begins)

- Flag the text (premark book for stopping and thinking points).
- Prepare an anchor chart and post.
- Prepare all materials (independent work, folders, pencils, crayons, and so on).

I Do

Teacher models exactly what the students will do
5–8 min

- State the objective with clear, precise language.
- Teach the skill or strategy with a preplanned think-aloud from a shared experience or text.
  - Break down the steps consistently.
  - Chart thinking.
  - Explain the rationale behind the strategy.
- Check for understanding: ask, "What did I just model for you?" (students articulate).

We Do

Teacher checks for understanding and gets
the students to share the work
10–15 min

- We Do mirrors the I Do: students practice the same skill that the teacher modeled.
- Students and teacher work together.
  - Teacher starts a think-aloud; students take over.
  - Teacher questions and prompts strategically.
  - Turn and Talk is followed by discussion.
  - Quick-writes follow discussion.

(continued)

(continued)

- Evaluate skill implementation.
  - ◦ Teacher assesses quality of skill implementation.
  - ◦ Students assess the quality of their peers' skill implementation.
- Keep this tightly timed: make sure students end promptly to move to You Do.

You Do

Students do the work; teacher monitors
15–20 min

- Make a clear connection to the skill that was just presented and practiced.
- Give clear directions for independent practice: reading task (plus a writing task for grades 1–4).
- For grades 2–4, use a separate text for students to apply the skill (articles, texts, excerpts).
- Monitor to check for understanding (move around, observe work).

Apply Your Habits: Improve Comprehension Instruction

Self-Assessment

Which of the comprehension instruction practices we described will have the biggest impact on student learning in your class?

_____

_____

_____

_____

_____

_____

Tools to Use

- Comprehension Skills Framework (also included in the Appendix and on the DVD)

Your Next Steps

_____

_____

_____

_____

_____

_____

Chapter 6

Teaching Phonics

Greasing the Wheel

Lesson Type	Group Size	What to Teach?
Read-Aloud	Whole class	Skills from yearlong syllabus
Comprehension Skills	Small group by reading level or whole class if necessary	Skills from yearlong syllabus
Phonics	**Small group or whole class if necessary**	**Skills from premade program**
Guided Reading	Small group by reading level	Skills determined by assessment analysis (Chapter Seven)
Independent Reading	Individual	Skills for all students

Elementary educators increasingly agree that rigorous phonics instruction is a crucial component of teaching reading. A student's ability to form and create the right sounds at the right time is absolutely essential to higher reading comprehension, and today phonics instruction is accepted by critics across the spectrum of reading theorists.[1] Unfortunately, a common misconception exists that phonics are swept under the rug by the CCSS. That is completely untrue. The Common Core separates out these standards into the section called Reading Foundations, because the Common Core authors assume—as we should—that these are the foundations on which strong comprehension can be built. By separating them out, however, the Common Core does exactly what this book is trying to do: highlight the increased importance of comprehension even in the earliest grades. You cannot sacrifice phonics for comprehension, but the inverse is equally unhelpful.

So what can we say about teaching phonics lessons? Our main counsel, though it may initially seem surprising, is simple: don't reinvent the wheel.

Appropriately enough, this advice is borrowed. Generations of teachers (ourselves included) have heard some version of it during their first weeks in the classroom. This adage has stood the test of time because it speaks to a powerful truth: it is easier to adapt what already works than to build something from scratch. That's why so few humans have the desire to spend time reinventing the fork, the chair, standard spelling, or any other invention that has already successfully resolved a problem. And in the classroom, this is why it is so helpful to draw from what already works, rather than to strike out on our own. In a busy day full of implementing lesson plans, managing fast-evolving conflicts, and determining whether two dozen students are on the right track to success, there are limits to how much any teacher can—or should—create on his or her own. In many ways, this is why we have written this book in the first place: to provide the systems and strategies that have already made read-aloud, comprehension skills, guided reading, and independent reading effective. That way, you can focus on bringing them to life.

In the case of phonics instruction, however, this work has largely been done for us. That's because there's already general consensus not only around the necessity of teaching phonics but also around the question of how to do it well. There are plenty of phonics programs available that have already taken the guesswork out of sound work and that can change your classroom. This does not mean that all phonics programs are created equal—indeed, the next thing you'll see in this chapter is a quick list of what to look for in the phonics program you choose—but how a teacher *implements* them is what really has the power to make phonics instruction great. Great phonics teachers make student achievement soar by bringing optimal rigor and joy to phonics lessons, rather than by creating groundbreaking new programs. In short, they don't spend their time reinventing the wheel: they spend it making the wheel turn faster.

Core Idea

When you teach phonics, don't reinvent the wheel. Just make it turn more quickly.

CHOOSING THE WHEEL: MAKE SURE IT'S A ROUND ONE

Despite the abundance of phonics programs that can lead to superb success, some are better than others, and there are several clear criteria that the system you ultimately pick needs to meet. You don't need to reinvent the wheel, but you do need to pick a round one.

Choosing a Phonics Program

A List for Starting

There are so many strong phonics programs—and so many new ones on the rise—that it would be difficult to generate a comprehensive list of programs. Here is a short list of programs to start your search:

- Reading Mastery
- Wilson Language Training: Wilson Reading, Fundations
- The 95% Group Phonics Lessons
- Phoneme-grapheme mapping (as described in *Phonics and Spelling Through Phoneme-Grapheme Mapping*, by Kathryn Grace)

Once again: don't take our word for it. Take a look at the programs yourself and see which one matches the basic criteria and your needs. For example, the schools with which we work have used Reading Mastery and Wilson.

It's no accident that we've focused on explaining how to choose a discrete phonics program, as opposed to how to integrate phonics with other types of reading work, such as comprehension. Too often, elementary reading teachers attempt to teach phonics and comprehension at the same time, only to find that they end up focusing so much on phonics that they don't give comprehension work the emphasis it needs. Teaching phonics and comprehension skills lessons separately, in contrast, gives teachers time to concentrate explicitly on teaching both types of skills. None of this is to say that teachers should not correct those phonics errors that impede comprehension outside the context of phonics lessons! It is to say, however, that both phonics and comprehension should be isolated in a way that allows for truly deep and repeated practice.

Here are the criteria we recommend for picking a phonics program:

- **Proven results.** Given the sheer quantity of phonics programs at your disposal, the program you choose should be able to prove results with children. Look not only at their research but at schools like yours that are having success with reading to see what they're using.

- **High-frequency practice.** As you review a phonics program you're considering, count the number of times each student would have to practice using phonics skills during any given lesson. Later in this chapter, we'll discuss how to build even more practice into phonics lessons, but if you don't select a practice-oriented program in the first place, those strategies are less likely to fit. The best phonics programs will also provide materials for independent practice. It's essential that students have time to practice phonics skills independently, and developing those materials yourself, though possible, is quite difficult and time-consuming.

- **Out, in, and in context.** The best way to master phonics is to practice sounds in every context: the sound by itself (outside of words), the sound within a word (in), and the sound when that word is in the fuller context of a story (in context). Many phonics programs teach only in one form—for example, a worksheet that has only letters or individual words. Or students only see the sound "at" in the word "cat" but not in the word "catastrophe." The best programs do all three.

- **Error driven.** What make the great phonics programs stand out from the average ones are the built-in protocols around what happens when a student makes an error. The top programs have a series of repetitive steps that push the teacher not to move on until the student has mastered that sound or skill.

- **Scripted lessons.** The more scripted and comprehensive a phonics program is, the more easily and readily it can be adapted to your classroom. When lesson materials have already been created, this saves a tremendous amount of time that can be better spent on perfecting instruction and execution. This last criterion becomes optional if you've already received extensive training in how to teach phonics lessons—in this case, you may not need materials with such a high level of detail.

- **Focus on patterns … and exceptions.** English is a particularly challenging language because of the vast range of sounds a particular letter or set of letters may produce. For this reason, the phonics program you select must expose students both to the rules of English and to the exceptions to those rules, early and often.

Once you've selected a phonics program that meets these six criteria, all that remains is to make it optimally successful for each of your students—that is, to grease whatever wheel you've chosen. That will be our focus for the remainder of this chapter.

GREASING THE WHEEL: THREE WAYS TO MAKE PHONICS SPIN FASTER

First-grade teacher Laura Fern dedicates a portion of every morning's reading time to phonics. Seconds after her students seat themselves around her, a lightning-quick exchange begins. Watch how it unfolds in this video.

 WATCH Clip 21: Laura Fern's More Practice

In the course of only twenty-six seconds, every student in her small group has practiced decoding eight words. And the students didn't just practice; they practiced effectively. When not every student pronounced "mope" correctly, Laura stopped and made sure to correct and check for understanding.

On paper, the phonics lessons that Laura delivers each day are not very different from any number of other phonics lessons. She uses a premade phonics program, not a brand-new one of her own design. Yet as even this brief excerpt shows, this isn't phonics-in-a-box but phonics on fire.

> ## Core Idea
>
> Don't deliver phonics-in-a-box: teach phonics on fire.

Laura has taken a familiar type of lesson and made it incredibly engaging — and extraordinarily effective. And we've discovered that after lessons like Laura's, phonics won't hold back students on assessments: they are able to focus much more fully on comprehension, and their accuracy scores are well above grade level. Put simply, Laura is spinning the wheel faster, increasing both student achievement and student excitement.

Perhaps more than any other lesson type in this book, phonics lessons put habit creation center stage. The basic sounds we use for our entire reading lives can only be truly and deeply mastered when they have become innate, a reflexive part of how we think. Recognizing this, teachers like Laura deliver their phonics lessons with a focus on three key principles:

1. **More practice.** Create as many opportunities for practice as possible for as many students as possible.

2. **More *effective* practice.** Use assessment data and on-the-spot checks for understanding to make sure that students are practicing just what they need to practice — and doing so correctly.

3. **More fun.** Bring excitement and joy to phonics lessons.

Let's see how to put each of these into action.

More Practice

Take another look at the start of Laura's lesson.

 REWATCH Clip 21: Laura Fern's More Practice

One of the most impressive features of Laura's lesson is the sheer level of student involvement it demands. The students were decoding and saying words at a rate over four hundred words per student in a twenty-five-minute lesson! Her emphasis on practice is entirely deliberate. In *Teach Like a Champion*, Doug Lemov listed increasing the number of "at bats" per student—in other words, the number of practice opportunities each student gets—as one of the most powerful tools of successful teachers.[2] (Not surprisingly, Doug's most recent book is titled *Practice Perfect!*[3]) When it comes to phonics, this means that the more times each student practices forming correct sounds, the better off he or she will be.

How, then, can a phonics instructor make sure that each student practices as many times as possible over the course of a single phonics lesson? Here are some techniques that Laura and others like her have used to great effect.

Choral Response

One logical way to create more practice opportunities for 100 percent of students is to call on 100 percent of your students at once. The strategy of choral response, also addressed in Chapter Four, is the most straightforward way to accomplish this. In phonics, choral response generally requires all students to repeat a sound or word together. Here's how this looks in Jessica Lisovicz's kindergarten classroom.

 WATCH Clip 22: Jessica Lisovicz's More Practice

The class practices at a rate as impressive as Laura's, and Jessica "punches" the words twice in a row to nail the practice. Jessica followed the choral response with an individual response for the sounds in the word "go," guaranteeing both collective and individual practice.

Whiteboard Work

Individual student whiteboards are also a great tool for getting all students to practice at once. If you would like students to practice spelling a word, for example, you can have each child write the word down on his or her whiteboard and then ask them all to hold up the whiteboards so that you can check their responses. The key to making student use of whiteboards effective is to plan and teach the procedure for how students will use them.

Individual Turns

Having each student practice a sound in turn is another way to get all students involved in practice. As you have each student practice, keep track of those who struggle to get the sound right on their first try, and give them a chance to practice it again.

Smaller Groups

It goes without saying that breaking students into smaller groups for phonics practice will greatly increase the quantity of practice possible, as each student can get many more at bats this way. It is better to have one shorter lesson with fewer students than a longer lesson with many, as deepest learning occurs from concentrated, high-quality repetitions. So, if you can, break phonics instruction into smaller groups.

Independent Practice

You probably saw this one coming when we recommended a phonics program that included independent practice materials! When a phonics lesson ends, students should be given high-quality independent practice opportunities that cement what they learned from repeated in-lesson practice. By using phonics programs that provide effective worksheets and other means of practicing, teachers build many more chances for students to acquire phonics skills—and keep them.

More *Effective* Practice

The techniques described in the preceding section will ensure that phonics lessons give all students many opportunities to practice. Yet as we mentioned in Chapter Five, just having a high quantity of practice isn't sufficient to build student achievement; the quality of the practice matters, too. Thus, top-notch instructors constantly seek ways to make practice perfect, getting students to practice the exact skills they most need to work on and, above all, to practice them correctly. How can we reach that goal in phonics lessons?

Start from Data

Nearly all early literacy assessments, from DRA to F&P to STEP, allow teachers to get a sense of which phonics skills students struggle with. Use these data! By conducting an analysis of the types of words and sounds students struggle with, teachers can ensure that the corrections they give and the lessons they emphasize are the ones that matter most. Let's see this in action. Consider Figure 6.1, an excerpt from an early assessment of letter identification and letter sounds, conducted in September by Annie Maline with her kindergarten class.

Looking at the data, Annie can quickly see that her students have generally mastered letter identification, and only "g" and "t" require significant work. On letter sounds, she can systematically target each of the sounds that needs work, and she'll work little by little to quickly reduce the percentage of letters in "red" (60 percent correct or less for the class). Why does this matter? Because when the time comes for the phonics lesson, Annie knows exactly which letters require more work than others; this means that every second in class is maximized for the biggest benefit for children. In addition to her whole-class focus, she can also provide individual support to students like Alexis, Jadyn, and Jason, who haven't yet mastered any sounds and could use extra practice to catch up to their peers. As noted in *Driven by Data*, using data isn't about teaching to the test but about testing the teaching. And that makes all the difference.

> ## Core Idea
>
> Using early assessment data isn't about teaching to the test; it's about testing the teaching.
> And that makes all the difference.

Know Each Sound … and Defend It

In everyday life, each of us speaks English with a slightly different inflection. This variety is natural and welcome, but for a student new to reading, it can be immensely confusing. If teachers don't provide a clear and consistent model each time they make a sound, then the chance for truly high-quality practice dwindles. Recognizing this, the very best phonics instructors take the time to learn exactly how each phoneme sounds before teaching their lessons. As important, they are consistent in their expectation that students will be precise in their own use of those sounds. Take another look at either Jessica's or Laura's previous videos and pay special attention to the moment when students' sounds are off. You'll see Laura make sure that her students read the word "mope" correctly, and you'll see Jessica hold her students accountable for the sound of the letter "g."

Figure 6.1 Annie Maline's Phonics Assessment Data

September

NYU–Kindergarten	Lower-Case Letter ID																									
	a	f	k	p	w	z	b	h	o	j	u	c	y	l	q	m	d	n	s	x	i	e	g	r	v	t
Alexis										x													x			x
Alfred																x							x			x
Al-Sunan		x						x		x					x	x	x						x			
Ani																				x						
Anja																										
Chanel							x																			
Christian					x	x							x													x
Devin																										
Haamid		x		x				x								x	x	x		x			x			x
Jada		x						x			x							x				x	x			x
Jason											x			x	x						x				x	x
Justin																	x				x				x	x
Kayla							x																			
Kevin							x			x													x			x
Kevin																							x			
Malachi																										
Maraad							x			x							x						x			
Michael																										
Mohammed														x			x	x					x			x
Moussa																										
Savannah																										
Sean					x																					
Shamry																							x			
Sy'Mone					x						x										x	x	x		x	x
Titi																										
Tyler										x	x															
CLASS AVG	100%	87%	97%	93%	90%	97%	83%	93%	97%	80%	83%	97%	93%	93%	90%	87%	80%	90%	97%	90%	87%	90%	60%	100%	83%	63%

Figure 6.1 Annie Maline's Phonics Assessment Data *(continued)*

September NYU–Kindergarten	Letter-Sound ID																									
	a	f	k	p	w	z	b	h	o	j	u	c	y	l	q	m	d	n	s	x	i	e	g	r	v	t
Alexis	x	x	x	x	x	x	x	x	x	x	x	x	x	x	x	x	x	x	x	x	x	x	x	x	x	x
Alfred			x	x	x								x							x			x		x	x
Al-Sunan		x	x	x	x					x	x	x	x	x	x	x	x	x	x	x	x	x	x	x		
Amirah	x	x			x	x	x	x			x	x	x	x	x		x	x	x	x	x	x	x	x		x
Ani	x					x					x		x	x		x	x				x		x			
Anja																										
Ariel									x		x				x							x		x		
Chanel		x			x	x	x		x	x	x	x	x	x	x	x		x	x	x	x	x	x	x	x	x
Christian		x	x	x	x		x	x	x	x	x	x	x	x	x	x		x	x	x	x	x	x	x	x	x
Devin																										
Haamid	x	x	x	x	x	x		x	x	x	x	x	x	x	x	x	x	x	x	x	x	x	x	x	x	x
Jada	x	x	x	x	x	x	x	x	x	x	x	x	x	x	x	x	x	x	x	x	x	x	x	x	x	x
Jason	x	x	x	x	x	x	x	x	x	x	x	x	x	x	x	x	x	x		x	x	x	x	x	x	x
Justin					x	x	x	x			x	x	x		x	x	x	x		x	x	x	x	x		x
Kayla											x	x	x	x	x						x	x				
Kevin									x		x	x	x	x	x	x	x	x	x	x	x	x	x	x	x	x
Kevin	x	x	x	x	x	x	x			x	x	x	x	x	x	x			x		x		x	x	x	x
Malachi		x	x	x		x	x				x	x	x	x	x	x			x				x	x	x	
Maraad		x					x		x		x	x	x	x	x		x						x			
Michael																										
Mohammed	x	x	x	x	x	x	x	x	x		x	x	x	x	x	x		x		x	x		x	x	x	x
Moussa																										
Nisiyah	x	x	x	x	x	x	x	x	x	x	x	x	x	x	x		x	x		x	x	x	x	x	x	x
Samiyah									x		x				x					x		x	x			
Savannah																										
Sean	x								x	x	x	x	x	x	x	x				x	x	x	x	x		x
Shamry	x	x	x					x	x	x	x	x	x	x	x	x	x	x	x	x	x	x	x	x		x
Sy'Mone	x	x	x	x	x	x	x	x	x	x	x	x	x	x	x	x	x	x	x	x	x	x	x	x	x	x
Titi	x	x	x	x		x	x	x	x	x	x	x	x	x	x	x	x	x		x	x	x		x	x	x
Tyler	x	x	x	x	x	x	x	x	x	x	x	x	x	x	x	x	x	x	x	x	x	x	x	x	x	x
CLASS AVG	57%	67%	67%	70%	53%	60%	67%	50%	50%	63%	30%	47%	30%	40%	27%	60%	53%	50%	60%	23%	30%	33%	23%	43%	57%	40%

REWATCH Clip 21: Laura Fern's More Practice

or

REWATCH Clip 22: Jessica Lisovicz's More Practice

Think of what would happen if either teacher *hadn't* corrected the students: the students would have learned the wrong habits. And as anyone who has ever set a New Year's resolution knows, it's far harder to break a bad habit than to start off by learning a good one. For this reason, it is vital that corrections happen instantly, before students internalize misunderstandings. Your knowing the right sound and defending it ensures that students will consistently practice the right habits.

Tap the Power of Visuals

Phonics is as much about seeing as it is about talking. To help students connect the signs they see with the sounds they make, the most effective phonics teachers use compelling visual displays. Through charts posted on classroom walls, for example, teachers can help students associate sounds with key sight words, building greater pattern recognition and key connections. These teachers may also look to phonics programs that provide chances for students to constantly see the sounds in text even as they are making them. Consider this page from a Reading Mastery practice book (Figure 6.2), a text that students in Laura's class would hold during the lesson.

Notice that each sound being made is faithfully reproduced in a clear, visually accessible form. The visual support the text provides doesn't just present the sounds: it gives students visual tools to learn them, such as a miniature *e* that indicates the silent "e." By paying as much attention to seeing as to speaking, champion instructors are able to reach more students and, in the process, teach phonics far more effectively.

Say It with Your Hands

When you want a phonics lesson to be "on fire," the key is to keep the whole student engaged, mind and body. To maintain momentum and increase engagement, the top teachers we've studied use nonverbal signals to accompany the lesson. In a previous clip, you saw Laura use nonverbal signals to transition:

Figure 6.2 Reading Mastery Excerpt

49

READING VOCABULARY
Do not touch small letters.
Get ready to read all the words on this page without making a mistake.

fin

TASK 3 Sound out first
a. Touch the ball for **fin**. Sound it out. Get ready. Quickly touch **f, i, n** as the childern say *ffffiiinnn*.
b. What word? (Signal.) *Fin*. Yes, **fin**.
c. Repeat task until firm.

fīne

TASK 4 Sound out first
a. Touch the ball for **fine**. Sound it out. Get ready. Quickly touch **f, ī, n** as the childern say *ffffiīnnn*.
b. What word? (Signal.) *Fine*. Yes, **fine**.
c. Repeat task until firm.

TASK 5 Teach final-e rule
a. Touch the ball for **fin**. Everybody, read this word the fast way. Get ready. (Signal.) *Fin*. Yes, **fin**.
b. Point to i in **fin**. Here's a rule. If there is an ē on the end of this word, you say the **name** of this letter. Remember that rule.
c. Point to i in **fine**. There's an ē on the end of this word. So tell me the **name** of this letter. Get ready. (Signal.) *ī*. Yes, **ī**.
d. Touch the ball for **fine**. Read this word the fast way and say the name ī. (Pause two seconds.) Get ready. (Signal.) *Fine*.
e. What word? (Signal.) *Fine*. Yes, **fine**.
f. Touch the ball for **fin**. Read the fast way. (Pause two seconds.) Get ready. (Signal.) *Fin*. Yes, **fin**. Repeat until firm.
g. Touch the ball for **fine**. Read the fast way. (Pause two seconds.) Get ready. (Signal.) *Fine*. Yes, **fine**. Repeat until firm.
h. Repeat f and g until firm.

TASK 6 Listen, sound out with me
a. Point to **children**. I'll tell you this word. (Pause.) **Children**. What word? (Signal.) *Children*. Yes, **children**.
b. Touch the ball for **children**. Sound it out with me. Get ready. Quickly touch each sound as you and the children say *chiilllldrrreeennn*.
c. What word? (Signal.) *Children*. Yes, **children**.
d. Repeat b and c until firm.

fin

fine

children

Repeat any troublesome words.

Individual test
Call on different childern. Each child reads a different word.

her silent three-finger countdown. In the following clip, Jessica uses hand signals to help students sound out a word. Watch as this helps a student get to the right answer after incorrectly identifying the number of sounds in "make".

WATCH Clip 23: Jessica Lisovicz's More Effective Practice

The utilization of hand gestures increases engagement, joy, and learning. This not only saves time but also prevents students' concentration from being broken, keeping them more focused on what their peers say and ultimately deepening their skills.

Make Phonics Fun

Given the sheer redundancy of the best phonics lessons, it's only logical to wonder if they leave students tired, frustrated, or even bored. But Jessica and teachers like her prove that fun can be embedded anywhere.

WATCH Clip 24: Jessica Lisovicz's Make Phonics Fun

Notice the enthusiasm in the students' voices, the energy of their movements, and their intensity as they vie to help peers. Jessica's students aren't just tolerating this phonics onslaught—they're loving it.

At first, the task of making phonics fun might seem insurmountable. Yet when we break great phonics lessons down a bit more, we find a set of surprisingly simple strategies that make them fun. What are these?

Precise Praise

This video clip is from a phonics lesson taught by Andrea Palmer. Watch how frequently Andrea praises her students.

WATCH Clip 25: Andrea Palmer's Make Phonics Fun

By the end of this quick video, Andrea has praised her students every time they have responded to a question correctly: twelve times in all. Moreover, she never failed to tell students specifically what they had done to earn her praise. In offering such frequent and focused praise, Andrea shows that she's paying *close* attention to her students and that her expectations for them are high. At the same time, she also lets students know how it feels to meet those expectations, and rewards their good work with approval. All this adds up to a significantly higher chance that Andrea will again and again see the behaviors she expects. Doug Lemov has referred to this technique as "precise praise," and although it reaps high dividends in any number of teaching scenarios, it can be a particularly powerful way to keep phonics fun and positive.[4]

Game On!

Another possibility for bringing the fun to phonics is to turn lessons into games or contests. Students may earn points as a group by chorally responding correctly and in unison, by answering questions correctly, or by giving excellent effort. The points are always earned as a group (and not against another group), so the students are super-motivated to help their peers and cheer on their success. As the game develops, students get more and more excited about "winning" points, and so are more engaged in the lesson.

Chants and Cheers

One of the dynamic moments of Laura's lesson is when the students finish the first part of the lesson and then break into an excited cheer: "Everybody say, 'Good job, me!'" "Good job, me!" For younger students, setting up chants or cheers for key moments is a great way to build joy and momentum during a phonics lesson. Ideally, the chants should be short and familiar to students, so that they keep instruction moving rather than distract from it. As was the case with the classroom transitions we discussed in Chapter One, the time invested in learning a chant can pay off tremendously in the level of engagement and joy students will bring to phonics.

Pacing

A fast pace also matters. Think about how quickly each video in this chapter went, shifting from a quick sound review to a group practice to individual practice and then back to group practice in the space of a few minutes. During this entire time, the pace is blistering. Note that the essence of great pacing is not to teach faster, but rather to give the *illusion* of speed. Fast and clear transitions between components of lessons and quickly calling on a variety of students will contribute to the sense that phonics is exciting and engaging, even as teachers lead students through twenty-five highly intensive minutes of instruction.[5]

The best elementary reading teachers don't just make phonics lessons palatable: they light them on fire, making them one of the most engaging and exciting parts of the day. When phonics lessons become a time for praise, friendly competition, and energy, students can't help but feel the joy—and learn the sounds.

CONCLUSION: PHONICS AND FOUNDATIONS

Although we began this chapter on phonics lessons by saying "Don't reinvent the wheel," we wouldn't want to end it without emphasizing that great phonics instruction need never be uncreative or routine. Instead, the best phonics instructors start with a familiar set of tools but constantly find ways to use them better. They start with the same wheel, but turn it incredibly fast.

The goal of turning the phonics wheel at top speed, of course, isn't merely to move faster: it's to get students to read more proficiently. By using data and visual supports to reach all learners, creating as many high-quality practice opportunities as possible, and keeping lessons fun, teachers can truly bring phonics lessons to life. In doing so, they pave the way for every student to engage with texts on the very highest levels. As we move on to guided reading, you'll see the rich array of reading accomplishments that students become capable of when great phonics instruction is firmly in place.

Phonics Instruction Framework

Purpose of Phonics Instruction

Give students the tools to accurately, fluently, and independently read a text, therefore allowing them to focus on the meaning of the story.

Introduction/Hook (3–4 min)

Opening chant

Conduct a quick review of a challenging skill (choose one or two of the following):

- **Sight word review (K and struggling grade 1)**
  - ◦ Flashcard review examples:

    "This word is [teacher gives]. What word?" (*Students repeat*)

    "This word is [students give]. What word?" (*Students repeat again*)

    "[Student name], what word is this? What word?" (*All students repeat*)

- **Vowel sounds**
  - ◦ Vowel chant:

    "A, E, I, O, U, and sometimes Y. AGAIN!" (*A, E, I, O, U, and sometimes Y*)

    "Short A says its sound [students give]. Long A says its name [students give]. Short E says its sound [students give]. Long E says its name [students give]." (*Continue with all vowels.*)

- **Consonant sounds**
  - ◦ Example: Blend flashcard review:

    "Sound check, sound check, 1-2-3. This sound is [students give]. What sound?" (*Students give*)

    "What sound is this? [*ch*] What sound is this? [*ch*] What word is this?" [*check*]

- **Decoding rules—final e, double consonant, vowel pairs . . .**
  - ◦ Sample chant—silent "e":

    "Silent E. Say my name. (*Students give.*) Silent E. Say my name." (*Students give.*)

    "An E at the end, makes the vowel say its—*NAME!*"

(continued)

(continued)

    ◦ Sample chant—double consonant:

    "Two say the sound, one says the name."

- **Fluency strategies**

Scripted Lesson (18 min)

- Lesson is derived from the teacher's manual.
- Students practice decoding skills and word-solving strategies.
- Teacher identifies student errors and guides students to self-correct.
- Teacher models how to use decoding skills and strategies.

Oral Reading (10 min)

- Students have their own storybooks.
- Students read aloud to practice decoding skills and word-solving strategies.
- Teacher identifies student errors and guides students to self-correct.
- Teacher models how to fluently read and word-solve in context.

Independent Work (10 min)

- Students complete "take-home" sheets that coincide with the scripted lesson.
- Teacher and students go over the answers and review work.

Great Habits, Great Readers: A Practical Guide for K–4 Reading in the Light of Common Core, by Paul Bambrick-Santoyo, Aja Settles, and Juliana Worrell. Copyright © 2013 Uncommon Schools and/or Paul Bambrick-Santoyo. Reproduced by permission.

Apply Your Habits: Improve Phonics Instruction

Self-Assessment

Which of the phonics instruction practices we described will have the biggest impact on student learning in your class?

_____

_____

_____

_____

_____

_____

Tools to Use

- Phonics Instruction Framework (also included in the Appendix and on the DVD)
- Phonics Prompting Guide (included in the Appendix and on the DVD)

Your Next Steps

_____

_____

_____

_____

_____

Build the Habits of Reading

| Set the Habits of Learning | Teach the Skills of Reading | **Build the Habits of Reading** | Lead by Habit |

Introduction: The Making of Magical Moments

"Magical moments," when a light goes on and a student genuinely begins to read, may be the single most rewarding part of an elementary teacher's job. Recall the moment from the clip in the introduction when Erin Michels's student exclaims, "They're juvenile delinquents!"

 REWATCH CLIP 1: Erin Michels's Comprehension—730L

Somehow, seemingly out of the blue, a student who before could not comprehend is now sailing through books, growing at an astounding rate. It's incredible to watch, and incredibly moving. Because these leaps seem so dramatic, it can sometimes seem as though the skills of reading are the product of spontaneous and random inspiration. Indeed, it is this very "miraculous" character that leads many to believe, publicly or privately, that teachers depend on those miraculous moments to occur on their own, and when they don't, their absence says more about the student than the educator. In our own experience as educators, however, we have learned something very different. In the chapters that follow, we will show that with the right combination of instructional strategies and tactics, magical moments will occur for every reader.

What's the first difference you notice in this clip compared to the examples of comprehension skills and phonics lessons? If you're like most observers, you'll note that the students are doing the work: the locus of activity has shifted fully from teacher to student. This is when the big picture of reading begins coming together: when students integrate the practice of specific skills into the act of reading for every aspect of meaning in a story.

This is also the culmination of all the excellent foundation work you do when you implement the lesson types we described in Part Two of this book (remember: without that foundation, the "magic" of the next several chapters will be attainable, but not nearly as powerful). Part Three describes the parts of reading instruction that truly make reading soar.

GUIDED READING (CHAPTERS 7–9)

Guided reading is the most complex—and most fruitful—aspect of our entire reading program. We will dive into this deeply in Chapters Seven through Nine. First, the teacher uses assessments effectively to determine each student's specific reading skills. In each guided reading lesson, the teacher then allows students time to read aloud to themselves, while correcting student errors as soon as they occur. Finally, teacher and students lead a comprehension conversation using the habits of discussion.

INDEPENDENT READING (CHAPTER 10)

Independent reading makes an enormous contribution to the success of any reading program. If read-aloud, comprehension skills, phonics, and guided reading lessons are the practice sessions of reading, then independent reading lessons are the scrimmages: students put all their reading skills into action at once, and although teachers still play a role, they retreat as much as possible to the sidelines. Of all classroom reading activities, it is independent reading that best simulates what students will have to do throughout their lives when they embark on *truly* independent reading—from avidly devouring mystery novels to conducting doctoral research—and for this reason, it's independent reading that most thoroughly prepares them for these ventures. In Chapter Ten, we'll explore just why independent reading is so important for students' development as readers, as well as some of the reasons it frequently doesn't deliver all it promises. Then we'll explain strategies for beating those pitfalls and sending students on their way to becoming truly independent readers—both inside the classroom and out.

Chapter 7

Analysis and Action

Mind the Journey

Let's imagine two reading teachers working in the same school with very similar students. As you observe both teachers, you see abundant signs of strong instruction: the habits of the classroom (Chapter One) are firmly in place, and the students have mastered the habits of discussion (Chapter Two). In addition, each teacher is following the core framework for a guided reading lesson (to be addressed in Chapters Eight and Nine): students are reading a text and then discussing it in a small group with the teacher. Everything about the teaching itself seems to be aligned to what it means to deliver a quality lesson. When you walk out of each classroom, however, you glance over the students' early literacy assessment data, and you see that the students in one of the two classrooms are dramatically outperforming the others, despite having similar reading performance at the beginning of the year. How is this possible? The answer is quite simple: it has everything to do with how well each teacher targeted the lesson to her students' learning needs.

This point cannot be overstated. Collectively we have observed thousands of hours of literacy instruction and seen countless lessons that looked very sharp on the surface. Yet when we looked more closely at some of those lessons, we found that certain teachers weren't getting results because the students weren't learning what they really needed in order to advance. Without proper analysis of student reading errors, your instruction, however polished it might be, will not have the same impact.

In Chapter Three, we addressed why assessments are the starting point for instruction—not the end point. If you don't have a clear map of where you're headed, your students won't, either. But that's only part of the process. Assessments don't only serve to inform your curriculum choices at the beginning of the year; they also tell you what each student in your class needs throughout the year. The most successful reading teachers are masters at gathering the data provided by their assessments and using that information to continuously tailor their curricula to the learning needs of their students. They share a valuable insight: assessment isn't just about the destination; it's about the journey.

Core Idea

Assessment can tell you not only the destination but also how to make the journey.

In *Driven by Data*, Paul delineates the keys to using assessment data to fuel achievement gains for students.[1] The components boil down to the following four:

1. **Assessment.** Use regular checks of student skills to define a road map for rigor.

2. **Analysis.** Determine which students are struggling and why.

3. **Action.** Implement new teaching plans to respond to this analysis.

4. **Systems.** Create systems and procedures to ensure continuous data-driven improvement.

Chapter Three addressed assessment; this chapter will address analysis and action—moving from the "what" to the "why" and the "how." (We'll touch on support systems, too. *Driven by Data* goes in depth on those if you find yourself interested.) Here are some guidelines for administering reading assessments and for analyzing the data you get from them.

ADMINISTERING ASSESSMENT

A major key to effective assessment is frequency. Because early readers develop so rapidly, it is vital that you conduct your assessment at least three times a year—ideally four to six times. This will ensure that you have an up-to-date understanding of precisely where students are struggling and what they need to do to get to the next level. Of course, giving a reading assessment to all students takes time and can be stressful. Fortunately, there are ways that some of the highest-performing schools have used to take some of this time pressure off, including the following:

- **Grabbing all hands on deck.** Training paraprofessionals, gym or specials teachers, or parent volunteers to supervise while you conduct assessments can free up valuable time.

- **Getting back to basics.** During the week of assessment, music, physical education, art, or dance time may be used to conduct assessments. Because the assessments are so integral to a school's core academic program, they have to take priority.

- **Working the calendar.** Change the schedule (the dates for a student presentation, a field trip, and so on) where possible to give teachers extra time to administer assessments.

Chapter Three delineated criteria for choosing a literacy assessment. No matter what assessment you use, you will need to be able to identify the precise skills that will drive each student to the next stage of reading ability. If your assessment system does not provide skill-level guidance, you will need to take the time to analyze the results of each small group and identify what steps would have allowed them to score higher. For example, if one of your guided reading groups clusters around 380L, you would consider what skill would most effectively drive the group higher. To determine this, you would ask the following questions:

- What were the students doing effectively with that text?

- What strategies were the students using ineffectively or not using at all?

- What will students need to do differently in order to read texts of that difficulty level?

- What will students need to do differently to comprehend more deeply?

- What previous instruction (or lack thereof) may have led to the confusion?

Remember: merely having the students reading at the proper text difficulty level is not an adequate action step. We need to target the weaknesses that are keeping students from moving forward. The result of this process should be a set of a few skills that you can target and focus on for each subgroup of students. And in order to identify those skills, the way you collect data will make all the difference.

COLLECTING DATA

Once you test your students, you need to make those data useful by gathering and analyzing them in one place. A basic spreadsheet can quickly give you a bird's-eye view of your class's performance, as well as which areas to target for follow-up. The most effective data reports we've seen collect data at the class and individual level, organizing them on one page per classroom. Such a spreadsheet—in this case the one used by Aja in her own school—might look as shown in Figure 7.1.

Notice the power in the simplicity of the chart. On one page, you have all the key information for each student: rate, accuracy, self-corrections, fluency, comprehension (factual, inference, critical thinking), and spelling. It allows you to quickly identify struggling students as well as check for overall patterns in the class's performance in certain aspects of reading.

Myths About Early Reading Assessment

Unfortunately, most early reading assessments do *not* give you this sort of guidance on your results. Beware of the following myths that do *not* lead to deep analysis of results.

Myth: A data wall showing students' progress up the reading levels is sufficient.

Reality: The level of the text students are reading is insufficient to understand what you need to work on. It's nice to see a pattern of students stagnating at 250L, but that doesn't give you an action step. Your analysis needs to go a level deeper, as the sample spreadsheet in Figure 7.1 shows: noting trends in performance

Figure 7.1 Aja's Data Spreadsheet

Analysis: Steps 10–12

November 2011 — Temple University-VES

Accuracy/Rate

Name	Step 10 %	Step 10 Rate (abv, tar, bel)	Step 10 SC	Step 11 %	Step 11 Rate (abv, tar, bel)	Step 11 SC	Step 12 %	Step 12 Rate (abv, tar, bel)	Step 12 SC	Fluency (1–4)	E=M (Meaning Error)	E=S (Syntax Error)	E=V (Visualization error)
Jasmine	99	TAR	1				99	TAR	2	3			1
Rachel							99	TAR		4	1	1	
Taijah				100	TAR	4				3		1	
Jason				99	TAR	4				3	1	1	1
Timeese				99	TAR	2				3	1	1	
Andrew	99	TAR	1							3			1
Jessica	98	BEL	2								8	8	
Genice	94	BEL	6							2	2	2	1
CLASS AVERAGE	91			99		3	99		3	3	3	2	3

Comprehension

Name	Step 10 Total	S10 Retell	S10 Factual	S10 Inferential	S10 Critical Thinking	Step 11 Total	S11 Retell	S11 Factual	S11 Inferential	S11 Critical Thinking	Step 12 Total	S12 Retell	S12 Factual	S12 Inferential	S12 Critical thinking	WR 1	WR 2	WR 3	Total	PE	F	C	LA	Q
Jasmine											4	2		3	2	1	2	3		2	1	1	4	
Rachel											4	3		3	2	1	2	1		2	4	1	4	1
Taijah						5	3		1	4								1		1	2	3	1	
Jason						3	2		1	2								1		1	1	1	2	
Timeese						4	4		1	3								1		1	2	2	2	
Andrew	6	2	1	4	2											1	1	1		2	2	1	3	2
Jessica	5	2	1	2	2											1	1	1		2		3	2	2
Genice	5	4	1	4	1													5		1	3	1	1	1
CLASS AVERAGE	1	3	1	1	1	0/3	3	#	#/1	3	0/3	3	#	3	2	7	12	13		1	2	2	2	2

Developmental Spelling

Name	Spelling TOTAL:	Lg Vowel	R-control	Diphtong	Comp. blend	-ed/-ing	Double cons	Lg V - 2 syl	R-con - 2 syl
Jasmine						5	4	4	4
Rachel						5	5	5	5
Taijah						5	5	5	5
Jason						5	5	4	4
Timeese						5	4	5	3
Andrew		5	5	5	5				
Jessica		5	5	3	4				
Genice		4	4	5	4				
CLASS AVERAGE		5	4	4	4	5	5	5	4

on fluency, accuracy, and different types of comprehension questions—at a minimum.

Myth: Analyzing reading accuracy is sufficient to determine when to increase text difficulty.

Reality: Although some noted leading literacy experts have argued that assessing students' reading accuracy is sufficient to determine when to move to a higher text level, that is a dangerous assumption. Someone can read accurately without comprehension, especially the level of deep comprehension required by the Common Core. If we don't assess that ability to comprehend, we won't be able to drive our teaching to improve it.

Myth: More pages of reading data are better.

Reality: As highlighted in both *Driven by Data* and *Leverage Leadership*, the quantity of data does not lead to better analysis; in fact, once you move beyond a page of data—two, at a maximum—for a classroom, it is difficult to focus and not have the "eyes glazing over" reaction. The importance of consolidating all the most important data in one place cannot be overstated.

Myth: Just knowing that comprehension is an issue is sufficient.

Reality: Of all the myths listed here, this is one of the most common. The power of a data report like the one we've shown is that it can immediately target your focus on a level deeper than simple comprehension. In the report, the data are coded in red wherever the results kept the students from passing that assessment level. We can see that in the 600L group of students (STEP 11), one student, Jason, is struggling with his retell; two of the three, Taijah and Timeese, have too many comprehension errors, particularly in the area of critical thinking questions. This allows the teacher to quickly move to those individual student records and to look directly at the critical thinking errors, rather than perusing every record in every area of the assessment or, even worse, just teaching at that reading level. If the teacher does this, she will discover that Taijah and Timeese were struggling with figurative language and moving beyond literal interpretations. Let's go back to the opening premise: if the teacher just kept teaching "comprehension" at 600L, Taijah and Timeese might not ever really advance, or at least not quickly; they wouldn't be getting practice in the place they needed it. This demonstrates the importance of deeper analysis.

Sadly, most of early literacy assessments do *not* provide this quality of summary data. We can speak personally to this challenge: the school leaders we work with ended up designing the data report shown here because none of the existing reports met student learning needs.

Acquiring or Making an Assessment Report That Works for You

So what do you do if you don't have an effective way to view the data for your students? Here are some solutions—some more quickly implemented, others requiring a larger time investment:

- **Use ours.** In the attached DVD, you will find the Excel template that was designed for analyzing assessment data. Here are the pros and cons of using our template:
  - **All reading levels in one place.** The template is built to allow you to look at data for students across varying reading levels on one page. It is conditionally formatted so that it automatically turns red (failing), yellow (close), or green (passing) when the data are entered.
  - **STEP aligned.** This spreadsheet was built for the STEP assessment. If you wanted to use it with another assessment, you would have to adjust it to match the data that you would receive from that assessment.
  - **Requires data entry.** The spreadsheet will calculate the results, but teachers still have to manually enter the data for each student.
- **Push your assessment provider to improve its reports.** Assessment providers are built to serve, and they are more responsive than you would imagine when there is a large demand for better reporting. Show them a template that you are looking for and push them to provide that type of data report. In most cases, the technical capacity is there; you just need to ask for it!
- **Get comfortable at the dining room table.** When neither of the previous options are practical or doable, get comfortable at a very large table and spread out your individual student assessments so that you can see them jointly. Line up the assessments of similar reading levels side by side and look for patterns visually. Then create a simple analysis template (we'll provide examples later in this chapter) that allows you to take notes on those trends. This is what the finest literacy teachers were doing for years before computer technology. Although you won't find it as easy to see patterns, this approach can still work!

So once you have your data for all areas of reading, what *does* deep, effective analysis look like?

FROM ASSESSMENT TO ANALYSIS

For analysis to be most effective, it should take place between forty-eight hours and one week following the assessment.[2] Yet quick analysis is not adequate; it must go deep enough as well.

Core Idea

Quick analysis is not sufficient; analysis must go deep enough.

What is the most efficient way to go deep? By analyzing the errors of your students on specific comprehension questions. The powerful insights don't come from knowing that students got inference questions wrong, for example; they come from seeing the type of errors students made in their answers.

Core Idea

At its root, deep analysis is about analyzing errors of students on individual questions.

It's not enough to know they got inference questions wrong; you need to know what type of errors they made in their answers.

Let's consider an example of what one piece of an analysis might look like for the comprehension section of an assessment. Here, students had difficulty understanding the perspective of multiple characters in a text. With the test in hand, the teacher is able to zoom in on student difficulties and their potential causes:

> The question that caused the greatest error was, "What does Buttercup mean when she thinks that Angela might look too nice to be a dog-napper?" This question required students to understand perspective

about other characters. Tracing characters: students are struggling to hold on to well-developed main and secondary characters. Until now, I have selected texts with one well-developed character instead of a text where the secondary characters were also well developed. Students needed to understand their perspectives to answer questions about the text. I will select texts that have well-developed secondary characters and ask questions about the perspectives of the secondary characters.

This level of analysis—focusing on the errors made by the students at a specific reading level—allows the teacher to craft an instructional plan that is tightly focused on the next step for these learners. Table 7.1 shows her entire action plan for that group of students.

Think about the power of this analysis. The teacher knows far more than what text difficulty should be used with her students—she also knows precisely where the comprehension errors are occurring. This depth of analysis is what leads to highly effective action plans, which we'll explore in the next section.

Core Idea

The impact of your action plan is determined by the depth of your analysis.

We realize that this level of analysis doesn't come naturally: it's built by an effective assessment and by coaching on how to analyze assessment data. We address the quality of the assessment in Chapter Three; in Chapter Twelve, we'll address the role of instructional leadership (which is worth reading even if you're not an instructional leader, as the guidelines there can be used by anyone).

FROM ANALYSIS TO ACTION

Understanding student mistakes is the first step of the process. The next core question we must ask ourselves as teachers is "What do I need to teach my students so they can master the questions they missed on the assessment?" The true beauty of carefully analyzing your results is that the effort will flesh out your

Table 7.1 Effective Analysis: Sample for a 450L– 500L Group

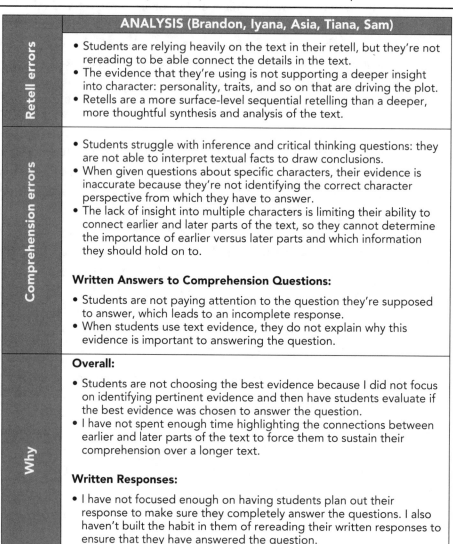

	ANALYSIS (Brandon, Iyana, Asia, Tiana, Sam)
Retell errors	• Students are relying heavily on the text in their retell, but they're not rereading to be able connect the details in the text. • The evidence that they're using is not supporting a deeper insight into character: personality, traits, and so on that are driving the plot. • Retells are a more surface-level sequential retelling than a deeper, more thoughtful synthesis and analysis of the text.
Comprehension errors	• Students struggle with inference and critical thinking questions: they are not able to interpret textual facts to draw conclusions. • When given questions about specific characters, their evidence is inaccurate because they're not identifying the correct character perspective from which they have to answer. • The lack of insight into multiple characters is limiting their ability to connect earlier and later parts of the text, so they cannot determine the importance of earlier versus later parts and which information they should hold on to. **Written Answers to Comprehension Questions:** • Students are not paying attention to the question they're supposed to answer, which leads to an incomplete response. • When students use text evidence, they do not explain why this evidence is important to answering the question.
Why	**Overall:** • Students are not choosing the best evidence because I did not focus on identifying pertinent evidence and then have students evaluate if the best evidence was chosen to answer the question. • I have not spent enough time highlighting the connections between earlier and later parts of the text to force them to sustain their comprehension over a longer text. **Written Responses:** • I have not focused enough on having students plan out their response to make sure they completely answer the questions. I also haven't built the habit in them of rereading their written responses to ensure that they have answered the question.

journey for the next few weeks. By identifying the skill deficiencies your students possess, you'll gain valuable guidance in three key areas:

1. **Grouping.** This information allows you not only to group students by ability level but also to tweak these groups so that each shares a common reading difficulty.

2. **Text selection.** You can now choose developmentally targeted texts that will specifically elicit the reading challenges with which your students need practice.

3. **Prompting.** The level of student proficiency also dictates what specific prompts you'll want to use with students as you conduct guided lessons. We'll discuss that in further detail in the Chapter Nine.

Using the deep analysis described in the previous section, a teacher can design an instructional plan for review with a peer, instructional leader, or literacy coach. Together, the team can review the analysis, investigate areas of struggle, and collaborate to design a multiweek action plan that will map out the curriculum until the next assessment.[3] Using your assessment data to target the right skills at the right times is what will drive student achievement.

Core Idea

Assessment-based action planning ensures that you will target the right skills at the right times.

Take a look at Table 7.2, the action plan for the first week of guided reading that corresponds to the analysis in the previous section. Notice how much detail the teacher is able to weave into the plan as a result of the analysis: the texts that will be used, the questions that will address this group's needs, and the plan for individual students who need extra attention.

The end result of the process should be a chart for what the next few weeks of guided reading instruction might look like overall for each of your guided reading

Table 7.2 Effective Action: Sample Action Plan for a 450L– 500L Group

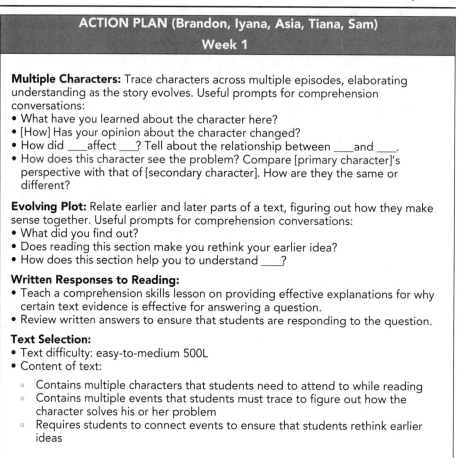

ACTION PLAN (Brandon, Iyana, Asia, Tiana, Sam)
Week 1

Multiple Characters: Trace characters across multiple episodes, elaborating understanding as the story evolves. Useful prompts for comprehension conversations:
• What have you learned about the character here?
• [How] Has your opinion about the character changed?
• How did ___affect ___? Tell about the relationship between ___and ___.
• How does this character see the problem? Compare [primary character]'s perspective with that of [secondary character]. How are they the same or different?

Evolving Plot: Relate earlier and later parts of a text, figuring out how they make sense together. Useful prompts for comprehension conversations:
• What did you find out?
• Does reading this section make you rethink your earlier idea?
• How does this section help you to understand ___?

Written Responses to Reading:
• Teach a comprehension skills lesson on providing effective explanations for why certain text evidence is effective for answering a question.
• Review written answers to ensure that students are responding to the question.

Text Selection:
• Text difficulty: easy-to-medium 500L
• Content of text:

  ○ Contains multiple characters that students need to attend to while reading
  ○ Contains multiple events that students must trace to figure out how the character solves his or her problem
  ○ Requires students to connect events to ensure that students rethink earlier ideas

groups. What might a week look like for a teacher with all his or her reading groups? Take a look at Table 7.3.

It's worth underscoring that the analysis process has allowed this teacher not only to be deliberate about grouping but also to determine what do with each group: what skills to target and what books to choose. Guided reading will be the ideal place for teachers to put this knowledge into action (see Chapters Eight and Nine).

Table 7.3 Effective Action: Sample Schedule for Guided Reading

WEEK 1 AT A GLANCE—GRADE 2				
Name of Group	**Eagles**	**Ospreys**	**Parrots, Hawks**	**Condors, Falcons**
Accuracy, Rate, Word Solving	Fluency: Read new 400L–520L texts in 3–4 word phrases with attention to punctuation in most texts.			
	Look for students to do the following: • Read quickly • Read smoothly • Read the punctuation	N/A	N/A	N/A
Comprehension	No written response work targeted for this level.	Written responses • Teacher will review written work to ensure that students are responding to the question. • Teacher will review written work to ensure that the students are explaining *why* the evidence from the text is important.		
	• Character motive • Sustained attention to meaning of longer text • Evidence	• Sustained attention to meaning of longer text • Character contrast: different characters' points of view	• Trace characters across multiple episodes • Relate earlier and later parts of a text	• Character perspective • Connect different parts of a text to build meaning • Identify pertinent information in a text when searching for answers • Compare the strength of different answers to a question

Table 7.3 Effective Action: Sample Schedule for Guided Reading (*continued*)

WEEK 1 AT A GLANCE—GRADE 2					
Text Selection		400L–450L	450L–500L	500L–550L	550L–650L
		Content: • Clear character motivations that explain character's actions • Clear cause-and-effect relationship within the text	Content: • Multiple characters that students need to attend to while reading • Multiple events that students must trace to figure out how the character solves his or her problem	Content: • Multiple characters that students need to attend to while reading • Multiple events that students must trace to figure out how the character solves his or her problem	Content: • Clear difference in perspective between characters • Requires students to revise their understanding of the character

A Word on ... Creating Small Groups for Targeted Instruction

Even with the help of assessment, teachers find that the question of *which* students should go in each small group for targeted instruction is much more complex than that of *how many* students should go in each group. During the process of determining the right group for each student in a class, a number of questions frequently come up that are worth addressing.

Question: We have a student who is on the "border" between two groups— he'd be easily the strongest reader in one group, but he'd be the weakest reader in the group the next level up. Where should we place him?

Answer: First, look at the sizes of the two groups. If one of the groups is fairly large, put this student in the smaller one: every student in both of those groups will get more practice opportunities that way, and you'll have more time to work with this student at his own level. If the two groups are the same size, put the student in the higher-level group to challenge him more.

Question: What if a student is very strong in some skills but weak in others (for example, a student with strong literal comprehension but weak inference skills)?

Answer: This is where the power of small reading groups and careful lesson planning comes into play. When you plan the questions you will ask during the comprehension conversation, you can write them with specific students in mind— for instance, you might plan an inference question specifically for the student described in this question— and then simply be sure to call on those students first when you ask those questions. Our most successful teachers took this a step further: they kept a notepad with them during guided reading and used it to record their individual students' responses to comprehension questions from day to day, so that they could better keep track of each student's growth and needs. (Note, however, that in the best assessment systems we have seen, such as STEP, the design of the test itself minimizes the chance that the situation described in this question can arise in the first place, as the levels are designed to group students with similar skill needs.)

Question: I teach a lot of students; is it really feasible for me to have groups as small as the ones you have suggested?

Answer: The size of your reading groups will depend on your schedule constraints and the size of your classroom. We'll address this head-on in Chapter Eleven. For now, it is sufficient to say that we have found that teaching between six and nine guided reading groups for your classroom is entirely feasible, meaning that even the largest elementary classrooms should be able to create these groups.

Question: We have a large group of students who all are on similar reading levels, and no other students are close to them. Should we still split them up into smaller groups?

Answer: Ideally, if many students are on the same level, you could split them into two groups. Even if the second group has the exact same needs as the first, each student would still get the chance for much more intensive coaching. However, if you can't do this, it's better to keep students of the same ability level together than to distribute some of those students into other groups, as groups of similar ability level are what will allow you to create effective lesson plans.

Dividing students into groups based on ability level remains controversial in many areas, due to fear of stigma or other unwanted consequences. When it comes to the focused practice used in guided reading, however, the specific needs of students differ so vastly that creating student groups based on other criteria, such as subject interest, would badly disserve instruction. In fact, we've found that it is precisely this differentiated, targeted instruction that has most allowed our lower-performing readers to catch up with their initially stronger peers. These students often benefit most from the chance to carefully and repeatedly practice the reading skills they need.

CONCLUSION: THE PATH FORWARD

Certainly, this process takes time and institutional commitment. The rewards, we have found, are worth every bit of it. Let's take a moment to reflect on what the assessment program we've described gives you and your students. With your action plan in hand, you know just what each student in your class needs to learn, and, perhaps even more important, you know how to teach it. You've ensured that your lessons will be at exactly the right level of rigor, and when you conduct your next assessment, you'll see right away what worked, what didn't, and where to go next.

Anyone who has even walked past the self-help section of a bookstore is familiar with the mantra, "It's not the destination; it's the journey." In the case of your assessment program, nothing could be truer. Results matter. What matters even more, however, is the way you use those results to help your students develop the right habits at every step of the way. The upshot is that you'll not only reach the destination you set out for but also get there much, much faster. Ultimately, the data from your assessments give you the tools you'll need to add precision and individualization to your reading program. In our next chapter, you'll see exactly what it looks like when the rubber hits the road, in the form of the guided reading lesson.

Apply Your Habits: Improve Analysis and Action Planning

Self-Assessment

Which aspect of data-driven instruction do you think will be most helpful for you to implement first?

- A calendar that supports assessment proctoring and grading
- A template for action planning from assessment data
- User-friendly mechanisms for collecting data
- A plan for meeting with an instructional coach to review data together

Tools to Use

- Early Literacy Analysis Template (included on the DVD)
- Early Literacy Results Sample: STEP Analysis (included on the DVD)
- Effective Action Sample Schedule for Guided Reading (included on the DVD)
- Effective Action: Sample Plan for Level 450– 480L Group (included on the DVD)
- Effective Analysis: Sample for Level 450– 480L Group (included on the DVD)
- Early Literacy Analysis Spreadsheet Template: STEP Analysis, Steps 8– 12 (included on the DVD)
- Additional examples and templates (available in *Driven by Data*)

Your Next Steps

Chapter 8

Guided Reading Planning

Move Beyond the Map

Lesson Type	Group Size	What to Teach?
Read-Aloud	Whole class	Skills from yearlong syllabus
Comprehension Skills	Small group by reading level or whole class if necessary	Skills from yearlong syllabus
Phonics	Small group or whole class if necessary	Skills from premade program
Guided Reading	**Small group by reading level**	**Skills determined by assessment analysis (Chapter Seven)**
Independent Reading	Individual	Skills for all students

Since 2003, map sales have been on the decline. Some states are dramatically cutting their production of road maps, once a staple of visitor centers.[1] Washington State has discontinued printing altogether. Why did maps fall so fast? It's not as if the GPS invents newer, faster routes to get us to our destinations—it tells us the same information a map would have. And it doesn't give us that information in more detail, either. Indeed, most navigation systems are extremely minimalist when compared to the sharp colors and elaborate byways seen on a traditional highway map.

The real difference, we think, is in-the-moment guidance. By now, many of us are familiar with the almost-human voice of the GPS narrator, telling us exactly what we need to do at precisely what time. More important, when we move off course, the system eagerly declares "Recalculating!" before correcting us and moving us forward. GPSs don't beat maps because they have different information: they beat maps because they guide our actions as we drive.

When it comes to reading instruction, the process we covered in the previous chapter is the equivalent of mapmaking. We work to choose assessments that will guarantee rigor; create comprehensive sets of the skills all students need; plan for days, weeks, and years; and chart our students' progress. When the dust settles, we have a deep understanding of what goals students should reach and what lessons they'll need to get there.

Yet as anyone who has ever been lost knows, maps aren't always enough. Whether an accident blocks the road, directions are misleading, or sudden events change our plans, a map-planned trip can draw us off course. If people have come to view the GPS as a driving necessity, it is because a GPS ensures that these mishaps cost us minutes, not hours.

As appealing as this is for anyone who drives a car, we find its implications yet more compelling for students who are "driving" toward reading proficiency. Learning to read is a deeply individual and dynamic process. After all, if all it took were well-designed materials and an established curriculum, the work we do wouldn't be so challenging! If maps were enough, people wouldn't buy GPSs. The very best reading teachers design opportunities for students to be coached and corrected in the moment as they learn to read, ensuring that they stay on course and practice the right habits — acting, in effect, as a "GPS" to mastering reading. How do these teachers do it? Through guided reading lessons.

Core Idea

Guided reading is the GPS of reading instruction: it gives students control of the wheel, while you make sure they stay on the road.

Because guided reading is a complex endeavor, we've divided our explanation of how to teach it into two chapters. This chapter is all about setting the course for a great guided reading experience; we'll take you through the process of designing a great guided reading lesson.

Chapter Nine focuses on execution. We'll cover the GPS work of providing in-the-moment coaching before, during, and after reading, keeping your students on track as they read and discuss a text — whether it is narrative or informational. And later on, in Chapter Eleven, we'll demonstrate how to organize your schedule to make ample time for both types.

STRUCTURING A GUIDED READING LESSON

At first glance, guided reading may seem similar to a comprehension skills lesson. After all, isn't teaching always about striking that balance between giving students increasing independence and keeping them on track? Certainly. But in guided reading, the principle is applied differently than in traditional I Do, We Do, You Do lessons. To see how, let's look at one example of guided reading in practice. Here, Aja Settles's students are discussing the story *Amber Brown Is Green with Envy*, by Paula Danziger, particularly the point at which Amber is very sad to hear that her mom is going to be having a baby. Watch what happens.

WATCH Clip 26: Aja Settles's Comprehension—600L

As you see here, guided reading takes the idea of coaching students to independence to a different level than a comprehension skills lesson. Whereas read-aloud, comprehension skills, and phonics lessons highlight specific skills of reading, guided reading lessons give students a chance to use all those skills at once — that is, to finally take the wheel from the start. They are applying all they've learned to understand a story — with the teacher's guiding questions along the way. What does the whole trajectory of such a guided reading lesson look like? Take a look at the box "Basic Structure of a Guided Reading Lesson."

Basic Structure of a Guided Reading Lesson

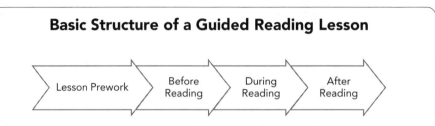

Lesson Prework → Before Reading → During Reading → After Reading

Guided reading lessons are flexible, small-group sessions that allow you to target the aspect of reading your students need support with most—even while they employ all the skills needed to make sense of a text. Use these lessons to address specific student needs while providing greater (but not total) reading independence.

Lesson Prework	Teacher analyzes student data to choose the appropriate text for each group, scripting prompts to focus practice on the skill(s) students need.
Before Reading	Teacher introduces students to the text and highlights the reading skill(s) of particular value for the text and lesson.
During Reading	Students read the text; where applicable, teacher uses word-solving prompts for students who need focus on accuracy and fluency.
After Reading	Teacher facilitates a comprehension conversation about what students have read, using prompts to target areas for student growth.

TOTAL LESSON TIME = 20–25 MINUTES*

*Note: If your schedule won't allow this much time for guided reading, you can reduce the time to 15 minutes by moving some of these components to other parts of the day (for example, having students read the text before gathering with you, reviewing the skills completely in read-aloud, and so on). For more details on scheduling, see Chapter Eleven.

Although we aim for twenty to twenty-five minutes for a guided reading lesson, you'll note that we didn't list timings for the different components of reading instruction. As your students develop, you'll want the flexibility to shift the timings of each section based on what skill you're addressing. Emerging

Table 8.1 Basic Structure of a Guided Reading Lesson: Adjusting to Your Students' Development

Reading Level	Before Reading	During Reading	After Reading
Up to 100L	5 minutes	17 minutes	3 minutes
100L – 300L	5 minutes	10 minutes	10 minutes
500L+	0 minutes	0 minutes (done during Independent Reading)	25 minutes

readers need to spend a lot of time word solving. If that's where your students are, you'll want to spend the bulk of your time with them reading in front of you. But at higher levels, you'll be working on comprehension skills, and the conversation after reading will be more important. Sometimes, in fact, students will have already done the reading, and your entire lesson can be an "after reading" conversation. The beauty of the guided reading format is that it can be adjusted quite precisely to the learning needs of your students. Consider the potential breakdowns shown in Table 8.1.

In life, when students embark on truly independent reading endeavors, their teachers won't be there to guide them any longer; they will, in effect, be driving without a GPS. To make sure that students can successfully transition from reading with a teacher to reading solo, the framework of guided reading lessons is flexible so as to make optimal use of teacher expertise while it's available. It's when the students need the most hand-holding that you need to be sure they're with you at the guided reading table. The bottom line? Guided reading lessons should match the *right reading skill* with the *right student* at the *right time*, no matter where the students are.

Core Idea

Guided reading lessons match the right skill with the right student at the right time.

To show how you can build this experience in your classroom, let's dive into our first task: choosing the right text.

PREWORK: SELECTING A TEXT TO MATCH THE DATA

Whether you're using narrative or informational selections, the texts you choose to use at the guided reading table are the gateway to conducting a lesson that is centered on your students' needs. As a quick review, the twofold core principle behind guided reading is as follows:

1. **Students take the wheel.** They use all their reading skills in tandem and do as much of the work of reading as possible.

2. **The teacher acts as a GPS—and students get plenty of opportunities to benefit from his or her presence.** As students read and analyze the text, the teacher prompts them to use their very best reading habits whenever they slip off track.

So when it comes to striking the correct balance between letting the students drive and giving them opportunities to be coached, choosing the right text is paramount. To help you, here are the two most important rules of thumb for making this happen at the guided reading table.

Look to the Reading Level—Shoot for 90 Percent Independence

One of the major instructional shifts embedded in the Common Core is the notion that schools must expose students to increasingly complex texts. Sometimes referred to as the "staircase of complexity," the CCSS are aligned to better prepare students for the challenges in texts they are likely to encounter in college. The key question, then, is how we choose the right texts to move students up that staircase. Although the Common Core does not endorse a single way to measure the quantitative complexity of texts, it does highlight Lexile scores as one of these methods, providing the following guidance on what, numerically, its expectations mean for text selection (see Figure 8.1).

So, the first step is to choose a text that is of an appropriate level of technical complexity for students. When you do this, keep in mind that your goal is not to pick texts at the highest end of your students' capacities. Remember: in guided reading, we don't only want to get students to practice the skill that is most challenging for them. We also want them to practice putting all their reading skills into play at once and, in doing so, to work toward being able to read independently. So when you look for the right text for students to read, you don't only want it to get them to practice that one tough skill; you also want them to be

Figure 8.1 Updated Text Complexity Grade Bands and Associated Ranges from Multiple Measures

Common Core Band	ATOS	Degrees of Reading Power®	Flesch-Kincaid	The Lexile Framework®	Reading Maturity	SourceRater
2nd–3rd	2.75–5.14	42–54	1.98–5.34	420–820	3.53–6.13	0.05–2.48
4th–5th	4.97–7.03	52–60	4.51–7.73	740–1010	5.42–7.92	0.84–5.75
6th–8th	7.00–9.98	57–67	6.51–10.34	925–1185	7.04–9.57	4.11–10.66
9th–10th	9.67–12.01	62–72	8.32–12.12	1050–1335	8.41–10.81	9.02–13.93
11th–CCR	11.20–14.10	67–74	10.34–14.2	1185–1385	9.57–12.00	12.30–14.50

Source: From "Supplemental Information for Appendix A of the Common Core State Standards for English Language Arts and Literacy: New Research on Text Complexity," Council of Chief State School Officers and the National Governors Association, http://www.corestandards.org/assets/E0813_Appendix_A_New_Research_on_Text_Complexity.pdf.

able to read the rest of the text mostly on their own. The ideal text to select, then, is one that your students will be able to read 90 percent independently, and the other 10 percent with your guidance on that specific skill. The assessment that you administer should point you to some good texts to use.

Look Beyond the Level—Target the Skill They Need

As the Common Core is quick to point out, the complexity of the texts you choose matters, but it's not the only thing you should keep in mind. Qualitative measures, as well as considerations about the reader and the task, also need to weigh in. Text level does matter; there's no question about that. But not every 500L text is created equal. It matters not only how difficult the text you choose is but also specifically which reading strategies it will require your students to use.

To make this clearer, let's briefly swap our GPS metaphor for an image of a ski resort. Typically, the trails at a ski resort are labeled with symbols to tell you how difficult they are: a green circle means the trail is easy to ski, a blue square means it requires an intermediate skill level, and a black diamond means it's tough. But as most skiers who have made use of those trail symbols know, a distinction between easy, medium, and hard doesn't tell you everything. One trail may be labeled with a blue square because it's steeper than your average green-circle trail; another may simply be longer and require more endurance. Therefore, if you've just graduated from a Skiing for Beginners class and want to get better at descending steep hills, the first trail will help you out, whereas the second — even though it's just as "difficult" as the first — won't.

Students who are moving up from one reading level to the next bear an unmistakable resemblance to skiers. Working with just any text whose "difficulty" matches the level at which they are reading won't truly help them advance to the next level or give you the most valuable chances to coach them. A text that gives them the opportunity to practice the specific skills they most need to work on (beyond the myriad other skills it takes to read a book) will.

This gap between text "difficulty" and the actual skills required to decode the text bears implications for which book you ultimately choose. Almost any book will give your students the chance to analyze character motivation, but the book you need is one for which understanding character motivation is critical to comprehending the big ideas in the text. Why? Because that will ensure that your students get authentic practice — making teaching the reading skill an exercise in purpose, not a forced and isolated application. We cannot stress this point enough: practice won't make perfect; only authentic practice will. Make sure the text you choose relies on the reading skill you want students to practice.

Core Idea

Be picky when you choose your texts. What matters isn't just text difficulty, but which skills the text demands.

The data analysis process we outlined in the previous chapter is your key to picking the text to teach in a guided reading lesson. With the data from your latest assessment and a curriculum that focuses on what your students ultimately need to master, you can determine exactly which strategy you most urgently need to teach your students. Pick your texts for both the level *and* the specific reading challenges to which you want to expose your students.

By way of example, imagine you have a group of readers at 125L. At this level of comprehension, students are focused on talking about primary story elements (main idea, setting, characters, problem and solution) and recalling story details to clarify ideas. Let's imagine that when you look at the data from your class's assessment, one of your groups is doing fine with primary story elements but has struggled recalling details from the text. Specifically, your assessment indicated that students weren't returning to the text to search for specific information.

The key to picking the right text for that guided reading lesson, then, would be to choose a text that would give the students as many opportunities as possible to practice recalling details—a book that was rich in important details would be far more valuable than one with a compelling but general plot. What's more, you'd want a text where recalling those details would be key to understanding the central ideas in the text. Working with any 125L text won't be enough. You'll want to pick the *right* 125L text. Once you've done that, you're well on your way to a successful guided reading lesson.

Your Turn! A Text Selection Exercise

Let's put these principles into action. You have a group of 450L students, and after administering the latest round of literacy assessments, you come to the following conclusions when analyzing their wrong answers:

Key Misunderstandings on the Last Assessment

- **Confusion around multiple characters:** students are struggling to keep track of more than two strong characters.
- **Too factual:** students use text evidence, but don't combine evidence with background knowledge to make complete inferences.
- **Difficulty keeping track of multiple events and settings:** students leave out important parts of the plot during their retell, normally around a new event or setting change.

March / New York University	Last STEP Administered	STEP Achieved	Reading Group (H, M, L)	Step 9 %	Rate (abv, tar, bel)	SC	Fluency (1–4)	Errors E=M (Meaning Error)	E=S (Syntax Error)	E=V (Visualization error)	Step 9 TOTAL	Step 9 Retell	Factual	Inferential	Critical Thinking	Written Response 1	2	3	4
Ahmari	9	8	L	99	abv				1	1	3	2		3		x			
Avante	9	8	L	99	abv				1	1	3	3	1	2					
Cyncere	9	8	L	99	tar	1				1	3	2	3	1		x	x		

(continued)

(continued)

On the basis of these data and your analysis, you go into your 400L–500L library and find the following three options: *A New Coat for Anna* (Harriet Ziefert), *Minerva's Dream* (Katherine Mead), and *Survivors of the Frozen North* (Beverley Randell).

Which one is the best choice? Why?

(Do *not* keep reading until you've made your choice! The answer is revealed below.)

_____

_____

_____

_____

_____

Why is this the best choice? Of the three options, this one stands out because it has multiple characters that are developed, and the book has a strong theme. Because this book is a beginning chapter book, the setting changes allow students to practice sustaining their understanding for longer stretches of time. In addition, this book is great for figuring out implicit cause-and-effect relationships, which would force students to move beyond factual responses to support their thinking.

Choosing the right text can make a world of difference in targeting what students need.

Correct Choice: *Minerva's Dream*

This example points to a clear conclusion: text selection is exceedingly important to the success of guided reading.

Core Idea

Text selection is half the battle: everything else flows from here.

But even with clear direction from your data, selecting the right books for your students can be time consuming and even overwhelming. We appreciate that your time is probably too limited to try to sort this out on your own. There are two solutions we'll suggest. First, we think the opportunity to get in-house coaching around text selection is valuable—so long as it is based on your students' data. Even a great text, if it's not aligned with the reading skill your class needs, will fail at the guided reading table. But if you don't have coaching readily available, we offer a list of books and their foci by level on the DVD that accompanies this book. For example, Table 8.2 lists a few of the texts for students that are normally tagged F&P Level K. You can find a full list of narrative texts from 50L to 700L on the DVD.[2]

A Word on . . . What Happened to Fountas and Pinnell?

Fountas and Pinnell (F&P), a leveling system that has long been a staple of many elementary reading programs, was conspicuously left unmentioned by the CCSS as a valid way to categorize text complexity. Although the standards note that no quantitative measure of text complexity is perfect, they point to systems like Lexile scores, Flesch-Kincaid, or ATOS as ways to identify complexity in a scientific manner. F&P, which levels books primarily along qualitative lines, fails this test.

Of course, the CCSS point out that qualitative measures do matter for leveling texts. In supplemental material to CCSS Appendix A, the Council of Chief State School Officers and National Governor's Association recommend that educators use quantitative measures to locate a text within a *grade band*, and qualitative ones to place a text within a specific *grade*. Once you level your texts using a quantitative system, the Reading-by-Habit model gives you the ability to precisely target your instruction to your students' qualitative needs.

If you are one of the many teachers using F&P right now, do not worry. Publishers will soon catch up to the CCSS and publish measures of their books' complexity scores; at this point, you'll be able to realign your class library. To help you get started, we offer the following chart. Keep in mind that the correlations between F&P levels and the Common Core are only general rules of thumb. Not all Level P texts are equal—or equally complex.

CCSS Grade Band	Lexile Aligned to CCSS	Corresponding F&P Levels
K–1	n/a	A–L
2–3	420L–820L	L–U
4–5	740L–1010L	U–Z

Note: These grade equivalencies reflect supplemental material to CCSS Appendix A, published by the Council of Chief State School Officers and National Governor's Association in August 2012. They argue that this update of the original text bands provided by the Common Core will provide "a more modulated climb toward college and career readiness and offer slightly more overlap between bands."

Table 8.2 A Guide to Selecting Level K Texts: Sample from the DVD—Narrative Texts

Lexile Level	Title	Author	Big Idea	Skill 1	Skill 2	Skill 3
310L	*Bear's Diet*	Annette Smith	Compassion, friendship (pet)	Mental state	Multiple episodes	—
340L	*Stone Soup*	Annette Smith	Cleverness, perseverance	Character motivation	Genre (fable)	Perspective (basic)
360L	*Bedtime for Frances*	Russell Hoban	Consequence, perseverance	Character motivation	Imagination	Overall meaning
360L	*Mr. Merton's Vacation*	Diana Noonan	Self-control, self-discipline (OK to lose)	Character motivation	Text features	Dialogue
380L	*The Frog Prince*	Edith H. Tarcov	Arrogance, cleverness	Character motivation	Secondary character	Dialogue
400L	*The Night Out*	Jack Gabolinscy	Acceptance (lack of)	Character perspective	Text features (thought bubbles)	Character development
420L	*But I Want It*	Linda M. Washington	Self-control and consideration	Character motivation	Character change	Dialogue
470L	*Nathan and Nicholas Alexander*	Lulu Delacre	Friendship, justice (fairness), gratitude	Character motivation	Character change	Perspective (basic)

Again, what makes this list effective is that it doesn't just target a book's Lexile level but that it identifies the focus that the text allows you to explore. The skills listed here aren't just applicable; they're key to understanding the central idea of the corresponding text.

GUIDED READING LESSON PLANNING — A SAMPLE

We've already presented a quick summary of what a guided reading lesson looks like:

Lesson Prework	Teacher analyzes student data to choose the appropriate text for each group, scripting prompts to focus practice on the skill(s) students need
Before Reading	Teacher introduces students to the text and highlights the reading skill(s) of particular value for the text and lesson
During Reading	Students read the text; where applicable, teacher uses word-solving prompts for students who need focus on accuracy and fluency
After Reading	Teacher facilitates a comprehension conversation about what students have read, using prompts to target areas for student growth

How does this look when we add in all the details? Here, illustrated in full in Table 8.3, is one sample lesson plan that reveals the answer. Notice how the text selection, which reflects the specific skills the students need to work on, sets the stage for an effective plan.

It's clear how the lesson plan in Table 8.3 reflects the overall trajectory of a guided reading lesson: it splits neatly into the categories of before, during, and after reading. What makes each part effective and well planned? Let's take a closer look at each section.

BEFORE READING

The most important concept to know about introducing a guided reading lesson is that you want to get students excited about the work they're about to do and make sure they know how to do it . . . without doing any of it for them. Accordingly, the Before Reading segment typically takes up less time than any other portion

Table 8.3 Guided Reading Lesson Plan: Sample for 450L

Group: Anaya, Anton, Karina, Elizabeth, Nevaeh, Luqman, Zauryn, E'Naisha	
Text and Author	*The Magic Finger,* by Roald Dahl
Reading Focus	**450L: Multiple Plots or Events** • Trace characters across multiple episodes, elaborating own understanding as the story progresses. • Relate earlier and later parts of a text, figuring out how they make sense together. CCSS RL.3.6
Before Reading (5 minutes)	**Introduction to the Book** Students, today we are beginning a new text by one of our favorite authors, Roald Dahl. We have already read books such as *Charlie and the Chocolate Factory,* and today we will read *The Magic Finger.* Take a moment and preview the text. What do you notice? What are you thinking this story will be about? *(Preview front and back covers.)* **Reading Strategy** Students, now that we have previewed the text, we need to set our focus for reading. As you read today, pay close attention to the characters and their motivation. How do we determine a character's motivation? *(Students recall definition learned in read-aloud and comprehension skills lessons)* Yes, we think about what they say, think, and do, and connect it to our schema to make an inference [point them to the anchor chart]. Remember, when we are reading a text of this level, we must include multiple pieces of evidence in our thinking about the characters, especially when identifying character motivation. When reading this chunk of text, also pay close attention to the motivation of the *secondary* characters. **Vocabulary in Context: N/A**
During Reading (13–15 minutes)	Students will read pages 1–21. **Task When Finished Reading** After reading the text, complete the following open-ended response. Be sure to include multiple pieces of evidence: ○ Why did Mr. Gregg walk past the narrator like she isn't there? ○ Why did Mr. Gregg go back inside on page 21?

Table 8.3   Guided Reading Lesson Plan: Sample for 450L (*continued*)

After Reading (5–7 minutes) • Inference: Adding up the clues to figure out what is not being said • Critical thinking: Adding up the clues from the whole text and combining that with personal experience and prior knowledge to make an interpretation	**Retell** (Students must include the following information.) • The narrator of this story is a girl who has a special power called the "magic finger." In the past, she has put the magic finger on people who make her very upset, like when her teacher called her stupid. • She lives on a farm next to the Gregg family, who likes to go hunting. The girl hates the fact that they go hunting. One day, as the Greggs are leaving their house, she gets so cross that she puts the magic finger on them. **Check for Understanding** Factual Questions: • How did Mrs. Winter turn into a cat? • Why does the narrator dislike hunting so much? • What did the Gregg family do the morning the magic finger was put on them? Inferential Questions: • Why do the boys go hunting? (p. 8) • **Why did Mr. Gregg walk past her like she isn't there? (p. 8)** • Why wouldn't the ducks leave the Greggs alone on page 18? **Key Answers to Inferential Questions:** (Look for these answers to the **bolded** question) • Mr. Gregg walked past the narrator like she wasn't there because he did not care about her opinion. In the story, the narrator tells Mr. Gregg not to go hunting, and he walks past her. I know if someone walks past another person and ignores them after being spoken to, they are not interested in that person's thoughts or opinion. Mr. Gregg's actions, therefore, tell the reader that he does not care about the narrator's perspective and will continue going hunting. Critical Thinking Questions: • Why won't Mrs. Winter be all right? (p. 13) • Why did Mr. Gregg want to go home? (p. 18) • **Why did Mr. Gregg go back inside on page 21?** • Why does Mr. Gregg not tell Mrs. Gregg what is going on with the ducks? **Key Answers to Critical Thinking Questions:** (Look for these answers to the **bolded** question) • Mr. Gregg goes back inside because he is afraid the ducks are pursuing him. When he had been hunting with his sons and shot at the birds, he was unable to kill them. Instead of the birds flying away from him, they flew toward him. I know that if an animal is being shot at, its instinct is to flee. This is the first sign that the ducks are after Mr. Gregg. When Mr. Gregg returns to his house, he sees the birds circling overhead. I know that birds do not typically follow people, and additionally would be in their nests at night, making the ducks' behavior even more concerning. For these reasons, Mr. Gregg believed the ducks were out to get him.

of a guided reading lesson. That does not mean it's the least important. To drive this point home, let us give you an example from an unlikely place: knitting.

Imagine you are learning how to knit (as is Paul's daughter). You show up to knitting class with your teacher, and there is a new stitch you have not tried before called "knit-two-together." Imagine if the teacher just said, "OK, start knitting!" You wouldn't know what the instruction meant, so you would take your best guess. You would probably get it wrong and then would have to start over and have the teacher redirect you.

Imagine a second scenario in which the teacher began the knitting class saying, "So you're going to use a new stitch today. Here it tells you that you need to knit-two-together. Instead of putting your needle into one stitch, you have to put your needle into two stitches and come out with one. So now you try it!" You try it once, the teacher affirms your attempt, and then you go on to knit the entire pattern that includes "knit-two-together" along with other knitting steps. There can be little doubt that the second knitting student will be far more successful, and finished much more quickly.

A book introduction serves the same purpose. If you cue students to the particular skill they need to focus on (based on your analysis) and remind them of how to use that skill, you dramatically increase the likelihood that they will use that skill correctly. Remember: guided reading isn't about just practicing but about practicing using a skill *correctly*. A well-crafted Before Reading section sets up students to succeed.

Core Idea

Guided reading isn't just about practicing but about practicing *correctly*. A well-drafted Before Reading section makes correct practice far more likely.

In fact, for a new teacher who has not done guided reading before, delivering the Before Reading section can be even more powerful than facilitating practice during the After Reading section. Why? For the precise reason demonstrated in our knitting analogy. If you didn't introduce the reading focus well, then your After Reading conversation becomes all about fixing errors that could have been addressed before they were made. Start the guided reading lesson well, and students have more chances to be successful.

Take a look at how the sample guided reading lesson plan in Table 8.3 accomplishes this goal. The final lines of the Before Reading section are as follows:

> Yes, we think about what they say, think, and do and connect it to our schema to make an inference [point them to the anchor chart]. Remember, when we are reading a text of this level, we must include multiple pieces of evidence in our thinking about the characters, especially when identifying character motivation. When reading this chunk of text, also pay close attention to the motivation of the *secondary* characters.

The teacher is not doing any of the heavy lifting of the comprehension, but she is reminding students to use the skills they learned about during their read-aloud, comprehension skills, or phonics lesson. What a difference that can make!

An effective Before Reading plan, then, includes two basic components:

1. Hook the reader, but don't "tip" the text.
2. Review the skills students need to succeed.

Hook the Reader, but Don't "Tip" the Text

As we mentioned earlier, the teacher's challenge here is to get the students excited about reading the text while not revealing much about it. Such a hook is even more important when working with students who have not yet experienced the joy of reading, such as early or struggling readers. There are a number of ways to accomplish this successfully. The table here lists some possible approaches.

Text Introduction Idea	Example
Pose a question to students that draws on their prior knowledge.	"Have you ever been to the beach? What are some things you do at the beach? Well, in this book..."
Have students preview the text and explain the clues they gather from the title, illustrations, back summary, author (if they have read prior texts from that author), the first two pages, or some combination of these.	"What did you notice when you previewed the text?"
Build suspense.	"This story will have a problem. It is your job to figure out what the problem is and why it is a problem..."

Remember, don't reveal too much of the story during your introduction, or you'll end up doing the comprehension work for the students.

Beware: many commercial programs make a text preview a part of every one of their packaged lesson plans. Previews—revealing part of the content of the text itself—are a dangerous way to lower the rigor of a text, which the Common Core authors have been wise to highlight in their trainings across the country. Ultimately, the students must do the cognitive work of figuring out the text.

Review the Skills Students Need to Succeed

If you take the time to align guided reading to read-aloud and comprehension skills lessons (as we recommend), you will likely have already taught the skills your students will need at the guided reading table. If occasionally you need to teach your students a skill that isn't already familiar to them, you can do a mini-lesson that follows the structure of the read-aloud skill introduction. Then, keep a visual display in your reading area to remind students how to apply the skill. The box "Sample Anchor Chart on Deep Retell" shows a second-grade teacher's example of how to retell effectively.

Sample Anchor Chart on Deep Retell

A Good Response Tells . . .

- *What* happened
- *Why* it happened
- *How* the character(s) feel about the event

Some Ways to Answer Thick Questions . . .

- I know _____ (information from text) so that tells me _____ (inference or critical thinking)
- _____ (information from text), so that tells me _____

What specific skills are you likely to focus on during the skill review? That will vary depending on your students' reading level. Typically, the most useful skills to focus on at each reading level follow the pattern shown in Table 8.4.

Table 8.4 Key Skills to Focus on at Each Reading Level

Reading Level	Skills to Focus on . . .
Up to 100L	Word-solving strategies
100L–300L	Citing evidence and tracking character development: struggles, motivations, triumphs, mental state
300L–500L	Choosing the best evidence and keeping track of multiple plotlines and secondary characters
500L–700L	Text features, author's craft, and metacognitive work: "What can I do to help myself as a reader?"
700L+	Connecting multiple sources or main ideas; write concise arguments about abstract concepts, themes, and figurative language

The next chapter will deal with the execution of Before Reading, but most of its success will come from the planning itself. If you craft a strong lesson plan for this section, you'll hook your readers and prime them for successful skill use during and after reading.

DURING READING

Once you have delivered your introduction, students should be prepared to spend time reading the text independently. In the early reading stages, you play an especially critical role here: students will read aloud in "whisper voices" so that you can provide individual, in-the-moment coaching based on each student's struggles and successes with the text. For more developed readers, During Reading will happen either silently or during time that they aren't at the guided reading table.

Regardless, this is a section that is much less about the planning and much more about the execution. (That's why you can notice in the sample lesson plan that all that is really indicated is which section of the text they will read.) We'll discuss how to coach this way in the next chapter. Meanwhile, though, when it comes to planning your lesson, you'll simply decide how much of the text students will read and for how long. If you're teaching younger students, this might be the most substantial and longest part of your lesson. Their texts at the earliest levels will be quite short, so they will have the opportunity to reread them three to five times in one lesson, getting to a fluency rate that will allow them to focus on comprehension. You will want to make a few notes in your lesson plan about what you'll look for when you coach these students. For later readers with longer texts, rereading will be more for close reading than for fluency, so your need to monitor their fluency will practically disappear.

AFTER READING

After Reading is often also called the comprehension conversation. This is arguably the part of the reading cycle where the teacher adds the highest value, checking for comprehension and guiding each student in the moment he or she makes an error. The comprehension conversation starts according to the development of the reader:

- K–2 (before they can capture their comprehension in writing): retell
- 2–4 (once they can efficiently write answers to comprehension questions): written response to a comprehension prompt

Let's look at each of these approaches in more detail.

Retell

In the early years, before students have mastered enough of writing to write answers to comprehension questions, After Reading begins with a fast retell of what was just read. Do not underestimate the value of an opening retell for kindergarten through second-grade students, who are good at remembering details but struggle to string them together into one coherent story. By scripting the key details that you want your students to recall during the retell, you can make sure that they aren't missing key parts that will sabotage the rest of your discussion. Having such an "answer key" allows you to check the level of their retell more effectively, especially when teaching guided reading in your initial years as a teacher.

Consider the power of retell in light of the CCSS. The standards push us to make our classrooms more text- and evidence-based. Retell, then, becomes the ultimate evidence-based tool for your classroom. Here is your students' chance to tell you what words, what evidence, and what passages matter in a text. And because they need to reason through this first, the cognitive work is totally theirs to do. You'll simply need to have your key points ready so that you'll be able to refocus students when they get stuck.

We should note that not all retells are alike. Just as the complexity of your texts will increase between grades, so too will the complexity of the retell you can expect from students. Up to 100L, students are focused on a basic explanation of the problem a story presents and its solution. By 300L, students need to be able to say what happened, why it happened, and the effect of the events on a character's mental state. Even in retell, there's a continuum of skills for readers to master as they develop. The box "Not All Retells Are Alike" is a quick reference on this progression that matches the increasing comprehension levels of the students.

Not All Retells Are Alike

A Guide to Retells of Increasing Complexity

- **Up to 100L:** Retell problem and solution.
- **100L–300L:** Retell what happened, why it happened, and the effect on characters' mental state.
- **300L–500L:** Retell what happened, why it happened, the effect on characters' mental state; emphasize connections between earlier and later parts in the story.
- **500L+:** Comprehension conversation starts from evidence-based written responses; conversation is fluid and based on data from written responses; retell with emphasis on character insight, touching on genre-specific elements and attempting to use the vocabulary or figurative language used in the text.

A Word on . . . Getting Past Retell

A common problem for guided reading teachers is that they get bogged down in the retell portion of their lesson. Eager to make sure that students have every possible fact of a story, they spend all of their time correcting small details. Doing this can be a mistake, however, because it can get a conversation stuck in a low-level discussion of facts. Great reading teachers give their students time to recall the key moments of a story, but recognize that the point of a conversation isn't mere recall. After the students have had their chance, these teachers add any missing points and move to the comprehension conversation—the heart of the After Reading component of their lesson.

Written Response to a Comprehension Prompt

Once a student's writing ability is strong enough that he or she can generate a written response to text in a reasonably short time, the focus of the comprehension conversation shifts. Why? Because reading a student's written response to a prompt is game-changing: for the first time, you can assess each student's level of comprehension before an oral comprehension conversation even begins. In some of the video clips in the next chapter, you'll see teachers who have looked at their students' work and gotten a head start on identifying comprehension errors, inappropriate evidence, and other areas of focus at the start of the conversation. When teachers do all this, the comprehension conversation becomes more fluid: it is a teacher's strategic launch based on written responses in which students have already cited evidence and summarized the story. If students have synthesized the story well, then the teacher can jump right into a close reading of a particular passage. If not, she or he can begin with a brief retell.

A Word on ... Close Reading and Written Responses

If you have recently attended training in the instructional "shifts" brought about by the Common Core, you might have been asked to read a passage like the Gettysburg Address and then to participate in a comprehension conversation: one in which you did close reading of the text and kept your discussion rooted in evidence from the text. One aspect of close reading that has been overlooked in most of the trainings we have attended, however, is the importance of students' writing responses to text *before* the conversation begins.

Once you hit the later years of early elementary school (the second through the fourth grades), beware the use of Common Core rubrics to evaluate conversations that don't include a teacher reviewing written responses prior to the conversation. Writing is the ultimate way in which students can demonstrate how well they comprehend a passage. Without including written responses, you won't have the same certainty about student mastery and student error. And that certainty is the key to being results driven—rather than simply process driven—in the teaching of reading.

In summary, the retell in the early grades and the written response in the second through fourth grades is the starting point. From there, the comprehension conversation must go much further to push student thinking.

> ### Launching "After Reading": Keys to Remember
>
> - **Up to 500L:** start with a retell
> - **500L+:** start with a written response to the text

Planning the Rest of the Comprehension Conversation

You probably noted in the sample plan in Table 8.3 that the teacher wrote out what comprehension questions she would ask after students read the text. These comprehension questions will be catalysts for student learning, and, just as important, they will be your primary checks for student understanding. When you craft questions for your lesson, you need to be driven by the particular skills that students will need at their reading level and based on your assessment analysis. For example, if you're working on character motivation, then you would prompt: "Why did character Y do this action?" And if you were asking about character perspective, you would ask, "How did character Y feel about that action?"

This is where the reading assessments we highlighted in Chapters Three and Seven will be especially powerful. You'll need to know more than a student's level: you'll need to know the precise type of error he or she is making. It won't be enough to know that your students are at 250L. If you've given the assessment even at the level on which students are failing, you'll know exactly where the skill breaks down for them, and you'll be able to use that information to generate your discussion questions. This way, you'll be able to target with expert precision the reading skill they need.

You'll also need to think about what types of questions you ask students and how you'll expect them to answer. You might have noticed that the questions in our sample plan were labeled "factual" (or "literal"), "inferential," and "critical thinking." The box "Types of Comprehension Questions" (on page 213) offers a quick definition of each of these types of questions.

It would be a mistake to conclude our definition here, though, because inferential questions are much like texts at any given difficulty level: *they are not created equal.* Strong inference questions must require that students utilize the skill that is the focus of the lesson, and we can't make that happen just by writing questions that start with the word "Why." Table 8.5 shows some examples of

Table 8.5 Not All Inference Questions Are Equal—a Case Study with the Narrative STEP Assessment

Text Level	Bottom Line	Question	What Question Requires of Students
Up to 100L (STEP 3)	Connect meaning found in pictures and words.	Which job will make her leave Earth?	Use pictures to support meaning; understand character actions, S-T connections.
300L (STEP 6)	Focus on character motivation, struggles, interactions.	Why doesn't Ashley know what to answer when Margo says, "I always know best"?	Understand how main character affects secondary characters; understand character personality; identify problem; add up details over time.
450L (STEP 9)	Focus on connecting earlier and later parts, figuring out how everything works together.	Why does Jeffrey's mother trust him to mail the letters?	Use details from the text; keep track of multiple characters and multiple points of view; identify character motive and theme.
650L (STEP 12)	Focus on figurative language, interpretation, genre.	Did Ella turn into a squirrel and a pigeon? How do you know?	Understand genre (fantasy); work to comprehend texts that are removed from personal experience; connect different parts of the text; hold on to multiple plots.

how inference questions and text and plot complexity evolve alongside students' reading abilities. The examples come from the STEP assessment, which provides a road map for increasing complexity of each of these types of questions via the "bottom lines" that are aligned to each assessment.

Types of Comprehension Questions

- **Factual thinking:** understanding the facts within the text
- **Inferential thinking:** adding clues within the text with prior or content knowledge to understand what is not being stated directly
- **Critical thinking:** adding up clues and inferences from throughout the text and combining them with prior or content knowledge to develop an interpretation

The differences between all these questions illustrate how inferential thinking is shaped by the particular skills students need to focus on at a given reading level. A helpful strategy for writing effective questions is to write the expected response for two or three essential questions in the plan. Working through the questions yourself will help you identify whether they address the skills you intend them to. What's more, this technique will help you gauge the effectiveness of the lesson by comparing students' answers to your desired response.

One of the keys to planning for your comprehension conversation is recognizing that there are moments for which you won't be able to plan. The best guided reading teachers we've seen are aware of their own biases and, in the moment, assess whether students really have demonstrated the targeted skill or not. How? By prompting further. Diving deep into a student answer isn't just for guiding the reader on the right path when he or she is incorrect; it's also a tool to reveal the student's thinking.

Core Idea

Prompting doesn't just highlight a new path for student thinking; it illuminates which path students have already taken.

We'll return to comprehension conversations in the next chapter, when we'll see prompting in action.

A Word on . . . Creating Lesson Plans of This Depth

At first glance, the lesson plan sample presented in this chapter looks very intricate: it has a high level of detail and required significant thought. How does a teacher build lesson plans with this much sophistication? The short answer: little by little, one by one.

Guided reading is the teacher's most important moment in the classroom, so these lesson plans are the most important of all. For this reason, it is better to build up effective lesson plans one at a time, creating a bank of lesson plans that can be simply adjusted to match students' learning needs. This doesn't happen overnight, but with a commitment to design a few lessons periodically, you will slowly build your own treasure of effective lesson plans!

CONCLUSION: WHEN YOU'VE SET THE COURSE

We've now gone over each component that sets up a great guided reading lesson plan. Once you've put all the pieces of this plan together, you've plotted the route of your guided reading lesson. But as anyone who has ever used a GPS knows, plotting the route is only the very beginning of any journey. From there, you need to actually make the trip without drifting off course. In the next chapter, we'll explain how to get your students to the right destination—executing the guided reading lesson plan. We'll particularly address what to do when students struggle to read or understand.

Guided Reading Lesson Planning: Key Standards to Focus on in Each Component of the Plan

Before Reading

Text Preview and Focus for Reading

- **Up to 100L:** word-solving strategies
- **100L–300L:** citing evidence and character development: struggles, motivations, triumphs, mental state
- **300L–500L:** choosing the best evidence; keeping track of multiple sections, plots, and characters
- **500L–700L:** text features, author's craft, and metacognitive work: What can I do to help myself as a reader?
- **700L+:** connecting multiple sources or main ideas; write concise arguments about abstract concepts, themes, and figurative language

During Reading

Word Solving

- **Up to 100L:** Students whisper-read; teacher uses word-solving problems to guide students in decoding challenging words.
- **100L+:** Teacher does targeted word-solving and fluency work with students who need particular support.

After Reading— Retells and Written Responses

What Happened, Why; Characters' Feeling or Thinking

- **Up to 100L:** Retell problem and solution.
- **100L–300L:** Retell what happened, why it happened, and the effect on characters' mental state.
- **300L–500L:** Retell what happened, why it happened, the effect on characters' mental state; emphasize connections between earlier and later parts in the story.
- **500L+:** Comprehension conversation starts from evidence-based written responses; conversation is fluid and based on data from written responses; retell with emphasis on character insight, touching on genre-specific elements and attempting to use the vocabulary or figurative language used in the text.

After Reading— Comprehension Questions

Factual, Inferential, Critical Thinking

- **Up to 100L:** Questions focus on basic understanding of the text.
- **100L–300L:** Questions focus on character motivation, struggles, interactions.
- **300L–500L:** Questions focus on connecting earlier and later parts and figuring out how everything works together.
- **500L–700L:** Questions focus on text features and author's craft.
- **700L+:** Questions focus on abstract concepts and figurative language, connecting multiple sources, evaluating quality of evidence and argument.

Apply Your Habits: Guided Reading
Prework and Introduction

Self-Assessment

What aspects of the guided reading model we present will have the biggest impact for your students?

_____

_____

_____

_____

_____

Tools to Use

- Guided Reading Lesson Planning (also included on the DVD)
- List of guided reading texts by level and reading focus (included on the DVD)
- Professional development materials

Your Next Steps

_____

_____

_____

_____

_____

Guided Reading Execution

Stay on Course

Once you've done all the prework and planning, you get to the heart of the work: the execution of the guided reading lesson.

What makes guided reading so valuable is also what makes it the most difficult to capture solely in a lesson plan: the in-the-moment coaching that addresses each student's most urgent needs as a reader, both in the During Reading and the After Reading portions of the lesson. As you saw in the opening video of the last chapter, successful coaching gets students to put excellent habits of discussion and reading into practice so that they are able to master both. It is when the teacher engages in coaching that he or she truly becomes the GPS for the students, leading them all the way to the destination of great reading.

If this sounds daunting, keep in mind that every teacher has one great advantage over a GPS: the ability to anticipate the ways in which students might veer off course. Using a developed curriculum and up-to-date assessment data, you can predict with great accuracy where your students will struggle in their reading. That means you'll enter class with a sense of how you will get your students over those hurdles. All of this goes to say that as difficult as it is to write in-the-moment coaching into your lesson plan, it is still possible to prepare for it.

Core Idea

Teachers are better than any GPS system: they can plan for exactly where students will get lost.

You've already learned what makes an effective guided reading lesson plan. Let's see what each component looks like in execution.

BEFORE READING

You'll recall from the previous chapter that the two keys to Before Reading are to

1. Hook the reader (when applicable).

2. Review the skills students will need to use when reading.

Let's take a look at the following example of Before Reading in a guided reading lesson, during which students are going to be focusing on character motivation in James Marshall's *Miss Nelson Has a Field Day*.

 WATCH Clip 27: Yasmin Vargas's Before Reading—390L

This introduction clearly met with success. Yasmin Vargas started with a simple chant, and then she kept her language *very* concise and student-friendly, priming her students to read as effectively as possible—all in the span of just a few minutes.

For beginning readers in kindergarten, your objective will often be focused on word solving. In most cases, these objectives were already learned in read-aloud, phonics, or both. For this reason, Before Reading is an especially short hook (it's more important to get students immediately into the text at this early stage than it is later) and a simple review: "Remember, students, that we learned about ___ strategy in read-aloud. What do we have to remember to do when . . . ?" This allows students to recall the strategy they should be using. You can see an example of this here.

 WATCH Clip 28: Shadell Purefoy's Before Reading—50L

Before Reading is the simplest to implement when you have a well-planned lesson. But don't underestimate its importance; as we stated in the previous chapter, this is your chance to point students in the right direction! Keep your language brief and concise, and you'll set up your class to succeed.

DURING AND AFTER READING: THE POWER OF PROMPTING

Now we've come to the heart of what makes guided reading execution effective: the decisions teachers make in the During and After Reading sections. They are separate components of a guided reading lesson, but this next section combines both. Why? Because the interventions a teacher uses follow a similar core idea: the power of prompting. Let's look at a case study that brings home this concept.

Imagine you are a second-grade teacher, and you have just finished assessing your students. Your assessment leads you to the following conclusion:

> Students can cite details (CCCS R.L.2.1) but cannot synthesize them to get at the main idea and character motive (CCCS R.L.2.2&3).

As we outlined in Chapter Seven, you dig a bit deeper, looking at the types of questions students struggled with most, and highlight these two specific reading problems:

- Students are using too much factual information from the text and struggle to synthesize it.

- Students retell the events of the story without interpreting events and inferring character motivation.

The assessment data here aren't hypothetical—they're from the class of a real second-grade teacher, Erin Michels. Let's see how Erin responds to these errors. The students have been asked to read Elizabeth Levy's story *Schoolyard Mystery*. After students have read independently, Erin begins the comprehension conversation. As you watch, you'll see that the students are still struggling to synthesize to a "big idea." Pay attention to what Erin does and says to guide students to the synthesis.

WATCH Clip 29: Erin Michels's Comprehension—410L

If we remove all of the student responses, we can focus on what Erin said and did during the conversation. Here are all her prompts:

- What's going on?
- Who was saying that?
- What am I going to say?
- I want big ideas.
- Try it again.
- How can we make that a big idea?
- How can we talk about important parts of the beginning of the chapter in the way of a big idea?
- She was giving a lot of detail; how can we give a big idea of what happened in the very beginning?
- So let's stop. That's the fact in the text, we know that happened. We need to understand the character's actions, understand the why. What is the motive? How do we better understand this by what they are doing?
- Do you see the difference? Now, after we worked through it, Briana brought it back to the big idea. Precious told us the clues in the text and then we worked to figure out why it was happening. We want to think about the why and the how. We want to make it thick and juicy.

It's clear that the students did all the comprehension work, but Erin played a vital role in improving Briana's ability to synthesize information and state the characters' motivation. For starters, Erin selected the appropriate text for practice (as mentioned in the Prework section in Chapter Eight). What's more remarkable is that she knew exactly the right prompt to use for the student error at exactly the right time. She could have done this by designing brand-new prompts to match the errors she'd identified as likely ones for her students to make, but imagine how long this would take if Erin had to do it every time she planned a guided reading lesson. Fortunately, we have a powerful tool to offer teachers like Erin: the guided reading prompting guides. (You can find these guides in the Appendix as well as on the DVD—all ready for you to print and use!)

The prompting guides—one for narrative texts, and one for informational—are lists of prompts you can use when specific student errors occur at specific reading levels. Each guide breaks down each level of proficiency into the most commonly made student errors and gives you the language to use when these occur. To be sure, others have come up with lists of strategies before.[1] What makes this list more nuanced, though, is that it was developed and tested by analyzing the most common student errors at each reading level. The result is that the guide is hyper-targeted on the skills your students need to work on, taking the guesswork out of conversations. In the context of rich, text-based discussions, it is a perfect complement to the CCSS.

Consider the curricular implications of a tool like the prompting guide. We know that we need to increase text complexity across grade spans, but simply increasing the Lexile score of our texts falls far short of that goal. As the Common Core points out, text complexity entails a battery of qualitative measures, too. What we need is a curriculum that anticipates the key qualitative shifts at each reading level, one that helps map the skills students must master to keep developing. This is the power of the prompting guides. As noted, we have included two full prompting guides for kindergarten through fourth graders in the Appendix: one for literary texts, one for informational selections. For now, let's look at just a segment of it (shown in Table 9.1), to see how it applied to Erin's class.

Do these prompts look familiar? That's right—a number of them are the precise prompts Erin used during her lesson. By analyzing her students' reading assessment data to identify the skills they needed to learn, and lining up that knowledge with the prompting guide, Erin was able to go into her guided reading lesson with a very clear sense of exactly how she'd need to prompt her students.

To be sure, there's a magic to Erin's teaching, and this clip showed it. But what it really shows is that the magic is replicable. With the guide, Erin didn't have to memorize scores of prompts or have fifteen years of experience: she could start

Table 9.1 Excerpt of Narrative Guided Reading Prompting Guide: 450L: Comprehension

Core Element and Ideal Student Actions	Typical Student Errors	Teacher-to-Student Prompts to Encourage These Actions
DEEP RETELL: Retell stories using some synthesis and interpretation of events—going beyond factual recall and sequencing and including character motivation, feelings, actions, thoughts RL.3.2, 4.2	Uses factual information to retell, excluding important details Is unable to synthesize info Does not include character motive in retell	• Using the events from the story, tell me the big ideas in this section. • You've given me the text evidence: now how can you give a big idea of what happened in the very beginning of the story? • Let's dig a little deeper about the part between ___ and ___; what's going on? • Why [does, doesn't] a character do an action? • What were the most important things this writer had to say? • Summarize the main events in this story. • What are you missing in your retell? [character development: motivation, feelings, actions, thoughts; setting; problem; solution] • How can you make that retell more concise? • When you retell, you need to include ___. You're missing ___ in your retell. • How can we make this important part of the text a big idea? • So let's stop . . . that's the fact in the text, we know that happens, those are the character's actions; why did they do that? We need to understand the why. (What are their motivations? How do we better understand this? What are they doing?)

prompting correctly from her very first lesson. You have in the Appendix all the prompts great teachers like Erin use in the moment. Want to know what to say when a student makes an error? Look no further. These teachers have a list that shows them what to do in the areas with which they know students will struggle most.

Core Idea

There *is* magic to effective prompting during guided reading, but that magic is replicable.

Follow the teachers who have done this well—and the prompting guide that comes from their actions—and you can create that magic yourself.

Let's pause for a moment to put this in the context of Common Core. One of the key messages of the standards is that when it comes to teaching reading, there's an order that works for students. Fundamentally, that insight is what guides a tool like the prompting guide in supporting the development of specific reading skills. The CCSS ask us all to accelerate the rate and rigor of instruction for our elementary readers. But from down in the trenches, we realize that you'll also need to meet your students where they are. Guided reading will allow you to manage both demands. We're about to show you a continuum of skills on the journey of reading, and how the instruction of those skills can be tailored according to the developmental needs of each child.

Core Idea

The Common Core asks us to accelerate our instruction. Our students need us to meet them where they are. Guided reading lets you do both.

Recall the very first core idea of this text: habits are built at the moment of error, not at the moment of success. It is in the moments that students struggle that we are most useful to them, because it's at those moments that we have the power to establish brand new habits—the right habits—for them as readers. This is the core strength of guided reading: your teaching changes to match the needs of the reader. For that reason, no matter the reading level of the students you teach, we recommend that you read this section straight through; we'll highlight different instructional and literacy techniques as we map out how you can use guided reading to coach your students to proficiency. What's more, we'll tell you some of the real-life stories of the teachers you see in our videos—so you can see how they themselves grew to become the experts they are now.

A Word on . . . Watching Guided Reading on Video

Guided reading is the most complex and flexible of all the instruction types, so the largest percentage of the video in this book is devoted to guided reading. To make viewing maximally beneficial, we recommend you have the full Narrative Guided Reading Prompting Guide by your side as you watch each video. Each of the teachers had those guides at the ready when they were teaching—it sits permanently at the guided reading table in their classrooms.

For quick reference, here's a breakdown of all the guided reading clips in this book.

Clip #/ Teacher	Text	Lexile	Lesson Component	Watch for . . .
28/ Purefoy	*Hello, Bingo!*	50L	Before Reading	Book Introduction
30/ Purefoy	*Mother Bird*	290L	During Reading	Word Solving
27/ Vargas	*Miss Nelson Has a Field Day*	390L	Before Reading	Book Introduction
31–32/ Worrell	*The Bully*	400L	After Reading	Comprehension Conversation
33/ Worrell	*Rosie and the Audition*	500L	After Reading	Comprehension Conversation
29/ Michels	*Schoolyard Mystery*	410L	After Reading	Comprehension Conversation
34/ Michels	*Schoolyard Mystery*	410L	After Reading	Comprehension Conversation
35/ Settles	*Minerva's Dream*	430L	After Reading	Comprehension Conversation
36/ Hoefling-Crouch	*Knots on a Counting Rope*	480L	After Reading	Comprehension Conversation
26/ Settles	*Amber Brown is Green With Envy*	600L	After Reading	Comprehension Conversation
1/ Michels	*J.T.*	730L	After Reading	Comprehension Conversation
37/ Michels	*A Jar of Dreams*	970L	After Reading	Comprehension Conversation

THE PROMPTING GUIDES FROM 0 TO 1000

The guided reading prompting guides presented in this book are not based on rhetoric or a particular approach to teaching, and therein lies their power. Instead, the prompting guides were built from observing common patterns in student errors at every reading level and then the types of prompts highly effective teachers used to "move the needle" for those students. The University of Chicago Urban Education Institute was generous to work closely with us to generate these prompting guides based on its extensive analysis of student error patterns.

What follows are examples of actual teachers guiding students to be more effective readers. As we take you on the journey from beginning reading to beyond Lexile 1000L, let's look at how prompting changes to meet the needs of the reader.

Up to 100L: Using Middle Vowels and Blends and Ends

Common Core Grade K

We'll start with our earliest readers. Here are the four major places we'd want to coach their reading:

- **Concepts about print (for emergent readers).** You may have watched a preschool student with a book and noticed him or her "reading" by making up a story using pictures or using memories from a previous experience with the text. In order to progress, they need to learn basic concepts about print, such as how to hold a book, the direction in which people read, and what people do when they get to the end of a line.

- **Word solving.** When students are first learning to read, they are learning many initial word-solving strategies, such as looking at the beginning, middle, and endings of words. They are learning high-frequency words that they can easily recognize in a continuous text, and they are developing strategies for understanding word meaning—not only through context but also by comparing the word to other words that they have encountered.

- **Fluency.** Reading is related to the way language operates—all systems working smoothly together.[2] When students slow down their reading, they struggle to maintain meaning. To avoid this, they must be capable of *fluent* reading: the ability to adjust their phrasing and speed, depending on the meaning in the text and their purpose for reading.

- **Comprehension.** Contrary to popular belief, early readers can also comprehend at high levels of complexity—we just have to expect that of them.

The first three aspects of reading will be readily apparent in the During Reading section of guided reading. Whereas older students will read silently, with your early readers you have the opportunity to listen to them read, and to correct their word solving and fluency on the spot. Again, this is where the flexibility of the guided reading structure is useful. Vary the length of time you spend with students before, during, and after reading to create a lesson that is most suited to their needs.

Let's look at how this could work for your class. Consider this actual assessment data spreadsheet (Figure 9.1) for students on Lexile 150L (STEP 4). Even when she saw that students were not going to pass, the teacher, Shadell Purefoy, finished the assessment. The data were revealing. Before continuing, determine for yourself the core error that you think the chart reveals.

Just from this snapshot of Shadell's students at 150L, she could quickly see that the number-one thing holding back most of her students was their reading accuracy—the number of word-solving errors they made while reading. Four of her five students failed to pass the STEP 4 (150L) assessment for that reason. By studying the rest of the errors students made, Shadell was able to determine that mastering middle sounds and blends are key for them to move to the next reading level. So where does Shadell focus next in her guided reading lessons? She targets her coaching on During Reading.

A month later, these students have improved their comprehension but are still struggling with the core skills of fluency. Shadell knows that she can't simply push students up the Lexile framework, though: as the prompting guide suggests, fluency deficiencies will get in the way of comprehension if she doesn't address them now. In this clip, Shadell brings her focus back to word solving. Here you'll see students struggle—and how she responds.

 WATCH Clip 30: Shadell Purefoy's Word Solving—290L

Figure 9.1 Shadell Purefoy's Data Spreadsheet

October Results / BOSTON COLLEGE	Last STEP Administered	STEP Analysis: Step 4 Sounds/Word Solving/Accuracy								Reading Comp			
		Sound ID TOTAL:	Segmentation	Step 4: Reading Accuracy (Enter %)	SC (Self-Corrections)	M Error: Relied too much on pictures and personal experience	S Error: Student word sounded right but was incorrect word (ball vs. basketball)	V Error: Student only looks at the print and not what makes sense	TOTAL # OF ERRORS	Step 4 Comprehension: # of Errors	Fact (# of errors)	Inference (# of errors)	Critical Thinking (# of errors)
Emanuel	3	27	6	98	3	0	0	1	1	4	2	1	1
Seona	3	23	8	89	2	6	2	2	10	0			
Kayla	3	24	10	89	0	4	4	2	10	1			1
Autumn	3	26	4	89	0	10	6	1	17	1		1	
Azia	3	25	5	89	0	5	2	4	11	2		1	1

Shadell's student needed her to guide her through the middle-vowel and end sounds in "baby." And although it's true that Shadell might have come up with some of these prompts in the moment, the power of her lesson was that she didn't have to. Because her students' data already told her where their skills would break down, Shadell knew exactly what she'd need to say to steer them on the right path. Without having to generate these questions on the fly, Shadell doesn't have to divide her focus during instruction, *and* she knows she has a strong starter set of questions. If you rewatch the video, in fact, you'll see that Shadell's exact prompts are featured in the prompting guide for emergent readers (see Table 9.2 for an excerpt).

Shadell doesn't have to spend hours creating question prompts or to generate these in the moment. By using the prompting guide, she can give her students highly targeted instruction without getting weighed down by the enormity of the task.

Table 9.2   Excerpt of Guided Reading Prompting Guide: 100L–150L: Word Solving and Fluency

Core Element and Ideal Student Actions	Typical Student Errors	Teacher-to-Student Prompts to Encourage These Actions
BLENDS AND ENDS: Attend to initial blends and inflectional endings: -ing, -ed, -s RF.K.3.A., RF.1.3.F	States initial blend but gets rest of the word wrong OR States correct root word but misses ending (e.g., *fish* vs. *fisher*, *run* vs., *runs*)	• Read through the word. • It could be ___, but look at ___. • Check the beginning and ending letters. • You made a mistake. Can you find it? • How does that word start? Try it again with the ending. • Read that again. • Try ___. Would that sound right? • Would that make sense?
MIDDLE VOWELS: Attending to middle vowel sounds RF.K.3.B	Does not pay attention to the middle of the word	• Ask student to quickly differentiate between words that have different short vowels—for example, *run* vs. *ran; then* vs. *thin.* • What sound does [vowel] make?

Shadell's Story . . . Freeing Your Mind

By now you've seen a few clips of Shadell in action. It'd be easy to watch her in action and just see a master teacher. But she'd be the first to tell you that only a few years ago she was just learning to execute guided reading. And she was struggling.

Shadell had established herself early on as a master of classroom management. As a kindergarten teacher, she planned out every detail of her classroom's procedures, and she maintained them with the combination of joy and order highlighted in Chapter One. Guided reading, however, didn't fit that structure. She tried to "control" the lesson, but what occurred was that she was doing the "comprehending" work more than the students. There were so many things for her students to do, and she tried to hit them all at once at her guided reading table. For example, if students were mastering the alphabet, she'd tell them to focus on recognizing letters, use their fingers as a pointer, focus on the plot of a story, and look for a character's actions—all in the same lesson.

The result? Both Shadell and her students were overwhelmed. Shadell was frustrated; she was unable to notice what problems her students were having, and her kindergarteners were unable to manage all of her expectations at once. She worked so hard—why wasn't she seeing results?

What made the difference for Shadell was a shift in the way she thought about guided reading. She realized that the goal of guided reading was to give her students practice on the skill they needed, and if she analyzed her data effectively, she could be confident about what that was. Instead of trying to focus on fifteen things at once, Shadell began to frame her lesson around one. Then she worked with her instructional leader to learn how to identify the right text to match the skill. This didn't happen quickly; it was almost a year before Shadell felt confident doing this independently. With the right text in hand, she used the prompting guide to put her questions on sticky notes in her text, so she wasn't flipping back and forth with her plans.

At that point, Shadell's mind was freed up to let her students grapple with the skill in her lesson. They were able to think and talk more because Shadell was available to listen carefully to their conversation—and only jump in if they really needed her. Molly Branson-Thayer, director of literacy at the University of Chicago's Urban Education Institute, was able to witness Shadell's transformation. "I remember going into her room and her just being so 'I don't think I have this,'" Molly says. But after the shift, Molly remembers a totally different tone in Shadell's classroom. "She was having the comprehension conversation around the story and looking at me and smiling. It clicked: she finally was feeling the joy of facilitating effective guided reading."

Shadell made the leap from novice to master guided reading teacher by using her data to select texts and come to the table as an expert. Once she was able to narrow down her lesson to the right skill, with the right prompts, her mind was freed to truly listen to what her students were saying. Ultimately, Shadell turned a weakness to a strength and finally to an exemplar.

"By the following year," Molly recalls, "Shadell's expertise actually skyrocketed. Each thing that she had struggled to master now served as a model for all her fellow kindergarten teachers." Molly adds, "There is only one path to mastery—lots and lots of practice."

380L – 450L: The Story of Bianca

Common Core Grade 2

Let's travel a little further down the path. As readers develop, the After Reading component of a guided reading lesson takes on greater importance as the focus shifts to their ability to comprehend the texts in question. The teacher's role is to make sure that this part of class still focuses on the skills students need to develop most.

In particular, Lexile 400L–500L is a critical transition period for your readers. They take a big step into the next phase of reading. At this point, students are proficient at word solving, and that allows them to focus more energy on comprehension. Now, readers must master the art of problem-solving a word *and* maintaining the meaning. In particular, they move from following one main character with one plot to understanding a more fully developed story with multiple characters and plotlines, connecting different parts of the text using evidence. Then they'll have to respond to others' opinions, starting to evaluate the validity of others' interpretations of the texts. This is no easy transition for most readers!

To help illuminate the actions that teachers can take to push students over this bar, we'd like to take the time to tell the story of a second grader named Bianca. Over the series of the next three clips, we will watch how her teacher Juliana Worrell systematically helps Bianca blossom with masterful teaching.

In the first clip, the students in question have just finished reading *The Bully*, and there is a confusion about the characters in the story. Juliana, however, is not surprised: her assessment analysis had told her that her 400L students were having difficulty holding on to multiple characters. In her plans, she is already prepared for this potential error by selecting the prompts from the Narrative Guided Reading Prompting Guide that will be most relevant.

The result? A beautiful teaching moment during which Juliana and her students work through the correction together, enriching their reading skill and deepening their understanding of *The Bully*. For this clip, we are going to encourage *you* to act as the teacher. The clip stops at the moment of student misunderstanding. Your job is to watch the clip and then select the appropriate prompt that you would use in this situation. Table 9.3 is an excerpt of your Narrative Guided Reading Prompting Guide for this reading level.

Table 9.3 Excerpt of Narrative Guided Reading Prompting Guide: 400L: Comprehension

Core Element and Ideal Student Actions	Typical Student Errors	Teacher-to-Student Prompts to Encourage These Actions
SUSTAIN: Sustain attention to the meaning of a longer text over several days RL.3.5	Is unable to recall details from previous reading	*Help children connect related parts of a text—for example:* • What happened in the [beginning, middle, end] of the story? • What did we read about yesterday? • What new information did you learn about ___?
CHARACTER CONTRAST: Compare different characters' points of view and discuss why they might see things differently RL.3.3, RL.4.3, RL.5.3	Has difficulty holding on to multiple characters	• Is there something that you know about this character that can help you understand him/her now? • Why don't these characters agree with each other? • Does it matter that one character is older than the other? • What is [character]'s main problem in the story? • Compare these characters: [character] and [character]. • And what did [character] say? • Who were the important characters in the story? • Who is telling the story?
CITING EVIDENCE IV: Cite the best evidence from a story to support answers to inferential and critical thinking questions RL 2.7, RL.4.1	Does not weigh the value of two pieces of evidence to determine which is stronger Relies primarily on the first evidence found	• Is there another piece of evidence that can be used to support your argument? • Compare your evidence to [another passage]. Which is stronger evidence? • How does that [word, phrase] make your evidence strong?

As we pick up the comprehension conversation, Bianca is retelling the story: Cal and Jack are both in line for their lunch when the bully arrives in the cafeteria. Bianca then confuses these two characters (Cal and Jack). In the actual story, Cal is afraid of the bully and wants to leave the line before the bully demands his lunch money, whereas Jack is brave and stands up to the bully. Bianca makes the first error, stating that Jack is afraid of the bully, which is a critical error for understanding what happens. Here's Bianca's error on video. We have stopped it at the point of the error.

 WATCH Clip 31: Juliana Worrell's Comprehension, Part 1—400L

Before you watch the end to this video, imagine you are Juliana: write down the prompts that you would use to support Bianca in her comprehension error:

In-the-Moment Reflection

Prompts I would use—or would encourage my students to use:

_____

_____

_____

Now compare your notes to what Juliana does in the continuation of this video.

 WATCH Clip 32: Juliana Worrell's Comprehension, Parts 1 and 2—400L

Juliana's first action, while the most subtle, is also the most significant: she simply repeats the error that Bianca said. Literacy teachers often refer to this technique as "roll back the answer." What's the value in that action?

The value of a "rollback" is twofold. First, Juliana allows the rest of the students to hear the error again, giving them time to identify the error themselves. In this way, she makes sure that her students are doing the heavy lifting of listening to each other and evaluating each other's answers. Second, and just as important, she gives *herself* time to think! Rather than try to think of the appropriate prompt right away, she rolls back the answer, which allows her to access her Narrative Guided Reading Prompting Guide and consider what the next best action should be. Don't underestimate the power of giving yourself—and your students—time to think.

Core Idea

Never underestimate the power—and ease—of the "rollback": repeat the student's error and give yourself—and your students—time to think.

How did Juliana's prompts compare with yours? If you used the prompting guide, they were likely pretty similar. When you think about the prompts you could use, Juliana's teaching no longer feels as unattainable. Juliana's discussion didn't take place by chance: it was the result of careful planning and the use of the prompting guide. Thus her students received the precise coaching they needed for the precise place in which they struggled. And you can do the same in your own classroom.

The power of these conversations can be seen in how quickly students grow. We pick up the story of Bianca just a few weeks later. She has now mastered not only holding on to the traits of multiple characters but also seeing how characters' feelings change during a story. In this discussion of Pamela Rushby's *Rosie and the Audition*, Bianca is now the protagonist helping Juliana guide her peers to use text evidence to identify the character's emotions.

 WATCH Clip 33: Juliana Worrell's Comprehension—500L

Because the prompting guide has been a staple of her classroom, not only does Juliana have the right questions on the tip of her tongue when an opportunity arrives, but so does Bianca herself. Juliana leveraged her instruction so effectively that Bianca is taking off as a reader.

These magical moments did not come naturally to Juliana—she worked at them. How did she achieve this level of expertise? Let's take a look at her story.

Juliana's Story . . . Step-by-Step

Juliana makes guided reading lessons look easy even when we know they aren't. Yet guided reading didn't always come easily for her; she had to work at it.

When she first started teaching guided reading, Juliana was pretty adept at implementing the Before Reading—During Reading—After Reading basic structure, but she still felt overwhelmed. "I didn't know what I was doing at the table," she said. "There were just too many kids here with different needs: I felt like I was constantly putting out fires." Essentially, as soon as students started giving incorrect answers, Juliana would freeze: she didn't know what to do. Then she would start answering the question herself and take over the comprehension conversation. The consequence? Student learning didn't advance.

The solution began to unfold as Juliana learned to group her students based on assessment data. She soon realized that her most challenging students were disengaging or misbehaving during her lessons not because of her lack of classroom management but because the books she was using weren't the right ones for their needs. That's where data came in.

Her first step was to learn how to analyze data and group students accordingly. Doing so clarified everything for Juliana. Then she was ready to more deliberately choose books and analyze them in advance so that she'd know what parts were important to highlight using the prompting guide. Juliana became a proponent of adding more guided reading texts for her school, and she began to become an expert on specifically what each book could offer her groups.

Juliana's next growth area was retell. If you recall from Chapter Eight, retell has the potential to dominate a conversation with low-level facts if it isn't managed. Juliana didn't want her students to leave with misunderstandings, but she got caught up in those facts and missed opportunities to build the higher-order thinking skills in the comprehension conversation.

With time, Juliana shortened her retells and gave more time to her comprehension conversation. But she still worried about her students. She'd ask questions, and they wouldn't immediately know the answers. Here's where the habits of discussion became a powerful tool for her. Juliana realized that, for her students' young minds, a little thought time was OK. She gave the students some space to think about and discuss her questions, and their answers grew stronger and stronger!

You've already seen the final result in Juliana's videos. She built her practice to the point that it looks natural, even simple. It didn't start out that way, though. It was the product of hard work, a lot of reflection, and the decision to build her practice step-by-step.

450L–500L: Deep Retell and Cross-Book Themes

Common Core Grade 2

Just as understanding characters is a critical growth area in reading development, so, too, is holding on to meaning in more sophisticated stories. Here the students are reading longer texts with more developed themes and multiple plots, so they need to start to synthesize information and add more inferential and critical thinking to their retells.

In this next clip, Erin's students are retelling *The Schoolyard Mystery*, by Elizabeth Levy, and the students are struggling to build an effective synthesis of the story. Erin's data have told her that her students are having difficulty connecting earlier and later parts of the text. Although they are accustomed to finding evidence on a certain page within a chapter, they are not yet used to finding evidence from earlier chapters. Table 9.4 is an excerpt of your Narrative Guided Reading Prompting Guide for this reading level.

 WATCH Clip 34: Erin Michels's Comprehension—410L

Erin leverages her understanding of student error to guide students to more sophisticated conversation—and better comprehension. In the context of the Common Core, this level presents a beautiful moment for children; as they become more developed in their comprehension conversations, your students will be able to use more sophisticated textual evidence to support them. A word of caution, though: beware the temptation to let the drive for evidence replace the need for the *right* evidence. At the guided reading table, the moment that students choose the wrong evidence is precisely when they need you to guide them. It is in this moment of intervention that students will grow most, because the guidance you're providing is exactly the guidance they need. Again, it's the

Table 9.4 Excerpt of Narrative Guided Reading Prompting Guide: 450L—500L: Comprehension

Core Element and Ideal Student Actions	Typical Student Errors	Teacher-to-Student Prompts to Encourage These Actions
MULTIPLE PLOTS, EVENTS: Trace characters across multiple episodes, elaborating own understanding as the story progresses Relate earlier and later parts of a text, figuring out how they make sense together RL.3.6	Focuses on one character and plot throughout story	• What have you learned about the character here? • Why are you [not] surprised about what the character does here? • How did _____ affect _____? Tell about the relationship between _____ and _____. • What did you find out? • Does reading this section make you rethink your earlier idea? • How does this section help you to understand _____? • What's going on? • We need to connect different parts. It's important for us to connect what happened earlier in the text to what is going on later in the text.
CROSS-BOOK THEMES: Connect general themes among books, discussing some similarities and differences RL.1.9, 2.9, 3.9, 4.9	Does not connect multiple parts of the text OR Does not extend and relate background knowledge to reading	• What other books have we read about [theme]? What are the similarities or differences? • Could we make a connection to another book that we have read? What were the perceptions in that book? • This book reminds me of _____. Can you think why? • Think of another book you read that is like this. • Have you ever read about other characters like this? How did they approach _____? • Do you know anyone that is like a character in this book? • How does that help you think about this _____?

| DEEP RETELL: Retell stories using some synthesis and interpretation of events—going beyond factual recall and sequencing and including character motivation, feelings, actions, thoughts RL.3.2, RL.4.2 | Uses factual information to retell, excluding important details Is unable to synthesize information Does not include character motive in retell | • Using the events from the story, tell me the big ideas in this section.
 • You've given me the text evidence: now how can you give a big idea of what happened in the very beginning of the story?
 • Let's dig a little deeper about the part between _____ and _____; what's going on?
 • Why [does, doesn't] a character do an action?
 • What were the most important things this writer had to say?
 • Summarize the main events in this story.
 • What are you missing in your retell? [character development: motivation, feelings, actions, thoughts; setting; problem; solution]
 • How can you make that retell more concise?
 • When you retell, you need to include _____. You're missing _____ in your retell.
 • How can we make this important part of the text a big idea?
 • So let's stop . . . that's the fact in the text, we know that happens, those are the character's actions; why did they do that? We need to understand the why. (What are their motivations? How do we better understand this? What are they doing?) |

prompting guide that will let you do this. If you go back and scan the prompts for deep retell, you'll see how teachers like Erin are always prepared to coach students when their evidence use goes off course.

Core Idea

Beware the temptation to let the drive for evidence replace the need for the *right* evidence.

Of course, at this skill level, there are other challenges for students to conquer. Aja's group, for example, is struggling with another of the core skills for this level: identifying cross-book themes. Watch as she gives her students a chance to think and then build off one another's answers.

 WATCH Clip 35: Aja Settles's Comprehension—430L

550L– 600L: Diving into Figurative Language

Common Core Grade 3

The beautiful thing about guided reading is that it allows students to continuously build from the skills they already have. And because assessments take the guesswork out of knowing precisely where to go next, teachers can confidently add skills to others to create powerful experiences for students. In a previous clip, Juliana Worrell's students were focused on learning to use evidence to support their views. Once they're using evidence properly, you can dive into figurative language with the level of attention the Common Core expects. The CCSS ask students to begin distinguishing literal from nonliteral language in third grade (CCSS.ELA-Literacy.RL.3.4). Let's look at one small example of this.

Emily Hoefling-Crouch's students are in the midst of reading *Knots on a Counting Rope*. In this passage, the authors write a unique description of the wind, which trips up a student's comprehension. Here is the passage in question:

Your mother and father and I were safe in the Hogan . . . and the sheep were safe in the pen . . . when a wild storm came out of the mountains . . . crying "Boy-eeeee! Boy-eeeee!" Yes, Boy, it was whipping up sand and sharp as claws and crying like a bobcat. I was much afraid.[3]

Watch how Emily Hoefling-Crouch works with the student to uncover the meaning of this passage.

 WATCH Clip 36: Emily Hoefling-Crouch's Comprehension—480L

Emily is able to dive deep on the personification of the wind because her students already have a strong handle on locating textual evidence. She not only prompts her student to understand the figurative language but also gives significant wait time so that the student can figure out the answer. Her guided reading lesson works because it is built on the shoulders of the literacy work that came before it. Now, when it comes time to talk about figurative language, that topic feels less like a challenge and more like a logical extension of students' reading growth.

700L+: Symbolism and Beyond

Common Core Grade 4

Let's consider a final prompting example. As student conversations become more advanced and nuanced, it's easy to see only the magic and not the mechanisms that make it happen. But even the most complicated conversations are the product of moves that can be scripted and learned.

We're going to move to Erin Michels's class, which is reading *A Jar of Dreams*, by Yushiko Uchida. In this video of Erin's classroom, it is clear that these students are eager to learn: excited about the book they've been reading and employing great habits of discussion. At this level of reading, the students already completed a written response to reading, in which they analyzed key passages from the book. After reviewing their written responses, Erin notes that all of them have missed the symbolism of a key line in the story. Take a look at Table 9.5 to see how the

Table 9.5 Excerpt of Narrative Guided Reading Prompting Guide: 900L+: Comprehension

Core Element and Ideal Student Actions	Typical Student Errors	Teacher-to-Student Prompts to Encourage These Actions
SYMBOLISM: Notice the writer's use of symbolism RL.4.4	Relies too heavily on the literal meaning of an object, setting, or person	• When you think of ___, what do you think of? • What does the ___ represent? • The author mentions ___ in the story. What is the meaning of this ___? • If ___ were not mentioned in the story, how would this story be different? • Have you seen or read about this symbol in any other works of art? How was it used? • I want you to bring it back to the symbolism of ___; how does that relate to themes in the story? • How does ___ help you better understand ___?

Narrative Guided Reading Prompting Guide looks at this level; then watch what happens.

 WATCH Clip 37: Erin Michels's Comprehension—970L

Here we see a master teacher at work. Erin asks her students questions to get them thinking about pictures so that then they can get to the "aha" moment of the symbolism of Mama locking her pictures in a trunk. This comprehension conversation is remarkably student driven. At the same time, though, it's entirely within Erin's control. Even as she turns the tough cognitive work over to the students, she's keeping them on the right path. How? With the right prompts at the right times.

CONCLUSION: A PATH FOR EVERY STUDENT

Although every reading lesson type we've described is an essential component of reading instruction, guided reading is truly the bread and butter of the reading program this book presents. And if you've ever taught guided reading before, you've probably had the experience of not being sure if you're doing it the right way. That's understandable; guided reading is complex. It's for those reasons that we've laid out Chapter Eight and this chapter with so much detail.

The complexity of guided reading may be daunting, but it's not insurmountable if you break down this instruction type into its composite parts. As we saw in each video and every vignette, once you build up each step of the process, you're going to increasingly feel like the expert your students see when you enter the room. As the GPS of a guided reading lesson, you're not just leading students along a path. You are, in fact, keeping them on course: taking them on the thrilling journey to truly independent reading.

Apply Your Habits: Guided Reading Execution

Self-Assessment

What changes to the execution of guided reading would have the most significant results for your students?

_____

_____

_____

_____

_____

Tools to Use

- Narrative Guided Reading Prompting Guide (included in the Appendix and on the DVD)
- Informational Guided Reading Prompting Guide (included in the Appendix and on the DVD)
- Guided Reading Note-Taking Template (included on the DVD)
- Professional development materials

Your Next Steps

_____

_____

_____

_____

_____

Chapter 10

Independent Reading

Don't Wait for a Hero's Quest

Lesson Type	Group Size	What to Teach?
Read-Aloud	Whole class	Skills from yearlong syllabus
Comprehension Skills	Small group by reading level or whole class if necessary	Skills from yearlong syllabus
Phonics	Small group or whole class if necessary	Skills from premade program
Guided Reading	Small group by reading level	Skills determined by assessment analysis (Chapter Seven)
Independent Reading	**Individual**	**Skills for all students**

After years spent reading the great epics of a dozen civilizations, theorist Joseph Campbell came to a startling insight: throughout human culture, most heroic stories follow a similar dramatic arc. Heroes receive a call to adventure, face various types of trials, and learn similar lessons. In short, there is a shared template for heroism.[1]

Campbell's insight is striking because it connects the trials, travails, and triumphs of so much of human literature. Yet it is also striking because it resonates with our own lived experiences. In almost every story of a heroically gifted or talented person, we see a familiar arc: a young woman or man has a deeply meaningful experience, is called to his or her passion, and then pursues it to the fullest. For author Ray Bradbury, it was an encounter with a carnival magician named Mr. Electrico.[2] For his colleague Walter Dean Myers, it was a fifth-grade teacher who sparked his love of writing.[3] In any case, once the call to adventure has been heard, it compels its charges to dedicate their minds and bodies to achieving incredibly ambitious goals.

On some level, this same call to adventure is what often seems to set the very best readers apart. Find someone who loves books, and chances are good that she can point to some moment, time, or memory when she realized that she truly loved reading, wanted to do it for its own sake, and could do it well. This realization is as powerful as any teaching technique or tactic, given that ultimately mastering reading requires individual work . . . and lots of it. Bradbury and Dean Myers realized early that they had a passion for writing, but it took years of ceaseless practice before they became the legendary authors we remember now. Reading is no different. Those who have been truly and deeply "hooked" on reading may have been caught early, but the skills, creativity, and insights they build only come from hours upon hours of dedicated and focused work. When it comes to becoming a truly great reader, love is not optional.

Yet if great drive and passion are required to build great reading, what role can teachers play? After all, if only those "called" to reading are meant to truly throw themselves in, then one could argue that being a truly great reader is simply not for all students. Fortunately, in our experience as educators, that's not quite how it works. A student's call to the adventure of enthusiastic reading is not issued by mythical beings, nor is it even the product of unique circumstances. Rather, this final component of reading excellence—the passion to read and the long stretches of time to practice reading well—can be built through a strong independent reading program. The very best teachers refuse to wait for destiny to call; instead, through independent reading, they give it a megaphone.

If guided reading is about coaching and practicing with young readers, then independent reading is about sending them into a crucial scrimmage. So what's the "big game" they're preparing for? A lifetime of both academic and extracurricular reading adventures: analyzing primary history sources, reviewing the findings of laboratory reports, or just picking up novels for pleasure. Students aren't ready for that unless they can engage in independent reading in the classroom—that is, unless they are able to read successfully when the teacher steps back to the sidelines, when they must use their whole inventory of essential reading skills at once. This doesn't mean that the teacher fades entirely from the picture when independent reading time rolls around; on the contrary, as we'll discuss presently, independent reading requires diligent teacher attention in order to be effective. It means, rather, that just as students need opportunities to practice the skills of reading with explicit guidance, they also need opportunities to practice those skills on their own *before* the big game begins.

Core Idea

Independent reading is the scrimmage that prepares students for the "big game" of reading.

That big game happens later—when no one is keeping score.

There's plenty of research to support the value of independent reading. When students at Leiden University in the Netherlands sought to investigate the common generalization that "practicing reading is the miracle drug for the prevention and treatment of reading problems," they found evidence to support the notion.[4] Indeed, the *NAEP 1998 Reading Report Card for the Nation and the States* found that fourth graders who were given significant time to select and read their own books scored significantly higher on average in reading than peers who reported that they did not.[5]

Given all of these benefits, independent reading time might seem like a no-brainer for schools to put into place. Have they? Not necessarily. In fact, one study in 1998 found that teachers were using only about a third of reading instruction time for actual reading.[6] Why is this trend occurring, and how can teachers reverse it?

To find out, let's visit the classroom of Mr. Snyder, a teacher who wants to increase the amount of time his students spend reading.

Case Study

Mr. Snyder's Independent Reading Lesson

Mr. Snyder has been teaching third grade at Smithfield Elementary for four years. A skillful teacher of reading, Mr. Snyder often shares his guided reading lesson plans with other teachers at Smithfield, and has even led workshops on read-aloud. However, he feels that there are still ways he could improve his independent reading lessons: although he knows that students need independent reading time to become truly adept readers, he's worried that the time he gives his students for this might not really be helping them.

At 11:00 each day, Mr. Snyder's students break into two groups: half of them work with him on guided reading, and the rest read independently. As he dives into a spirited book introduction, his independent reading students congregate around the class library. The library is a colorful space where plenty of well-maintained books are stored. Because Mr. Snyder has set the expectation that reading time is silent time, these students are quiet and do not disrupt the guided reading lesson. Each student selects a text of interest and returns to his or her desk.

After a few minutes, Mr. Snyder glances in the direction of the desks and sees a familiar pattern. A handful of students seem super-engaged in their books, not distracted by anything going on around them. Another group appear to be reading, but only when they know Mr. Snyder is watching. And a few of the remaining students are quietly but clearly off task. Tianna has zoned out and is staring out the window, and Clark is turning pages so quickly that it's clear he's looking at pictures, not words.

As time goes on, students fill out logs that prompt them to record the title and author of the book they've read and to write a few sentences about whether they liked the book. Then, after twenty-five minutes total, the groups switch. The independent readers go to the guided reading table, and the guided reading students prepare for an independent reading session of their own.

Stop and Jot

Having read this summary of Mr. Snyder's independent reading lesson, what do you think he could do to allay some of his concerns about whether his independent reading lessons are effective? Jot down the advice you'd give Mr. Snyder.

_____

_____

_____

_____

_____

Mr. Snyder's independent reading lesson gives him a lot to be proud of. He has set up a great library, established a quiet time for students to read, and required students to fill out a reading log. Yet if you asked Mr. Snyder's students a series of comprehension questions about what they'd read during independent reading time, how many would answer proficiently? The answer is simple: we don't know. Tianna may have lacked focus because she picked out a text well above her reading level and was unable to struggle through it on her own. Clark appeared to be reading after he stopped flipping pages, but he might have found some other way to be off task behind an open book. And although it's certainly relevant to ask a student whether he or she liked a book, it doesn't tell you how well the student read the book — or, in some cases, whether the student really read the book at all. The lesson of Mr. Snyder's class is an important one: it's possible to give students independent reading time without being completely sure whether students are using that time to the fullest. And if students aren't reading, they won't get the practice they need to get better at reading — let alone to fall in love with it.

Core Idea

Students can't fall in love with reading if they aren't reading to begin with.

Now let's consider a different setting, Valerie Samples's third-grade classroom. Like Mr. Snyder, Valerie splits up her class each morning between guided reading and independent reading. During independent reading time, each student takes a book from a bin labeled with his or her reading level. While reading, they hold their books flat on the desk surface, making it easy for Valerie to check whether they are making progress. Finally, each student completes a brief comprehension-based written response on the book he or she read.

The differences between Valerie's independent reading lesson and Mr. Snyder's are subtle, but what sets Valerie's apart is that she knows for certain that each of her students is engaging with a text at exactly the right level for him or her, and spending twenty-five full minutes reading. And she can check to see not just whether they were reading but whether they comprehended what they read. In short, Valerie's students are truly being prepared to reap the knowledge and the joy that come from reading.

So what made the difference in Valerie's classroom? Three factors:

1.   Choosing and organizing texts for success

2.   Setting expectations for independence

3.   Insisting on intellectual accountability

We'll spend the remainder of this chapter exploring these game-changers one by one.

> ### Independent Reading—a Definition
>
> **Independent reading:** a carefully designed, accountable moment for students to read a book without your support. There are three keys to creating that moment:
>
> 1. Choose and organize texts for success.
> 2. Set expectations for independence.
> 3. Insist on intellectual accountability.

CHOOSE AND ORGANIZE TEXTS FOR SUCCESS

One of the most common beliefs about independent reading is that it is a time for students to read any book they want in any way they want. It's not hard to see where this idea comes from: there's undeniable value to giving students the opportunity to choose what they read, especially when it comes to teaching students to love reading. Yet if we give our very earliest readers this level of freedom, we're forgetting that the ability to choose the right book to read is a skill that must be developed, just like any other reading skill. Even as adult readers, we can all think of times when we have purchased a novel that turned out to be disappointing, or read an article that didn't address the topic we had hoped to learn about. We know enough about reading to take these setbacks in stride, holding on to the faith that our future reading experiences will still be fruitful. For very young readers, however, being disappointed by a book can be a much bigger roadblock to better reading experiences in the future.

By way of example, imagine Gabriel, a third grader reading at the beginning third-grade level, whose teacher allows students to select any book from the classroom library during independent reading. An avid fan of trucks, Gabriel initially chooses *Craig Jeffries and the Mega Truck Mystery*, a book with an exciting cover that is at the fifth-grade level. For ten minutes, Gabriel runs into wall after wall: words he cannot decode, a narrative structure he does not understand, and, on some level, a sense that books are closed to him. Disheartened, he switches his book for *Monster Trucks*, a kindergarten-level picture book. He gets more fun out of the last part of independent reading, but he doesn't get productive practice time out of any of it.

Stories like Gabriel's are an incredibly common result of independent reading as it is often structured. Again, that's not to say that student choice doesn't matter in independent reading. Providing students with a variety of books from which to choose plays a vital role in making independent reading worthwhile. But in order to make independent reading time truly valuable for every reader, teachers must combine the support that comes from meeting each student at his or her level with the freedom of choice that comes from a great classroom library.

To secure these appealing results, great teachers don't just let kids rummage among books at random: they organize independent reading to set up students with the right books for them. How?

Target Choices

Dividing your independent reading library by reading skill level is a vital step to ensuring that students actually benefit from reading time. As Gabriel's story showed, when students are not pointed toward books that will meet them at the right level, they often end up feeling frustrated, bored, or just not challenged.

Kylene Beers reminds us that presenting students with books that are too challenging can turn them off to reading.[7]

So what's the ideal? In our experience, the best independent reading happens at around half a grade level (or a few reading levels) below a student's current reading capacity.

Core Idea

The best independent reading occurs at around half a grade level below students' capacity.

They've practiced flapping elsewhere; this is their time to fly.

At this point, it is important to address a key concern: whether this approach is sufficiently rigorous. Some have argued that independent reading should take place at or *above* each child's reading level—not below. They argue that it is through such adaptation that students learn the skills they most need.

It's true that students needn't be entirely separated from books above their grade level. For many struggling readers, for example, it can be extremely motivating to see the exciting books he or she will be able to read after a few more months of instruction. These students will benefit from being able to pick these books up in the library and spend time looking through them, getting a sense of what it will take to be able to read, for example, a whole chapter book independently. However, the systems outlined in this book ensure that students have multiple rich opportunities to read at and above grade level outside of independent reading. In guided reading, students work with texts directly at their level, and comprehension skills and read-aloud lessons expose them to texts anywhere from a half to two full grade levels beyond—all with the support of a teacher. Overall, then, the "choice" to pick an independent reading book two grade levels too high is not a freedom that benefits most students, so book selection should be organized to avoid this. That way, students can be assured of both learning from independent reading and partaking in sufficiently rigorous reading instruction.

Meet Student Interests

Gabriel's excitement when he began reading is a testament to one positive decision his teacher made: keeping high-interest books in the classroom. As you build your library, there is great benefit to picking books that reflect the diverse interests and aspirations of your students, making sure that everyone in your class can find multiple books to love.

Embed Informational Options

One of the most striking findings in a study of Boston-area first-grade classrooms was that the typical student library comprised only 10 percent informational texts. That study found that students spent an average of only 3.6 minutes daily working with nonfiction.[8] This dearth of informational material is of grave concern. Presenting students with engaging informational texts is a vital way to help reinforce certain reading skills that are extremely crucial—and that feature largely in the CCSS. Although it's true that 60 to 70 percent of the informational text work you do will happen in your content-area instruction, this still needs to be a focus within your independent reading lessons. For many students, being exposed to informational texts will also be a key step to finding the reading material that is of greatest interest to them. A 50–50 split between narrative and informational texts in your class library, then, is a much better target to aim for.

Don't Be Afraid to Assign

Finally, it is important to remember that letting students choose their books is not the *goal* of independent reading: it is a means to achieve the bigger goal of creating a joyful and focused time for students to practice reading. With this in mind, don't be afraid to assign students to read certain books during their independent reading time, especially when students are younger and need more guidance. Indeed, in earlier grades, one of the most simple and effective strategies for independent reading text selection is for students to use the book that they have previously used for guided reading. This provides a very easy logistical transition from guided reading text to independent reading text. Another option—one that strikes a great balance between letting students choose books and guiding them toward the right books—is to give each student a choice among five specific books that you think would be of high interest *and* high learning benefit to that student.

SET EXPECTATIONS FOR INDEPENDENCE

In our chapter on routines and procedures, we worked to underscore the importance of setting high and consistent standards for students to make the most of classroom time. Although this is crucial to all aspects of an effective reading classroom, it is particularly important in the context of independent reading. Given the complexity of independent reading—that is, the challenge of ensuring that each student is focused, considering that they are all engaged in a somewhat private activity—creating the expectation that students will use this time to the fullest requires forethought and planning. The best place to turn for the creation of such systems is Chapter One. However, once you have reviewed these strategies, there are a number of more specific actions and systems you can put into place to ensure that independent reading time is as productive and focused as possible.

Library Systems

We have already discussed the value of a well-designed classroom library. It is also important to note that a strong set of "library procedures"—like the overall classroom procedures we highlighted in Chapter One—can create a highly effective experience for students. See the box "Key Tips: Library Systems" for a few basic techniques for "library time" that can help ensure that it is as productive as possible.

Key Tips: Library Systems

- **Position the library away from class activity.** Ideally, your class library will be far away from the main centers of classroom activity, such as where you normally speak from. This will minimize unnecessary movement.
- **Chart "classmate-free" paths to and from the library.** Training students in how to reach the library without moving among student desks will greatly reduce the "friction" that such a transition could cause, which could derail reading time.
- **Make clear labels.** Clearly labeling the library section will help ensure that students can very quickly find books of the level they are looking for.
- **Limit the number of students up at one time.** To ensure that the class remains focused during independent reading time, it is vital to limit the number of students who are selecting books at any one time.

When the Reading Starts

In order for independent reading to yield the many benefits it promises, students need to actually read. The trouble is that independent reading can be extremely difficult to enforce. For comparison, consider the teacher's expectations of students during guided reading. If students are off task, they will be easy to spot because they will be talking out of turn, physically looking away from the page, or unable to respond to basic questions. Perhaps most important, there are relatively few students in each guided reading group, and the students all sit close to the teacher.

By contrast, independent reading can feature many more subtle forms of noncompliance, any of which can greatly reduce the effectiveness of the lesson as a whole. It only takes a few students daydreaming, napping, or only looking at pictures for the entire independent reading system to break down. Fortunately, there are some key expectations that can be set and strategies that can be put in place to make sure that students remain fully focused during this time (see the box "Key Expectations for Independent Reading Time").

Key Expectations for Independent Reading Time

- **Have books kept flat.** When students keep books flat on their desks, it is much easier to track whether students are actually reading or are engaged in off-task behaviors.
- **Check page numbers.** When monitoring the classroom, a quick and easy way to keep students on track is to monitor the page number each is on.
- **Insist on silence when reading.** Quickly and consistently responding to talking during reading time is especially important, as this is a part of class time that can easily be disrupted by student misconduct.

From the foundation of the expectations outlined in this section, it is possible to begin building a strong independent reading classroom. Yet although strong routines and procedures are one key to ensuring that great independent reading *can* happen, they are not sufficient to ensure that great independent reading *will* happen. For this, we must move on to the next step: establishing intellectual accountability.

INSIST ON INTELLECTUAL ACCOUNTABILITY

Just as students should be held to a high behavioral standard during independent reading, it is also important to hold them accountable for rigorous thinking. One of the greatest challenges of independent reading is that the "action" you are looking for is occurring inside each student's mind, not in his or her responses to teacher questions or peer comments. Without a check for intellectual understanding, it is impossible to tell an independent reader from a zoned-out student.

Core Idea

Zoned-out students look just like independent readers—unless you know how to check.

The good news: holding students intellectually accountable need not be challenging. By designing standard assignments to gauge student thinking, great teachers can ensure that each period of independent reading is filled with meaningful work. And, as an added benefit, teachers can gain a much greater insight into what skills students have truly mastered and where they may still be struggling. These assignments can include "reading reports" like the one in the box "Accountability for Independent Reading: Sample First- Through Third-Grade Reading Report—Narrative Stories."

Accountability for Independent Reading

Sample First- Through Third-Grade Reading Report— Narrative Stories

Title: _____

Select one key quote from the passage you read:

Quote from Novel	What is happening in this quote?	How does this quote contribute to the central meaning of the novel?

Synthesize the main events of the section that you read:

_____

_____

_____

_____

This can be used for nearly any narrative story, which makes it work well for all independent readers. A similar report can be used for informational texts; the box "Accountability for Independent Reading: Sample Third-Grade Reading Report—Informational Texts" shows how that might look.

Accountability for Independent Reading

Sample Third-Grade Reading Report— Informational Texts

Title: _____

Name three important facts or arguments from the text:

_____

_____

_____

_____

Why are these important to the text?

_____

_____

_____

_____

Once again, this kind of report allows for students to select their own texts and for you to still have a common accountability tool. It also allows you to prepare students to work deeply within texts, one of the signature expectations of the Common Core. There's no need to create a new tool for each book students read.

One word of caution: beware the overinvolved worksheet. When students only have twenty-five minutes for independent reading, it's important to think carefully about anything that might take some of those minutes away, especially for students who need a lot of time to complete either a reading assignment or a written assignment. Whatever intellectual accountability work you assign for independent reading should be substantive enough for you to confirm that your students made productive use of independent reading time, but not much more substantive than that. Think quality of questions, not quantity.

Another way of ensuring intellectual accountability is to create a class challenge that celebrates every book a student finishes during independent reading time with some kind of award. For this to be effective, the award must be a matter of recognition, not of material gifts—for example, having a board where every student's name gets posted when he or she has read twenty-five books in all, rather than rewarding each student with a pencil for the same achievement. Challenges like these create an atmosphere of friendly competition and support not unlike what you may remember from summer reading challenges at your local library.

A Word on . . . Independent Reading 201

Setting up a productive independent reading period like the one this chapter describes, including making sure all students are reading books and completing comprehension assignments, is in and of itself a significant accomplishment that paves the way for incredible gains in student achievement. If, however, you've got great independent reading lessons up and running and want to take them to an even higher level, here are some ideas that have worked well for many successful reading instructors:

- **For students reading at a kindergarten level:** These students aren't yet prepared to spend twenty-five full minutes on independent reading. Instead, have them spend about ten minutes rereading texts they've read at the read-aloud table. If you need something more for these students to do while their peers work with you in small groups, assign them independent literacy practice—either on worksheets or at computer workstations—that focuses on phonics, word solving, or vocabulary. (For more information about independent literacy practice, see the "Independent Reading" box.)

- **For students reading at a first-grade level:** Now students are more prepared for independent reading—but not for quite as much of it as older students need. Have them do independent reading for two days of every week, and independent literacy practice the other three.
- **For students reading at a second-grade level:** Add a personal reading log to the standard independent reading pattern (that is, reading and a basic comprehension worksheet). Throughout the year, students will use this log to track the books they read. You may also allow students at this level to choose which type of comprehension work they'll do for each book they read: summarizing the book, identifying the theme, or describing a character's motivation.
- **For students reading at a third-grade level or above:** For these students, it may sometimes be beneficial to have them read the texts they're reading for guided reading during independent reading time. Why? Because they're often reading chapter books or other long texts in guided reading, and won't be able to get all the way through them if guided reading time is the only time they have to read them. You can use the same accountability worksheets as the ones referenced earlier.

A Word on . . . Resources for Independent Literacy Practice

Besides its immense advantages for students, independent reading has one extremely important benefit for you as the teacher: it gives students something to do while you work with other students in a small group. But what if you're working with early readers who aren't yet prepared to spend twenty-five minutes reading independently? What work could you assign to these students?

We call the assignments that fall into this category *independent literacy practice*. Independent literacy practice must be silent and easy for you to monitor, and—most important—it must still help students build great reading habits. Here are some resources you can leverage to create meaningful independent literacy assignments for early readers:

- **Option 1: Purchase a computer-based literacy program.** These are the strongest resources available for student independent work. If you are able to purchase such a program, you can have students use it independently at

(continued)

computer workstations, where ideally they will have headsets to keep them from getting distracted.

- **Option 2: Acquire a phonics workbook.** A phonics or literacy workbook is a great alternative to a computer-based literacy program. The great advantage of both this option and option 1 is that they are premade: they save you the labor of designing independent work for your students so that you can focus on planning the other types of reading lessons.
- **Option 3: Develop your own series of independent literacy practice assignments.** If you do not have the ability to purchase either a computer-based literacy program or literacy workbooks for your students, then you will need to develop your own series of independent practice assignments. However, as this is a time-consuming project, we suggest that if possible, you borrow these from another teacher who has done it before. Independent work is important, but your time is better leveraged working on the lessons you will be teaching.

CONCLUSION: LOVE MATTERS

The benefits of a rigorous independent reading system can be expressed in many concrete terms: the number of books students have read, hours they've spent reading, or the test scores they've achieved through all this practice. By setting up the right texts, building the right classroom procedures, and developing deeper student learning through intellectual accountability, great reading teachers can use independent reading to achieve all these things. Equally important, though, is the love for reading that independent reading builds. A student does not truly have the opportunity to fall in love with reading until he or she spends enough time alone with an interesting text to discover that he or she is capable of reading it. Moreover, the value of this development reaches far beyond the joy of reading for pleasure. Regardless of what other subjects elementary students fall in love with over the course of their lives—from history to psychology, from theater to advanced physics—the love of reading is a love that will matter.

Independent Reading

Guidelines to Remember

Key Tips: Library Systems

- **Position library away from class activity.** Ideally, your class library can be far away from the main centers of classroom activity, such as where the teacher normally speaks from. This will minimize unnecessary movement.
- **Chart "classmate-free" paths to and from the library.** Training students in how to reach the library without going through student desks will greatly reduce the "friction" that such a transition could cause, which could derail reading time.
- **Make clear labels.** Clearly labeling the library section will help ensure that students can very quickly find books of the level they are looking for.
- **Limit the number of students up at one time.** Finally, it is vital to limit the number of students who, at any one time, are selecting books. This will be vital to ensuring that the class remains focused during independent reading time.

Key Expectations for Independent Reading Time

- **Have books kept flat.** When students keep books flat on their desks, it is much easier to track whether students are actually reading or are engaged in off-task behaviors.
- **Check page numbers.** When monitoring the classroom, a quick and easy way to keep students on track is to monitor the page number each is on.
- **Insist on silence when reading.** Quickly and consistently responding to talking during reading time is especially important, as this is a part of class time that can easily be quickly disrupted by student misconduct.

Apply Your Habits: Independent Reading

Self-Assessment

Which of the practices we described will help your students get the most out of independent reading time?

_____

_____

_____

_____

_____

_____

Tool to Use

• Independent Reading: Guidelines to Remember (also included on the DVD)

Your Next Steps

_____

_____

_____

_____

_____

_____

_____

Great Habits, Great Readers: A Practical Guide for K–4 Reading in the Light of Common Core, by Paul Bambrick-Santoyo, Aja Settles, and Juliana Worrell. Copyright © 2013 Uncommon Schools and/or Paul Bambrick-Santoyo. Reproduced by permission.

Lead by Habit

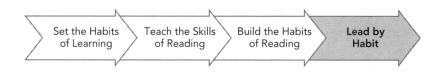

| Set the Habits of Learning | Teach the Skills of Reading | Build the Habits of Reading | **Lead by Habit** |

Part 4

Introduction: Script the Change You Need

It is tough to change our habits. Whether doing so as an individual, a classroom, or a district, adopting a new way of thinking and working can be incredibly challenging. Up to this point, we've discussed many different ways to change the way reading is taught. We hope that by now you have at least some ways in which you would want to change your classroom.

Yet as we've seen again and again, being shown the right path is not enough. Almost everyone in education has had the experience of encountering a big idea to redesign their teaching. Sometimes, it comes from a charismatic and engaging professional development setting. At other times, it comes from books that lay out great ideas. Years later, we may even remember catchy anecdotes, clever turns of phrase, or key concepts. But once we leave the session or put the book down, how many of these changes do we actually put into place? The answer, if we're being honest, is not many.

In *Switch*, professors Chip and Dan Heath explored exactly this disconnect between the ideas we want to put into practice and actually doing so. The Heaths found that when people need to redesign a complex endeavor, whether a business, a government, or eating habits, they tend to become paralyzed by the choices ahead. Without a clear sense of precisely what change looked like, a "switch" can simply seem too difficult to pull off.[1]

Fortunately, the Heaths found that dramatic changes are, in fact, possible, provided that we start with an incredibly specific and direct set of "critical moves." Terminally failing businesses that were unable to rally workers around a general sense of thriftiness created vast change by creating simple and clear rules: make no new purchases, reuse equipment, always give higher priority to older gear. Health officials who had unsuccessfully warned of the dangers of unhealthy eating in general terms created vast changes when they pushed a clear action: replace whole milk with 2 percent milk.

Scripting the next steps is just as important for changing a school, a classroom, or a student's life. In Chapter Eleven, we present the specific and concrete ways to design your schedule to fit in all of the lessons we've discussed in this book, regardless of your specific school conditions. Chapter Twelve offers a comprehensive guide for school leaders and instructional coaches on how to support and develop teachers to make them effective instructors of reading.

Chapter 11

The Schedule

Getting It All on the Table

Imagine two cooks: the manager of a dining hall and a novice chef who's been assigned to make lunch himself for the first time. Eager to put his best culinary school skills into action, the less experienced cook gets to work preparing shrimp scampi with fresh linguine. Although he has excelled at serving fine dishes in a small setting, he has never prepared food for an entire lunch shift. Still, he's working with top-notch ingredients and state-of-the-art kitchen equipment, and he is eager to please. Quickly he runs into a setback when he has not finished preparing the linguine dough to put in the pasta press, yet the shrimp still needs to be peeled. He works even harder, and throws the fresh pasta into a large vat of water, even though the water isn't yet boiling. As he hastily chops vegetables for the dish, his manager notes with concern that the lunch hour is drawing dangerously near. Though the novice chef works increasingly harder to get back on track, his problem isn't a lack of work ethic: it's a lack of efficiency. Twenty minutes before the beginning of lunch hour, he has no choice but to throw chicken breasts onto the grill and serve it with his homemade pasta, which didn't cook terribly well given how rushed he was. He started with a great plan, but ran out of time to deliver a great lunch.

What if the manager himself had been preparing the meal? The story would have gone entirely differently. The manager would have known to begin boiling the water for the pasta earlier, so that it would be ready when the pasta was. He'd have had a keen sense of when to begin preparing the shrimp so that it would be done promptly but would also be optimally fresh. By lunch time, he'd have created a complete, nourishing gourmet meal — not to mention arranged it appetizingly on plates. The complex choreography of cooking on a schedule is likely second nature to a chef of his experience; he can both get everything done on time and make it all worth savoring.

The moral of this tale of two chefs is that knowing which components to include in a reading program — or a meal — is just part of the challenge of creating something extraordinary. When we constantly spend time and energy deciding how to fit those components together, we find ourselves not having enough time left to serve up a quality finished product. If the previous chapters of this book were about the meat, potatoes, and vegetables of our reading program — our five types of reading lessons — then this chapter is about getting it all on the table by lunch time. Without an effective schedule, students will never actually receive the reading instruction they need.

Core Idea

Good teachers know how to deliver all the reading lesson types; master teachers—and leaders—build a schedule that guarantees they will.

We will spend the rest of this chapter detailing how to create a set schedule that makes every essential component of reading happen every day. Too often, for teachers at the elementary level, it can be tempting to avoid following such a schedule in favor of coming up with a different plan every day. Yet think of how much thought and energy it takes to schedule each day of literacy instruction this way. For one thing, it's extremely difficult to keep some element or another from falling through the cracks. For another, it leaves you with far less energy to devote to your students' individual needs as you plan and deliver the lesson. Coming up with a set schedule like the one we'll propose doesn't just protect your time; it also protects that much more of your energy for the most important work: teaching and learning.

THE SCHEDULING PROCESS: AN OVERVIEW

What are we going to need to put into our elementary reading schedule? Let's look at Figure 11.1 to review what we learned about that at the very beginning of this book.

The process of fitting these five types of lessons together into a schedule is similar for any elementary classroom. However, the exact amount of time you end up spending on each in your classroom will vary depending on a number of factors, from the time you have available for reading instruction to the level at which your students are reading. As we walk through the scheduling process, we'll unpack the most crucial of these variables.

Here's a quick preview of what the scheduling process looks like:

Quick Preview: The Scheduling Process

1. Determine how much time you *can* spend on reading instruction.
2. Identify which components of reading need to be taught during that time.
3. Build each of these components into your schedule.

Let's walk through it step-by-step.

Figure 11.1 Lessons in the Reading-by-Habit Model

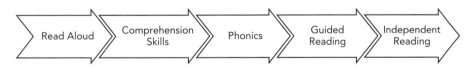

HOW MUCH TIME *CAN* YOU MAKE FOR READING?

The most obvious issue at stake here is how long a reading block you are able to create. The reason we ask how much time you *can* make for reading—not how much time you already have—is that, overall, more time spent on reading means greater gains in student achievement. Although it's possible to fit every lesson type we've covered in this book into a daily reading block of around two hours, the top-performing classrooms we have examined have a reading schedule that runs around two-and-a-half hours a day. So if the time you already spend on reading adds up to less than this, we recommend you consider some ways to stretch it further. Even in a world where instructional time generally feels like a candy bar that's never quite as big as you want it to be, many teachers find that a little creativity can make that candy bar supersized.

Some of the time-expanding tactics that have worked for teachers we know include changing "homeroom time" into "homeroom and independent reading" time, or "snack time" into "snacks and read-aloud" time. As you consider what might work in your classroom, be aware that all components of reading instruction need not happen consecutively: they can be split up across the day. For example, there is no harm whatsoever in completing the first part of reading instruction in the morning and then picking up after lunch or after a mathematics block. The only caveat here is that it's best not to cut off in the middle of any single activity (for example, you wouldn't want to stop students in the middle of guided reading and then bring them back to it after lunch). The only exception is independent reading, which can be more easily interrupted.

A key determining factor in how much time you really have for reading instruction is whether any other adults are available in your classroom during reading time. Any time during which you can invite an additional adult into the classroom, even if it's just for an hour, allows for more students to be receiving direct small-group instruction simultaneously. For example, when one group of students engages in guided reading practice with one teacher, a second group could be receiving a phonics lesson from a second teacher or teacher's aide. For this reason, the schedules you would design for a class with two adults differ significantly from those you'd create for a class with one.

It can be tempting to make an immediate mental response to this question about the number of adults in your reading classroom—either, "Great, I already have another teacher working with me" or "Oh, well, I guess I'll make it work with just me in the classroom"—and then move on. But if you're in the latter camp, the potential benefits to students make it worth considering ways to make a two-teacher reading classroom possible at your school, even if you have to think outside the box to do it. Here are a couple of suggestions:

- **Split the time of a grade-level assistant.** Some school districts we have worked with have only one assistant per grade level, or one assistant per several teachers. Inviting this assistant into each classroom during its reading instruction time ensures that all classes would have two literacy instructors when it counted most.

- **Ask for help from physical education teachers, art teachers, social workers, parent volunteers . . .** Although it would be great if the second adult in your classroom were a fully trained elementary reading teacher, he or she will be immensely valuable even without such training. You'd simply need to train any such adults with the materials in this book and delegate them to phonics or scripted lessons, while retaining control of lessons that require as much teacher expertise as possible, such as guided reading.

Even if you can add another adult to your classroom only a couple of times per week, you still greatly increase the amount of time your students spend on reading. Of course, though, if you find yourself unable to add a second adult to your classroom at any point, your students will progress even without that extra one-on-one practice time.

Once you've determined how much time you have for reading, the next step in the planning process is to figure out what needs to be taught during that time.

HOW SHOULD YOU SPEND READING TIME?

Read-aloud, comprehension skills, phonics, guided reading, and independent reading lessons are the key ingredients as you build a reading schedule. However, the particular menu that you'll serve to your students will need to be adjusted according to two main factors: the level at which your students read and the resources you are able to tap into for student independent work.

The amount of time you'll spend on each component of reading instruction will vary depending on where your students are on their reading journey. The question is a complex one, considering how quickly students can progress from

Table 11.1 Reading Ingredients by Level

Emergent, Early, and Transitional Readers (Up to 500L)	Extended Readers (500L+)
Phonics	—
Read-aloud	—
Comprehension skills (80% narrative, 20% informational)	Comprehension skills (50% narrative, 50% informational)
Independent reading and literacy practice	Independent reading
Guided reading	Guided reading

one reading level to the next—and how much this rate varies from student to student. However, by reviewing your assessment data, you can determine which of the instructional models shown in Table 11.1 would best suit the majority of your particular students.

Let's take a closer look at how each model works. The distinguishing characteristics of the *early reading model* are as follows:

- **Phonics.** As we noted in Chapter Six, phonics plays a major role in beginning reading instruction. This *does not* mean that an early reading program should exclude comprehension—on the contrary, as the early elementary curriculum we've outlined reflects, comprehension skills lessons are vital as well. Early readers must spend significant daily time on both of these aspects of reading.

- **Read-aloud.** As we detailed in Chapter Four, read-aloud is invaluable to early readers who still need great reading explicitly modeled for them. Thus, at the early reading levels, read-aloud happens every day.

- **Comprehension skills: 80 percent narrative texts, 20 percent informational texts.** Early readers should be exposed to informational as well as narrative texts, but the overall focus should be on narrative. That's because learning to understand the structure of a story—beginning, middle, and end—is crucial for the development of reading and writing skills for students at this stage. As a result, the comprehension skills lessons you teach early readers should focus on narrative texts 80 percent of the time and informational texts 20 percent of the time. (Because students do further informational reading in their science and social studies lessons, they are still focusing on informational texts frequently enough to meet the informational text requirements set forth by the CCSS.)

- **Independent reading and independent literacy practice.** As we mentioned in Chapter Ten on independent reading, it's valuable for early readers to have opportunities for independent practice in phonics, word solving, and vocabulary. For emergent readers (who cannot fully read on their own yet), independent literacy practice serves to supplement independent reading time, which isn't productive for such long periods of time for these students.

- **Guided reading in smaller groups.** Finally, because early readers develop faster than their older cohorts, it is important to create smaller guided reading groups for these students (as detailed in Chapter Six).

Here are the distinguishing characteristics of the *extended reading model*:

- **No phonics necessary.** At the extended reading levels, students have mastered phonics well enough to benefit from a more comprehension-focused program.

- **No explicit read-aloud necessary.** Similarly, explicit read-aloud time can be phased out as students approach extended reading levels. Without a doubt, there are still benefits to reading aloud with older students, so you can keep this lesson type in play if desired — and even if you don't, there may be isolated times when you need to read aloud to your students to teach them some specific skill or concept. Overall, however, it's less critical to include an explicit daily read-aloud at the later reading levels than at the earlier ones, and many teachers find that they need to use the time that read-aloud takes up to teach other lessons that students need more urgently.

- **Comprehension skills: 50 percent narrative texts, 50 percent informational texts.** The Common Core specifies that as students reach higher reading levels, they must spend more time reading informational texts. This is also a vital part of college-ready reading preparation. Thus, for extended readers, we recommend splitting comprehension instruction between narrative texts and informational texts.

- **Independent reading.** Also emphasized in the Common Core is that extended readers need increasing amounts of time to practice sustained reading of both narrative and informational texts. They no longer need to spend time on independent literacy practice.

- **Larger guided reading groups.** For older students, larger groups will work for guided reading, as these students are likely to be reading at more similar levels.

When you know how much time you have to teach reading and what pieces of reading instruction need to fit into that time, you're ready to build a schedule that pins down a specific time for everything. The best way to show how this works is to do it. Let's get started!

BUILDING THE SCHEDULE: ONE TEACHER, TWO HOURS

For the sample schedule we're about to build, imagine that you are the only adult in an early reading classroom with two hours to spend on reading. First, as a reminder, let's review everything that needs to fit into the early reading schedule:

Emergent, Early, and Transitional Readers	Extended Readers
Phonics	—
Read-aloud	—
Comprehension skills (80% narrative, 20% informational)	Comprehension skills (50% narrative, 50% informational)
Independent reading and literacy practice	Independent reading
Guided reading	Guided reading

Next, we'll break down how much time each of these gets in a single day of early reading instruction (see Figure 11.2).

As you can see, comprehension skills and guided reading lessons share a twenty-five-minute time block. That's because students will alternate daily

Figure 11.2 Early Reading Instruction

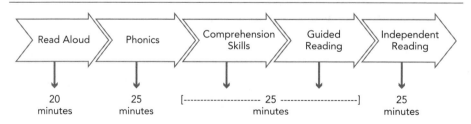

Figure 11.3 Early Reading Instruction

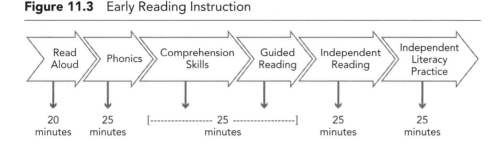

between comprehension skills lessons and guided reading lessons. In Figure 11.2, then, we've accounted for most of what happens during reading time at the early reading level . . . but you may have noticed that we still haven't filled up two full hours. That's because there's one more piece to fill in: each student will also spend twenty-five minutes daily on independent literacy practice (illustrated in Figure 11.3).

A Word on . . . Alternating Daily Between Comprehension Skills and Guided Reading Lessons

For many elementary school teachers, it's all too easy to lose sight of how essential it is to teach both comprehension skills lessons and guided reading lessons. Unfortunately, if you don't make a distinct separation between teaching comprehension skills and turning over the work of using those skills to students, it's extremely difficult for students truly to be able to use the skills independently. When the lines blur, the work of reading tends to rest on the teacher's shoulders for too long.

It's in order to avoid this outcome that we recommend alternating explicitly between days that are for teaching comprehension skills and days that are for guided reading. At the early reading levels, when students have the most to learn about reading comprehension, the best option is to designate three days for comprehension skills lessons and two for guided reading lessons. For later readers, it's still necessary to teach comprehension skills lessons, but it's not necessary to teach as many of them. For this reason, we recommend switching to two days of comprehension skills and three of guided reading when students reach later reading levels.

You'll notice that although the schedule shown in Figure 11.3 emphasizes read-aloud, phonics, comprehension skills, and guided reading lessons, it dedicates the biggest time chunk of all to independent reading and independent literacy practice. This is wholly intentional. It ensures that practice time — the time that leads to the concretizing of exemplary habits — is the major focus of each student's time.

So how do we transform all this information into a daily calendar? Here are the steps:

1. **Set aside twenty minutes for read-aloud.** A whole-class read-aloud is a great way to kick off a day of reading instruction, so let's begin by leaving time for that. As outlined in Chapter Four, read-aloud lessons take at least twenty minutes. Let's see how this looks in a schedule.

Sample One-Teacher Schedule, Step 1

	Group 1 Higher Readers	Group 2 Middle Readers	Group 3 Lower Readers
9:00–9:20	Whole-class read-aloud		

2. **Set aside twenty-five minutes for a daily whole-class phonics lesson.** If you have an extra adult in the room, phonics can become a small-group activity. For the one-teacher classroom, however, we recommend a whole-group phonics lesson of around twenty to twenty-five minutes every single day.

Sample One-Teacher Schedule, Step 2

	Group 1 Higher Readers	Group 2 Middle Readers	Group 3 Lower Readers
9:00–9:20	Whole-class read-aloud		
9:20–9:45	Whole-class phonics lesson		

3. **Create rotations for guided reading, comprehension skills, independent literacy practice, and independent reading.** Once early readers have participated in a read-aloud and a phonics lesson, it's time for them to apply the skills they've been practicing there. This takes place over the course of your remaining reading time, in three small-group rotations. Table 11.2 shows the complete schedule.

Table 11.2 Sample One-Teacher Schedule—Complete

	Group 1 Higher Readers	Group 2 Middle Readers	Group 3 Lower Readers
9:00–9:20	Whole-class read-aloud		
9:20–9:45	Whole-class phonics lesson		
9:45–10:10	Guided reading (T, Th) Comprehension skills (M, W, F)	Independent reading*	Independent literacy practice
10:10–10:25	Snack		
10:25–10:50	Independent literacy practice	Guided reading (T, Th) Comprehension skills (M, W, F)	Independent reading*
10:50–11:15	Independent reading*	Independent literacy practice	Guided reading (T, Th) Comprehension skills (M, W, F)

*Pre-readers do extra independent literacy practice.

What do you notice about this schedule?

- **One group for either comprehension skills or guided reading lessons.** Remember, these will alternate from day to day. At the early reading level, we recommend spending three days per week on comprehension skills lessons and two days per week on guided reading.

- **One group for independent literacy practice.**

- **One group for independent reading.** (Pre-readers will spend ten minutes of this time on independent reading, and the rest on extra independent literacy practice instead.)

What are the benefits of creating these small-group rotations? For one thing, you will see all students in a small group every day, which allows you to tailor each lesson specifically for each student's needs as well as give as many practice opportunities as possible.

Take a moment to think about what this schedule accomplishes. We have now fit everything we've covered in this book into a two-hour schedule. You've locked in twenty-five minutes per day of targeted small-group instruction for each student—that's *seventy-five hours* in a 180-day school year—and twice as much again for independent practice. Because you no longer need to make daily decisions about which vital components of reading instruction will happen when, you've given yourself considerably more time to focus on planning and teaching each of those components. And to help you accomplish this, you have multiple extremely powerful tools at your disposal: a great reading curriculum, your students' assessment data, and the guided reading prompting guides, to name just a few. Scheduling is about prioritizing, and when you have created a schedule like this one, you have given top priority to the specific needs of every single one of your students.

Core Idea

Scheduling is about prioritizing. A balanced schedule gives your students access to all the types of reading instruction—and gives you more time to plan for them.

Now we need to account for the ways in which this schedule might need to change in other situations. Let's look at a few of these variations.

THREE VARIATIONS TO THE SCHEDULE

If we were to attempt to show every possible way this schedule could be adjusted to fit the specific needs of every elementary reading teacher, we'd have a much larger book on our hands. Instead, we've outlined the three variations most likely to address your scheduling needs: one for when you're teaching later readers, one for when you have two adults in your classroom, and one for when you have extra time for reading instruction. At the end of the chapter, we'll present a blank schedule template that you can use to make any other adjustments, so that your schedule works just right in your classroom.

Variation 1: Teaching Extended Readers, One Teacher

Let's review how reading instruction changes when you're teaching extended readers with one teacher:

Emergent, Early, and Transitional Readers	Extended Readers
Phonics	—
Read-aloud	—
Comprehension skills (80% narrative, 20% informational)	Comprehension skills (50% narrative, 50% informational)
Independent reading and literacy practice	Independent reading
Guided reading	Guided reading

What does all this mean in terms of changes to a two-hour reading schedule? Table 11.3 shows what it would look like.

What do you notice?

- **Read-aloud, phonics lessons, and independent literacy practice can be cut from the schedule altogether.** As we've already noted, there are many

Table 11.3 Variation 1: One-Teacher Schedule—Extended Readers

	GUIDED READING DAYS (M, W, F)		COMPREHENSION SKILLS DAYS (T, Th)
	Group 1 Higher Readers	Group 2 Middle Readers	Whole Class
9:00– 9:15 9:15– 9:30	**Guided reading** Informational	**Independent reading** Informational	**Comprehension skills** Informational
9:30– 9:45 9:45– 10:00	**Independent reading** Informational	**Guided reading** Informational	**Comprehension skills** Narrative
10:00– 10:15 10:15– 10:30	**Guided reading** Narrative	**Independent reading** Narrative	
10:30– 11:00	**Independent reading** Narrative	**Guided reading** Narrative	**Independent reading** Narrative or informational

situations in which your students may still benefit from these types of lessons, but they don't require a permanent spot in your schedule. This allows you to spend more time on the types of lessons that remain.

- **Comprehension skills lessons, guided reading, and independent reading time will be split every day between work on narrative texts and work on informational texts.** Just as with early reading, comprehension skills and guided reading lessons occur on alternating days. For extended readers, we recommend spending only two days on comprehension skills lessons and the other three on guided reading. Moreover, they will spend half their time working on narrative texts and the other half working on informational texts. On guided reading days, *the same split happens with independent reading*, with students spending half their time independently reading narrative texts and the other half independently reading informational texts. Extra work on informational texts won't be valuable if students don't have this time to practice the skills independently. Informational text work is so critical at the later reading levels that this emphasis on informational texts is extremely beneficial.

Remember when we noted that guided reading groups can be larger at later reading levels because students' reading skill levels aren't generally as varied? That's why, in this schedule, we've shifted from three student groups to two. In this way, as well as in the phasing out of read-aloud and phonics lessons in favor of more time for both guided and independent practice, this schedule reflects the evolving importance of each component of reading as students gain more reading experience. When the students' priorities change, the schedule's priorities change, too.

Variation 2: Early Readers, Two Teachers

Let's see what the payoff of adding another adult to your reading classroom can look like. We'll focus on early reading, as that's where this change has the greatest impact, and assume we still have two hours. The changes a second adult's presence makes to the early reading schedule are illustrated in Table 11.4.

What are the benefits of this schedule?

- **Phonics in small groups.** With a second adult, you can move phonics from whole-group to small-group instruction, giving all students more chances

Table 11.4 Variation 2: Two-Teacher Schedule—Early Readers

	Group 1 Higher Readers	Group 2 Middle Readers	Group 3 Lower Readers
9:00– 9:25	Whole-class read-aloud		
9:25– 9:55	**Hi ½ Group** Guided reading/ Comprehension skills **Lo ½ Group** Independent guided reading practice **Lo ½ Group** Guided reading/ Comprehension skills **Hi ½ Group** Independent guided reading practice	**Independent reading***	**Phonics** Led by Teacher 2
9:55– 10:10	Snack		
10:10– 10:35	**Phonics** Led by Teacher 2	**Hi ½ Group** Guided reading/ Comprehension skills **Lo ½ Group** Independent guided reading practice **Lo ½ Group** Guided reading/ Comprehension skills **Hi ½ Group** Independent guided reading practice	**Independent reading***
10:35– 11:00	**Independent reading***	**Phonics** Led by Teacher 2	**Hi ½ Group** Guided reading/ Comprehension skills **Lo ½ Group** Independent Guided Reading practice **Lo ½ Group** Guided Reading/ Comprehension Skills **Hi ½ Group** Independent guided reading practice

*Pre-readers do extra independent literacy practice.

to practice. This schedule also allows for the less developed teacher in the classroom to do phonics for all students; the more experienced teacher teaches the more challenging guided reading component for all students. This is a great way for a novice teacher to transition into literacy instruction.

- **More time.** By cutting both whole-group phonics and independent literacy work in this situation, you are able to devote more time to the other reading blocks: twenty-five minutes instead of twenty minutes for read-aloud, and thirty minutes instead of twenty-five minutes for all small-group rotations.

- **Even smaller guiding reading groups.** Guided reading becomes more effective in smaller groups. With the thirty-minute rotation you get by having an extra adult in the classroom, you can divide small guided reading groups into two smaller subgroups and spend fifteen minutes with each. This creates more individualized instruction and a greater number of practice opportunities for each student.

- **Independent guided reading practice.** When you add in subgroups for guided reading, you need to give the other two subgroups something to do while you work with each group individually. Independent guided reading practice solves this problem without putting student learning on hold. At the earliest reading levels, independent guided reading might consist solely of having students reread what they read at the guided reading table; at extended reading levels, they might have a comprehension worksheet or even an open-ended response question to complete as well.

Variation 3: Early Readers, Two Teachers, More Time

What if you not only have two adults in your early reading classroom but also are able to spend more time on reading—what's the best way to use that time? Here are our recommendations for what the schedule could look like:

- **Don't spend more than twenty-five minutes on read-aloud.** Because read-aloud lessons focus on the I Do and We Do of reading, spending extra instructional time on them isn't fruitful. You're better off getting as quickly as you can to comprehension skills, guided reading, independent reading, and independent literacy practice, as these are the points at which students begin to do the work of reading.

- **Expand rotation blocks to forty-five or fifty minutes each.** This will give each group of students more time for the practice that matters most to their development as readers.

- **Make guided reading subgroups even smaller.** Within a forty-five-minute guided reading rotation, you can spend fifteen minutes with each of *three* student subgroups, rather than two. This way, you can meet each student's needs even more specifically and give each student even more opportunities to practice.

- **Don't add any more time than that!** At this point, students' reading will actually be helped more by applying reading to other subjects—such as math, science, and social studies—than by spending more time on reading instruction specifically.

Table 11.5 shows how all this looks.

Table 11.5 Variation 3: Two Teachers, Early Readers, More Time

	Group 1 Higher Readers	Group 2 Middle Readers	Group 3 Lower Readers
8:00– 8:25	Whole-class read-aloud		
8:25– 9:10	**Hi ⅓ Group** Guided reading/ Comprehension skills **Lo and Med ⅓ Groups** Independent Guided reading practice **Med ⅓ Group** Guided reading/ Comprehension skills **Hi and Lo ⅓ Groups** Independent guided reading practice **Lo ⅓ Group** Guided reading/ Comprehension skills **Med and Hi ⅓ Groups** Independent guided reading practice	**Independent reading***	**Phonics** Led by Teacher 2

(continued)

Table 11.5 Variation 3: Two Teachers, Early Readers, More Time *(continued)*

	Group 1 Higher Readers	Group 2 Middle Readers	Group 3 Lower Readers
9:10–9:25	Snack		
9:25–10:10	**Phonics** Led by Teacher 2	**Hi ⅓ Group** Guided reading/ Comprehension skills **Lo and Med ⅓ Groups** Independent guided reading practice<hr>**Med ⅓ Group** Guided reading/ Comprehension skills **Hi and Lo ⅓ Groups** Independent guided reading practice<hr>**Lo ⅓ Group** Guided reading/ Comprehension skills **Med and Hi ⅓ Groups** Independent guided reading practice	**Independent reading***
10:10–10:55	**Independent reading***	**Phonics** Led by Teacher 2	**Hi ⅓ Group** Guided reading/ Comprehension skills **Lo and Med ⅓ Groups** Independent Guided Reading practice<hr>**Med ⅓ Group** Guided reading/ Comprehension skills **Hi and Lo ⅓ Groups** Independent guided reading practice<hr>**Lo ⅓ Group** Guided Reading/ Comprehension Skills **Med and Hi ⅓ Groups** Independent guided reading practice

*Pre-readers do extra independent literacy practice.

CONCLUSION: ALL IN GOOD TIME

For anyone passionately committed to teaching students to read, it's not enough to hope that they'll learn "all in good time." You need to be *sure* that they will — that each of your students will master the skills he or she needs for a lifetime of great reading. And in order to know how you'll get them to do that, you need to know *when*.

The ultimate tribute to the schedule presented in this chapter is that it guarantees that students are spending the right amount of time on every component of reading instruction. Just as the chef who knows his schedule knows he'll have every meal plated in time for the lunch-hour rush, a teacher using this schedule can know that every student will get the reading instruction he or she needs by the right time every morning. And just like the chef, the teacher will be able to focus on delivering everything *well*. Building a great reading schedule doesn't just ensure that reading instruction will happen: it ensures that the product — student achievement — will be many times better.

Apply Your Habits: Build Your Schedule and Plan for Growth

Now you have all the information you need in order to build your own game-changing elementary reading schedule. Here we've provided the templates for both early and later reading schedules. If you prefer, you can, of course, also use Microsoft Excel or your own calendar to make the reading schedule we've presented in this chapter your own.

MY EARLY READING SCHEDULE		
	Group 1 **Higher Readers**	**Group 2** **Middle Readers**	**Group 3** **Lower Readers**
9:00–9:20			
9:20–9:40			
9:40–10:00			
10:00–10:20			
10:20–10:40			
10:40–11:00			
11:00–11:20			
11:20–11:40			

Great Habits, Great Readers: A Practical Guide for K–4 Reading in the Light of Common Core, by Paul Bambrick-Santoyo, Aja Settles, and Juliana Worrell. Copyright © 2013 Uncommon Schools and/or Paul Bambrick-Santoyo. Reproduced by permission.

MY EXTENDED READING SCHEDULE				
	GUIDED READING DAYS (M, W, F)		COMPREHENSION SKILLS DAYS (T, Th)	
	Group 1 Higher Readers	Group 2 Lower Readers	Group 1 Higher Readers	Group 3 Lower Readers
9:00–9:20				
9:20–9:40				
9:40–10:00				
10:00–10:20				
10:20–10:40				
10:40–11:00				
11:00–11:20				
11:20–11:40				

Your Next Steps

Review the next steps you've written at the end of each chapter. You can't do all of these at once, so now's the time to plan which you will tackle first. Order your changes by which will make the biggest difference for your students.

Next Step	Date

Chapter 12

Coaching Teachers

A Guide for School Leaders and Coaches

In your hands is our guide to what a strong reading classroom should look like. We've seen how great readers are built, not born. We've watched how, by developing the right habits, any child can master the fundamentals of reading and put themselves on the fast track to a successful academic experience. The same can be said of teachers. The fundamental insight of this book is that there are specific, concrete actions that every K–4 teacher can take to enhance the literacy instruction in his or her classroom. And that means that all teachers can be coached to take those actions.

If you're an instructional coach or a principal, this coaching process can seem extremely daunting. You may be starting the year with someone who has never taught before, let alone mastered the finer points of reading instruction. No one could master all these techniques at once, so the question remains: What does it take to develop someone, little by little, to become a proficient reading teacher?

Let's look at how this happened for Valerie Samples, a third-year teacher at the time of the writing of this book. Valerie's story—from the moment she started teaching right out of college—will give us a concrete feel for how you can launch a teacher training program for instructors at any level. Once we've done that, we'll unpack some of the principles that made Valerie's growth possible and give you a few tools to help you hit the ground running at your own school.

Valerie's Story

In Her Own Words

My first year at North Star as a third-grade teacher was also my first year ever teaching. I had no understanding of guided reading at all, as I had never taught it in any of my student teaching experiences. Without question, I felt in over my head when I initially sat down at the guided reading table and tried to facilitate a discussion with my students. During conversations, I often felt like a toddler learning to walk and was unsure what steps to take and what direction to go.

The first thing that started to make me feel more at ease was when my instructional leader, Juliana Worrell, spent a day team teaching with me. Being able to see how she diagnosed student confusion and prompted in the moment made me determined to be able to do the same thing one day. Then came many more professional development sessions: what helped me the most was watching guided reading video footage. During the video, when a student would give a response, we would pause the video and would have to determine what prompt we would say to the student to get him or her to the correct answer. Getting to practice prompting with real student responses, while still being afforded the time to discuss and think about the prompts, helped me start to more fully understand what the prompts meant and what exactly I was prompting for. I started to feel a little bit better about the guided reading structure, and started to more deeply understand my role as the teacher within these discussions.

Once I felt like I further understood what guided reading was "supposed" to look like, the next difficult process for me was literacy assessment analysis. I soon realized that my teaching wouldn't advance without being able to do a deep analysis of my students' errors on their assessments. The initial struggle for me was that I oftentimes was not identifying what I myself would do as a reader when answering comprehension questions. Therefore, when trying to analyze my students' mistakes, I was unable to diagnose their deep-rooted confusion.

Sitting in analysis meetings with Juliana proved to be more beneficial than I ever could have imagined. She helped me self-reflect on my own reading process as an adult to more deeply understand the process that I want my students to go through as readers.

Now that I am in my third year of teaching, I finally feel like I "know what I'm doing." I've had the chance to go through an assessment analysis meeting at each level I have taught—Levels 380L through 800L. I have gone through the reading process myself, and therefore have analyzed these questions and have evaluated my own reading strategies. Now that my analysis is much more targeted, I align my instructional plans to this more directly. This allows me to know exactly where my students are going to make mistakes in the guided reading conversation, and I have already prepared for how I am going to prompt them to help them get at the correct answer.

All of these things combined make me feel more prepared than ever when I sit in front of my third graders at the green table and begin our guided reading discussion.

In the Words of Her Coach

When Valerie began teaching guided reading, she was very eager and open to all feedback. Initially, she struggled with common rookie teacher errors, such as not utilizing the habits of discussion to drive the comprehension conversation. Oftentimes, one student would share the thinking, and there would be no input from others. In addition, Valerie did not have a keen awareness of the bottom lines for each reading level and how to target individual student needs. Therefore, her beginning lessons weren't always driven by data, and student growth at certain reading levels was stagnant. Valerie and I had many analysis meetings, in which we'd discuss the bottom lines and determine which reading strategies would push students further along in their reading.

Once her planning became stronger, we began videotaping her lessons. Through video analysis, Valerie was able to see when her conversation was more "Ping-Pong" versus "volleyball." With this knowledge, she would go into the next lesson being even more aware of who she needed to involve in the conversation.

Eventually, we moved our focus away from habits of discussion and to strategic prompting for comprehension errors. In order to do this, Valerie had to get better at diagnosing student error in the moment. At the beginning of her teaching career, we did not have the videos in this book to support Valerie in seeing what it looked like. So we would co-teach lessons in which she would observe me teaching and write down all of the prompts I used to get students to critically think about a text. We'd then debrief these prompts, and she would put them in her upcoming lesson plans.

Eventually we had access to the videos in this book, and the cycle of video analysis, team teaching, and strategic planning led to huge gains in Valerie's teaching. Now she is able to actively engage students in the comprehension conversation using habits of discussion and to use strategic prompting to get students to do all the thinking. Valerie's planning became so strategic that by the beginning of her second year, she was able to write plans that other teachers on her team could also use.

The end result? Valerie is now a highly accomplished teacher. On the latest state literacy assessment, her students ranked first in *Advanced* Proficiency among all twelve hundred elementary schools in New Jersey, regardless of income level.

THE GROWTH MIND-SET

Valerie's story is not an anomaly; it's just one example of what can happen for a reading teacher when the right supports are in place. We know this works because we've seen it in action. At all the schools where we have worked, teachers run the gamut from seasoned veterans to newly minted novices. Nevertheless, the strong results mentioned in the Introduction are consistent across all schools, each with different leaders and different staffs. As Paul noted in *Leverage Leadership*, you cannot get these results by recruitment or by placing your best teachers in strategic grades. You get them by coaching every teacher's habits to excellence.

> ### Core Idea
>
> You cannot get standout results by recruitment or by placing your best teachers in strategic grades. You get them by coaching every teacher's habits to excellence.

It's true that some teachers will be ready on their own to work step-by-step and make these changes happen. Most, however, will benefit from a highly skilled instructional leader. When you make the choice to do this, you make the statement that every teacher is capable of learning and mastery. This is the heart of our profession; if we don't believe that about adults, we don't really believe it about children, either.

Core Idea

Effective coaching is at the heart of great reading results. If you don't believe that adults can grow, you don't really believe it about children, either.

In this book, we've given you a vision of what effective reading instruction looks like. Now it's time to train your eyes so that you can help teachers spot where to adjust their own instruction to match it. Valerie's story highlights the four levers that will make literacy coaching work in your school:

1. Data-driven instruction
2. Observation and feedback
3. Planning
4. Leading professional development

You'll notice that these are precisely the four instructional levers mentioned in *Leverage Leadership*. These can be broken down into a cycle of actions that can be replicated anywhere:

1. Lead professional development focused on K–4 reading.
2. Regularly observe teachers.
3. Drive teaching with data.
4. Choose the right action step to guide a teacher's growth.
5. Give effective feedback, including time to practice and plan ahead.

Once you see how accessible these steps are, the door is wide open to making any change you need in a reading classroom. Let's take a look at each step in detail.

LEAD PROFESSIONAL DEVELOPMENT

Professional development (PD) is often the first coaching you'll give teachers—right at the start of the year. Imagine teachers like Valerie walking into your school for the first time. Your PD is your opening statement about what's going to matter most this year.

To make PD a manageable process, strategic leaders tend to pick one or two reading focus points for a school year and then develop their staff trainings around them. Some of the techniques in this book may be new to you; others may be things you've been doing for years. But, as a whole, your staff will ultimately need practice with all of them if you want to build the sort of aligned, consistent instruction that will develop your school's reading program. In *Leverage Leadership*, Paul outlines principles of effective PD that could be applied to any reading topic. To make life easier, though, we've included step-by-step plans and materials for this book's key topics in Part Five. The following clip is an example of what these materials look like in action. Here Aja is leading a PD session on Chapter One, Habits of the Classroom. You'll notice very little lecture in this PD session.

 WATCH Clip 38: Aja Settles's Leading Professional Development

Aja follows the principles of "Living the Learning" that are highlighted in *Leverage Leadership* and *Driven by Data*: she takes advantages of the videos provided in this book to design a PD session during which teachers not only see what best practices look like but also have the chance to practice. As you'll see in Part Five, you have all the resources you need—agendas, videos, PowerPoints, and handouts—to replicate this caliber of PD.

Remember: PD without follow-up is meaningless. But PD as a starting point can create a vision for excellence that your teachers can follow.

Core Idea

Remember: PD without follow-up is meaningless. But PD as a starting point can create a vision for excellence that your teachers can follow.

Once you've led PD, it's time to make it translate to action.

OBSERVE REGULARLY

No PD session, no matter how well delivered, is alone enough to drive teacher growth. Teachers will need our continued support and follow-up if we want to make changes stick. And the only way we'll know what's happening in a teacher's class is if we're there to see it ourselves.

To keep teacher growth aligned to your PD goals and responsive to student needs, it's vital that instructional leaders build time to observe teachers consistently. Just as we wouldn't coach our kids in reading twice a year, we cannot count on midyear and end-of-year evaluations to meaningfully support teacher growth. This means that to make great coaching work, you need to commit the time to make it happen. Fortunately, there are many feasible ways that instructional leaders can put this into place. In *Leverage Leadership*, Paul outlined these ways in much greater detail. In brief, however, some of the keys to making routine observation and feedback feasible are

- **Shorter visits.** Top coaches observe, not for the traditional, hourlong block, but for only fifteen minutes per teacher. So long as leaders are strategic about what they are looking for, this shorter length of time is sufficient for thorough and direct feedback. Indeed, significantly longer observations are often inefficient, especially when they come with the cost of observing far fewer teachers.

- **Observation blocks.** Grouping observations across the same hourlong block reduces inefficiencies in traveling between rooms and transitioning between tasks.

- **Locked-in feedback meetings.** Great instructional leaders lock in regular check-ins at the start of the year. Teachers know when they'll meet, and there is no wasted time in email exchanges or tracking down teachers to deliver the feedback.

What might this observation and feedback schedule look like? Table 12.1 shows an example.

Further, it's important that you vary the time within each block that you observe teachers so that you can see them demonstrate a variety of types of reading instruction. If we only observe a teacher's guided reading instruction, we'll have no sense of whether read-aloud is functioning effectively or not. The

Table 12.1 Sample Observation and Feedback Schedule

	Monday	Tuesday	Wednesday	Thursday	Friday
6:00am					
:30	Greeting and breakfast	Greeting and breakfast		Greeting and breakfast	Greeting and breakfast
7:00am					
:30	Staff culture check	Morning assembly			Morning assembly
8:00am		Meet Wilson	Meet Bradley		Staff culture check
:30		Meet Vargas	Meet Frint		
9:00am	Observe Wilson, Vargas, Jenkins	Meet Jenkins			
:30					
10:00am			Observe Mitzia, Boykin, Devin		Observe Hoyt, Settles, Palma
:30					
11:00am		Staff culture check			
:30	Lunch	Lunch	Lunch		Lunch
12:00pm	Observe Henry, Bernales, Christian				Meet Bradley
:30		Meet Worrell		Leadership team meeting	Meet Palma
1:00pm	Meeting with principal supervisor	Meet Christian			Meet Settles
:30		Meet Bernales	Meet Boykin		Meet Hoyt
2:00pm		Observe Bradley, Frint, Worrell	Meet Devin		Large-project work time
:30			Meet Mitzia		
3:00pm					
:30			Professional development session	Staff culture check	
4:00pm	Dismissal	Dismissal		Dismissal	Dismissal
:30					
5:00pm					
:30					

☐ Work Time   ☐ School Culture   ☐ Observations   ☐ Meetings

easiest way to do this is to change up the order that you see teachers within an observation block. If that doesn't give you enough of an opportunity to see different reading lessons, adjust your schedule weekly or monthly so that you have a chance to observe at different parts of the day.

Think back to our chapter on class scheduling. Your schedule is a reflection of your priorities, so making time for observation and coaching sends a very strong signal about what matters to you as a leader.

> ## Core Idea
>
> Your schedule is a reflection of your priorities. Making time for observation and feedback means making reading results a top priority.

DRIVE IT WITH DATA

Imagine walking into a classroom and observing the perfectly executed guided reading lesson: the teacher has a tight, concise book introduction and an appropriately monitored During Reading; and in the After Reading section, she pulls her questions straight from the guided reading prompting guide. Even more, the students are nailing the lesson. Everything is perfect, right?

Wrong. When you look at the lesson plan, you see that the teacher is using a 150L text and is focused on middle vowels and blends. Yet when you look at the most recent round of assessment data, these same students have already mastered 300L texts that use middle vowels, blends, *and* syllable chunks. What's the lesson here? The teaching can be great; it can even be stronger than the teaching represented in the videos in this book. But if the teaching isn't grounded in the data — in what students need the most — your students' reading performance will go nowhere.

This is the most overlooked aspect of early literacy instruction. It is so basic but absolutely essential: Have you paid attention to what students have learned?

The next time you walk into the classroom and see a teacher who on the surface looks phenomenal but isn't making the reading gains you would expect, look no further than his or her data analysis. Without the match, the teaching will always be hollow.

> ## Core Idea
>
> Match the teaching to the data, or the teaching will be hollow.

IDENTIFY THE KEY ACTION STEPS

So when you enter a teacher's room, what sorts of things are you looking for? We think it boils down to a few questions:

- Are students practicing the skill that is most valuable for them? (Does what I see match what the data say we should be focusing on?)
- How effectively does the teacher implement the lesson?
- Are all students engaged in learning?

Oh, but there are so many ways to answer these questions! In fact, one of the biggest fears of principals is the lack of content knowledge around K–4 reading. And one of the biggest concerns of trained literacy coaches is, *I see so many things to work on—where do I start?*

Although it's true that the more coaching you do, the easier this will become, we wrote this book precisely so that both principals and reading coaches can feel more confident about the feedback they give. Each chapter is designed to provide you with the vision for what that particular aspect of literacy instruction should look like. Why? Because once you have a picture of excellence, it's a lot easier to notice deviations from it. By way of example, you don't need to be a Renaissance master to know what's "wrong" with Marcel Duchamp's version of the Mona Lisa, *L.H.O.O.Q.*

You can see the alteration in this painting immediately because you know what to expect. And although we know it takes time and practice to feel confident "spotting the mustache," the good news is that the further you develop your expectations for how a class should look, the easier it'll become to notice any disparities. To help you get a running start, later in this chapter we'll go into a bit more detail about what action steps you're likely to use.

There are, of course, myriad things a teacher can develop at a given time. And, in our experience, many will be eager to take them all on at once. This is where the support of an instructional leader is vital, as taking on everything simultaneously would be both exhausting and ineffective.

Great instructional leaders coach teachers on the one or two key changes they can make immediately to see class improvement. Rome wasn't built in a day, and it certainly wasn't built in a single step. Rather than forcing the teacher to figure out how to prioritize, great leaders limit the feedback to what is most important. That is, the action step they choose is the one that promises to have the greatest impact on instruction.

But identifying key changes isn't enough. In fact, instructional feedback often deteriorates at this point — when a coach gives broad feedback instead of breaking down the coaching into smaller steps. "Students need to be more engaged during independent reading" means little to a teacher who is struggling with this aspect of class. In contrast, "During independent reading, require that students keep books flat, and check student page numbers when you circulate in the classroom" are two concrete steps a teacher can make to immediately improve that experience.

> ## Core Idea
>
> People grow in steps, not leaps. Effective leaders coach them in concrete, bite-sized steps.

Instead of addressing broad, long-term goals, coach in the minutia, giving teachers a series of short-term, manageable changes. Over time, these add up to substantial growth.

The benefit of having experience with this type of coaching is that, after a while, patterns begin to emerge. We asked the highly effective principals accustomed to giving bite-sized feedback to tell us the most commonly provided action steps for guided reading, as that is the lesson type that is the most difficult to master. The box that follows lists the top twelve action steps for developing outstanding reading teachers, one step at a time.

Top Twelve Action Steps for Guided Reading

Highest-Leverage Action Steps for Reading Results

Text Selection and Prework/Planning

1. Early reader—selecting text
   - Select a text that allows the student to practice the identified word-solving focus at least once per page.

2. Aligning the text to the data
   - Select the reading skill or standard based on the struggles revealed in the student learning data.
   - Select a text where students must use that skill or standard to get to the big idea of the text.
     - Example: If your students are struggling with character contrast, there should be two strong characters evident in the text.

3. Early reader—designing word-solving questions
   - Pre-identify and plan for words that may be unfamiliar to students during the reading, and script the appropriate prompt from the guided reading prompting guide into your lesson.
     - Example: If your student struggles with vowel rules, ask, "What vowel pattern can you use?" (*not* "Use the long 'a'")

4. Designing comprehension questions
   - Design factual, inference, and critical thinking comprehension questions that align to the guided reading prompting guides and the data for that group of students.

- Anticipate wrong responses to inference and critical thinking questions and script into your lesson plan two to three prompts to address these wrong responses. (Use the guided reading prompting guides as your starting point.)
- Ensure that the questions align to the reading focus you selected from the data.

Before Reading (Book Introduction)

5. Reading focus
During the book introduction . . .

   - Use clear and concise language to state the reading focus and how you apply it.
   - Ask students to state their purpose for reading: "As I'm reading, I am thinking about [character motivation]."

6. Early reader word-solving
When dealing with early readers with word-solving struggles . . .

   - Prior to reading the text, model the word-solving strategies that students will need the most.

7. Text preview
When introducing the text . . .

   - For early readers: lead guided preview using the front cover and title.
   - For first grade and beyond: have students own the text preview— let them generate the preview themselves (using the front cover, back cover, title, first pages).

During Reading

8. Word-solving challenges
When a student stumbles on an unfamiliar word . . .

   - Use a universal word-solving prompt that allows the student to do the majority of the work:
     - Roll back the response: "You said ___."
     - "Read through the word."
     - "Does that make sense?"
     - "Get your mouth ready."

(continued)

(continued)

- Have the guided reading prompting guide open on your desk or clipboard to the level of the students, and choose the appropriate prompt from the prompting guide.
  - Example: If your student struggles with vowel rules, ask, "What vowel pattern can you use?" (*not* "Use the long 'a'")
- Lean in to prompt one student's word-solving struggles, then lean back out to listen to errors in the whole group, then lean in again with the next student who is struggling.
- Have note-taking binder open and take notes on whether students are self-correcting without being prompted.

After Reading (Comprehension Conversation)

9. Retell (100L–500L)

- Start the comprehension discussion with a retell:
  - "Tell me what happened in the [story, chapter] as if I've never read it before."
- When the student reaches a natural break in the retell, call on another student to continue; repeat this process to include as many students as possible.
- Refrain from making such comments as "My next question is . . ."— that's not a conversation or discussion.
- Prompt the students to include the key reading focus within their retell.
  - Example: If the reading focus is character motivation, say, "Remember to include the characters' motivation in your retell."
- Infuse inference and critical thinking questions within the retell.

When the students are struggling with the retell . . .

- Factual: If total understanding has broken down, use a factual question—get back to the basics of the story:
  - "What did Tommy ask the teacher?" "What did Tommy want to be when he grows up?"
- Inference: If there is confusion about the key action in part of the story (if, for example, there are parts of the story where students

don't understand Tommy's motivation), focus on a more specific chunk of the text and ask students to make an inference:

- ○ "Why did Tommy ask his teacher if he could skip math time?"

- Critical thinking: If students have a general understanding of the story (if, for example, the skill focus is motivation and they can identify Tommy's motivation throughout each part of the text), start with a critical thinking question:

  - ○ "How did Tommy's motivation change throughout the text?"

10. Written response to text (500L+)

- Review all written responses before beginning conversation: start the conversation with the error that you found in the written responses.

11. Increasing students' ownership of their own comprehension

- Prompt students to use the habits of discussion (see prompts in Habits of Discussion Scope and Sequence: Teacher Training and Prompting Guide)

  - ○ Build off each other: "Who has a different point?" "Who can add to what [student] just said?"

  - ○ Have students talk to members of their group instead of to the teacher (hand gesture)

- Implement Turn and Talk.

- Prompt students to give complete responses: don't assume what the student means or finish his or her thought.

- Have students name the comprehension strategy they used to help them understand the text.

12. Student misunderstanding

- Using the guided reading prompting guide, select the prompt that matches the student error.

- Roll back the student misunderstanding to give you time to look at your preplanned prompts in your lesson plan or those in the guided reading prompting guide.

- If you had to prompt more than twice to guide them to the right answer, ask the original question again so that students can practice putting it all together without prompting.

(continued)

(*continued*)

- If 100 percent of the students are confused and no student is on the right track, do a think-aloud to model the thinking.
- Narrate the positive of strategies students are using: "I like the way Jimmy went back into the text."

As we have hinted throughout the book, the best teachers and instructional leaders don't try to create everything new from scratch. They build by borrowing, and the result is a much stronger house. Leverage these action steps to tighten your own feedback in whatever areas need the most growth. That is what builds your instructional leadership expertise.[1]

And once you have those action steps ready, your next challenge will be to deliver them in a way that makes them stick.

GIVE EFFECTIVE FEEDBACK

So let's suppose we've identified the key action step for a teacher. Now our charge is to get the teacher to implement it. And what makes the difference is how well we provide the feedback. The teachers you coach need to have a clear vision of the action step, understand the rationale behind it, and be comfortable and ready to implement it in class. Paul outlines a six-step system for feedback meetings in *Leverage Leadership*, but there are two principles for coaching reading teachers that we'll highlight here.

Seeing Is Believing

The first challenge in giving feedback is helping the teacher recognize the gap between their instruction and where they're headed. There is no better tool to do so than the use of video—thus the inclusion of so much video in this book! Video also allows the teacher to do the heavy lifting, just as you want to push your students to do the majority of thinking in class. For that reason, great coaching looks a lot like great guided reading instruction—with the coach intervening with targeted questions to push a teacher to discover the key insights for himself or herself.

Video is particularly powerful when it's of a teacher teaching the exact same skill that you are developing in your own teaching. In the next video clip, Kristi's kindergarten students are trying to master these two 50L–100L skills (from the Narrative Guided Reading Prompting Guide):

- Retell the story in the proper sequence.
- Make a connection to understand characters' feelings.

(Once again, witness the power of your assessment to create a road map for what to teach!) In this clip, Aja has observed Kristi struggle with the retell portion of her guided reading lesson to these 100L students. Watch how she uses a video of Shadell Purefoy to help Kristi build a better start to her After Reading section.

 WATCH Clip 39: Aja Settles's Effective Feedback

You can see the power of video: Kristi was immediately able to identify the flaws in her retell and start to improve it. Seeing the model video was the turning point in her own development. Seeing is believing.

Core Idea

Watching a model lesson on video gives you a road map to excellence. Seeing is believing.

Perfect Practice (Not Just Any Practice) Makes Perfect

If you've ever tried to improve your golf swing, you know that good coaches will observe you; film you; stop you and tweak your stance, follow-through, and posture until you've got it right—long before you ever get out on the green. Likewise, it's unfair to expect teachers to grow quickly if the only time they get to try new techniques is in the middle of class. As we've noted, a coaching meeting follows many of the same instructional principles you follow in your classroom. This means that even when a teacher understands and can articulate an action step, you will want him or her to model and practice it to make sure it gets stored in muscle memory. Creating a space for a teacher to try things out may feel inauthentic at first, but this dress rehearsal time before taking the technique "live" with students makes all the difference. If there are problems with execution, here's a perfect place to correct and retry them. Watch how elementary school leader Juliana Worrell helps one of her teachers gain valuable experience before her next phonics lesson.

 WATCH Clip 40: Juliana Worrell's and Julia Thompson's Effective Feedback—Practice

Just imagine how much stronger the teaching will be with so much effective practice ahead of time!

As mentioned in Valerie Samples's case study, effective practice doesn't have to end in the meeting. Some of the most transformative experiences can be co-teaching with a teacher to model the skill you would like him or her to implement. Then the teacher can step in and teach right after you've modeled, to imitate your approach. Co-teaching has such an impact on instruction!

Once you've observed, figured out the key action step, and coached the teacher to make the change in his or her instruction, one step remains: coaching him or her through the process of planning his or her actual lessons.

COACH PLANNING

Even if you carry out all the previous steps in instructional leadership, one of the easiest places for great coaching to break down is in the translation from the feedback session to the actual lesson. Even great feedback is useless if it isn't translated into daily practice. The way to make that happen is to reserve time specifically to start planning out the week with the teachers you coach. For example, let's revisit Aja's feedback to Kristi around her retell. Watch the end of the meeting where they engage in the simple act of locking the action step into Kristi's lesson plans.

 WATCH Clip 41: Aja Settles's and Kristi Costanzo's Planning

Coaching a teacher through lesson planning not only validates the work he or she has done, but, because such coaching does not have to be done face-to-face, it can fit into your schedule more simply. Think of providing planning feedback as being a lot like editing an aspiring writer's rough draft: revisions won't just make the final product stronger but will help the author become a better writer in general. The box "Common Planning Errors for Guided Reading" lists some common errors to look for when you coach a teacher through guided reading lesson planning.

Common Planning Errors for Guided Reading

- Setting an objective that is not aligned to student literacy assessment data
- Picking a text that doesn't allow students to practice the skills identified by the assessment data
- Lacking concise, student-friendly language around the reading strategy
- Not anticipating the errors students will make in their guided reading text

---

YOUR NEXT STEPS

Students and adults learn in similar ways. Just as students learn to read by being coached at precise points, teachers learn most quickly when we break professional development down into precise, bite-sized steps. We know that great reading teachers are made, not born. But too often we've tried to "make" them the way we make diamonds: with lots of time and pressure. As professionals, teachers like Kristi deserve not to have to wait for the tools they need to become great; and in today's information-based society, their students simply cannot afford to.

Great instructional leaders are the lynchpins in making this change work for your school. With the right coaching, teachers can supercharge their instruction. And once they see that success, they'll be hungry for more. As you continue to develop as a community, we strongly recommend that you consider working with books like *Leverage Leadership, Teach Like a Champion, The Skillful Teacher*, and *Driven by Data* as the next step for putting teachers on track for success.

CONCLUSION: WHY IT MATTERS

At the very start of this book, we introduced you to four students: Ade'shyah, Braelynn, Yihanna, and Nasiyr. In fifth grade at the time of this publishing, all remain passionate about reading, both inside the classroom and out. Braelynn cites fiction, especially realistic fiction, as her favorite genre to read; Yihanna concurs, but is also quick to mention a well-loved informational text about dogs.

Ask these students what they want to be when they grow up, and they offer answers that are every bit as eager and confident as the responses you saw them provide during Erin Michels's guided reading lesson. Braelynn wants to be a lawyer because her friends and family often praise her ability to make a strong point. Yihanna dreams of becoming a songwriter; when she writes lyrics in her notebook, she loves any opportunity to use vocabulary words she's learned in school. "They make the songs come alive," she says. Ade'shyah thinks she'd like to be either a doctor, a teacher, or a dancer.

How will reading help them pursue their goals? "Reading can help you be exceptional in your career," Ade'shyah says. "If someone hands you a paper to sign, you need to be able to read to know what's on the paper"—not just to be able to read each word, she explains, but to be able to analyze what you're reading so that you know what you're promising to do. Braelynn agrees. "At our school," she adds, "they have taught us how to break down books and understand them. That's what I need in order to go to the top college that I really want to go to."

Throughout this book, we have focused on strategies, tools, and techniques to help students build the habits of reading. Through creating the time and space for constant practice and by teaching the precise skills they need to master, reading teachers can radically change how students learn. Yet at the end of the day, the reason this book matters is that students like Ade'shyah, Braelynn, Yihanna, and Nasiyr need to read well in order to realize their dreams. The ability to read critically, deeply, and skillfully isn't an innate talent for teachers to "discover" in their students. It is a set of habits and experiences that can be given to—and change the life of—any child. Changing the way that we teach reading is never easy. Yet we owe it to our students to help them build the skills they need to be who they want to be.

Apply Your Habits: Developing Reading Teachers

Self-Assessment

What aspect of our coaching model do you think would have the biggest impact on the teachers you serve?

- A professional development curriculum aligned to your reading goals
- A feedback system that provides opportunities for teachers to practice new instructional techniques
- A regular feedback and observation cycle that allows you to target bite-sized action steps for your teachers
- A system for co-analyzing and planning from student data
- The ability to choose the right action step to guide a teacher's growth
- A cycle of lesson plan review and co-planning to hold teachers accountable

Tools to Use

- Top Twelve Action Steps for Guided Reading (also included in the Appendix)
- PD plans and materials for each component of reading instruction (see Part Five)
- Additional resources in *Leverage Leadership*

Your Next Steps

_____

_____

_____

_____

_____

_____

_____

_____

_____

_____

Part 5

Professional Development Workshops— Overview and Highlights

Introduction: Workshops Included with This Book

Use these professional development (PD) workshops to train other educators to implement the literacy instruction strategies presented in this book.

The professional workshops we've included with this book are

- Habits of the Classroom (Chapter One)
- Habits of Discussion (Chapter Two)
- Read-Aloud (Chapter Four)
- Comprehension Skills (Chapter Five)
- Guided Reading Planning (Chapter Eight)
- Guided Reading Prompting (Chapter Nine)

  Note:

- If you want PD materials for assessment, analysis, and action (Chapters Three and Seven), you can find them in *Driven by Data*.

- If you want PD materials for developing leadership (Chapter Twelve), you can find them in *Leverage Leadership*.

WORKSHOP MATERIALS IN THE TEXT

The workshop materials you'll see in the pages that follow are

- A **cover page** that highlights each workshop's goals and intended audience
- A **workshop preparation sheet** that shows what materials you need for the workshop, how long the workshop runs, and how to assess the workshop's success
- A **workshop overview** that outlines the agenda the workshop will follow

WORKSHOP MATERIALS ON THE DVD

You can find more workshop materials on the DVD that comes with this book. These are

- The full-length presenter's notes to be used while running each workshop
- The PowerPoint presentation that accompanies each workshop
- The handouts you'll need to provide for each workshop

Chapter 13

Habits of the Classroom Workshop

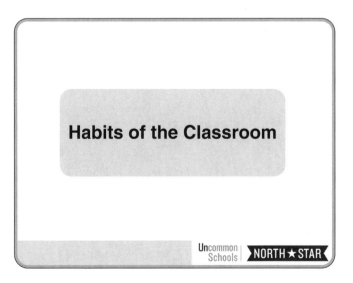

WHAT'S THE GOAL?

Use the habits of the classroom to drive their students' progress in reading. By the end of the workshop, participants will know how to

- Design classroom routines and systems that will maximize instructional time.
- Plan and lead lessons that will teach students excellent habits of the classroom.

WHO'S THE AUDIENCE?

Anyone who teaches K–4 reading. This could mean coaches or school leaders, as well as teachers.

WHEN TO USE IT

Best Time

Right before the school year begins. That's the easiest time for participants to begin building great habits of the classroom.

Other Times That Work

Any time during the school year! Teachers can use improved habits of the classroom to increase instructional time at any point in the year.

HABITS OF THE CLASSROOM

WORKSHOP PREPARATION SHEET

Workshop Objectives

1. Participants will design classroom routines and systems that will maximize instructional time.
2. Participants will plan and lead lessons that will teach students to use Habits of the Classroom.

Running Time

- 3 hours

Materials

Materials on Disc

Video Clips

- 2, 3, 4, 5

Habits of the Classroom PowerPoint Presentation

Handouts

- Printout of Habits of the Classroom PowerPoint
- Habits of the Classroom: Systems and Routines Handout
- Habits of the Classroom Reflection Template: Reading Routines
- Keys to Effective Habits of the Classroom
- Lesson Plan Template

Other Materials

- One name tent per participant.
- One binder per participant. (To organize each binder, print out the handouts listed above and arrange handouts in the order they are listed.)

Setup

Of the materials listed above, you'll need the following to start the workshop:
- One name tent per participant
- One binder per participant
Here's how to set up the workshop:
- Groups

  - Divide participants into groups of three. Ideally, the participants in each group should be from the same school and teach similar grade levels, subjects, or both.

- Tables

  - Seat each group of three participants at one table together, labeling each participant's seat with a name tent.
  - Place a binder at each participant's seat.

HABITS OF THE CLASSROOM

COMPLETE WORKSHOP OVERVIEW

Living the Learning Components Legend

AA = **Airtight activity** that leads participants to the right conclusion mostly on their own

R = **Reflection** during which participants quietly generate and record conclusions or takeaways

S = Small- or large-group **sharing**

F = **Framing** that gives participants a common vocabulary to use to describe what they learn

A = **Application** of learned principles

Section	Time	Activities	Type
1: Why Habits of the Classroom Matter for Reading	40 minutes	Introduction and objectives	F
		Case study: system breakdowns	AA, S
		Video: small group to small group transition	AA, S, F
2: Successful Transitions	1 hour, 15 minutes	Quick write: successful transitions	AA, S, F
		Video: midlesson transition	AA, S, R
		Video: independent reading transition	AA, S, F
		Application: transition design	R, S, A
3: Teaching Transitions	55 minutes	Video: teaching transitions	AA, S, F
		Application: teaching transitions	A, S, A
		Application: transition role play	A, S
4: Reflection	10 minutes	Reflection: key takeaways	R, S
		Conclusion	F

Chapter 14

Habits of Discussion Workshop

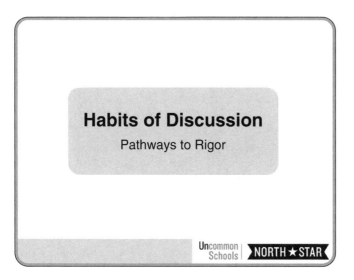

Habits of Discussion

Pathways to Rigor

Un common Schools | NORTH★STAR

WHAT'S THE GOAL?

Use discussion to increase the rigor of the classroom and to see evidence of student learning. By the end of the workshop, participants will know how to

- Utilize the habits of discussion to shift learning to the students.
- Create a scope of sequence for implementing the habits of discussion in your school.

WHO'S THE AUDIENCE?

Although focused on K–4 reading teachers, these habits apply to any teacher!

WHEN TO USE IT

Best Time

Right before the school year begins. That's the easiest time for participants to implement great habits of discussion in their classrooms.

Other Times That Work

Any time during the school year! Teachers can use improved habits of discussion to increase instructional time at any point in the year.

HABITS OF DISCUSSION

WORKSHOP PREPARATION SHEET

Workshop Objectives

1. Participants observe and analyze Habits of Discussion in practice and explain how these shift higher-order thinking to students.
2. Participants will analyze a scope of sequence for implementing the Habits of Discussion in your school.

Running Time

- 2 hours

Materials

Materials on Disc

Video Clips

- 6

Habits of Discussion PowerPoint Presentation

Handouts

- Printout of Habits of Discussion PowerPoint
- Habits of Discussion handout
- Habits of Discussion Scope and Sequence: Teacher Training and Prompting Guide
- Monthly Map Template
- Universal Prompting Guide (see Table 2.1 in *Great Habits, Great Readers*)

Other Materials

- One name tent per participant.
- One binder per participant. (To organize each binder, print out the handouts listed above and arrange handouts in the order they are listed.)
- One copy of the same text for each participant: Select a text that corresponds with the average grade level the teachers in the room teach. Depending on the text you have selected, you'll also need to decide on a few questions you'd like the teachers to discuss that will require the use of evidence from the text. Print out these questions and include it with the other handouts listed above.
- One sentence strip for each participant.
- Masking tape for each group of participants.

Setup

Of the materials listed above, you'll need the following to start the workshop:
- One name tent per participant
- One binder per participant
Here's how to set up the workshop:
- Groups

  ○ Divide participants into groups of three. Ideally, the participants in each group should be from the same school and teach similar grade levels, subjects, or both.

- Tables

  ○ Seat each group of three participants at one table together, labeling each participant's seat with a name tent.
  ○ Place a binder at each participant's seat.

HABITS OF DISCUSSION

COMPLETE WORKSHOP OVERVIEW

Living the Learning Components Legend

AA = **Airtight activity** that leads participants to the right conclusion mostly on their own

R = **Reflection** during which participants quietly generate and record conclusions or takeaways

S = Small- or large-group **sharing**

F = **Framing** that gives participants a common vocabulary to use to describe what they learn

A = **Application** of learned principles

Section	Time	Activities	Type
1: Case Study Comparison	40 minutes	Quick read: habits of discussion case study	AA, S, F
		Video: habits of discussion case study	AA, S, F
2: Identifying the Roadblocks to Habits of Discussion	10 minutes	Activity: identifying the roadblocks to habits of discussion	AA, S, F
3: Prompting vs. Leading	34 minutes	Prompting versus leading	AA, S, F
4: Team Review	26 minutes	Reflection: one-pager markup	F, R, S
		Application: laying out the monthly map	A, R
5: Conclusion	10 minutes	Reflection: key takeaways	R, S, F

Chapter 15

Read-Aloud Workshop

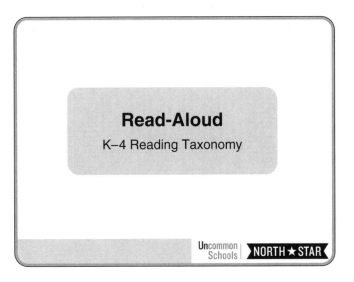

Read-Aloud
K–4 Reading Taxonomy

Un common | Schools | NORTH ★ STAR

WHAT'S THE GOAL?

Plan and implement effective read-aloud lessons. By the end of the workshop, participants will know how to

- Identify actions and strategies that make read-aloud lessons optimal learning opportunities for all students.

WHO'S THE AUDIENCE?

Anyone who teaches K–4 reading. This could mean coaches or school leaders as well as teachers.

WHEN TO USE IT

Best Time

Before the school year begins. That way, teachers can spend all year using read-aloud lessons to teach what's in the curriculum.

Other Times That Work

Any time during the school year! Although it's ideal if teachers can spend all year teaching read-aloud lessons that maximize student learning, it's never too late for students to benefit from such lessons.

READ-ALOUD

WORKSHOP PREPARATION SHEET

Workshop Objectives

1. Plan and implement effective read-aloud lessons.
2. Develop a roll-out plan to implement Read-Aloud instruction in their schools.

Running Time

- 2 hours, 5 minutes

Materials

Materials on Disc

Video Clips

- 13, 14, 15

Read-Aloud PowerPoint Presentation

Handouts

- Printout of Read-Aloud PowerPoint
- Read-Aloud handout: Before, During, and After Reading
- Read-Aloud Reflection Template: Before, During, and After Reading
- Read-Aloud: Key Guidelines to Remember
- Lesson Plan Template (with an objective that you determine and fill in)
- Model read-aloud lesson plan (may be reproduced from *Great Habits, Great Readers*, Chapter Four)

Other Materials

- One name tent per participant.
- One binder per participant. (To organize each binder, print out the handouts listed above and arrange handouts in the order they are listed.)

Setup

Of the materials listed above, you'll need the following to start the workshop:
- One name tent per participant.
- One binder per participant. Print out the handouts listed above and arrange them in the binder.
- A read-aloud text of your choosing (that can be used to teach the objective you write into the Lesson Plan Template).

Here's how to set up the workshop:
- Tables

  - Seat participants so that they can easily both see the presenter and turn and talk in small groups of three or four.
  - Place a binder and a name tent at each participant's seat.

READ-ALOUD

COMPLETE WORKSHOP OVERVIEW

Living the Learning Components Legend

AA = **Airtight activity** that leads participants to the right conclusion mostly on their own

R = **Reflection** during which participants quietly generate and record conclusions or takeaways

S = Small- or large-group **sharing**

F = **Framing** that gives participants a common vocabulary to use to describe what they learn

A = **Application** of learned principles

Section	Time	Activities	Type
1: Read-Aloud Lesson Introductions	30 minutes	Introduction and objectives	F
		Video: read-aloud lesson introduction	AA, S, F, A
2: I Do and We Do	50 minutes	Video: I Do	AA, S
		Video : We Do	AA, S, F
		Application: I Do, We Do	A, S
3: Final Check for Understanding	35 minutes	Role Play: errors in checking for understanding	AA, S, F
		Application: planning the final check for understanding	A, S
4: Reflection	10 minutes	Reflection: one-pager markup	R, S
		Conclusion	F

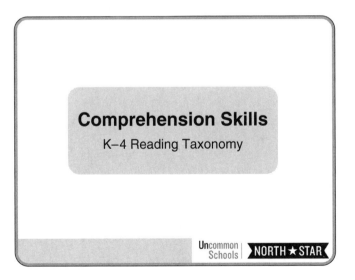

Chapter 16

Comprehension Skills Workshop

WHAT'S THE GOAL?

Teach the skills of reading comprehension in a traditional guided practice lesson format. By the end of the workshop, participants will know how to

- Utilize the actions and strategies that make each component of a comprehension skills lesson effective.

WHO'S THE AUDIENCE?

Anyone who teaches K–4 reading. This could mean coaches or school leaders as well as teachers.

WHEN TO USE IT

Best Time

Before the school year begins, after the read-aloud workshop. That way, teachers can spend all year using great comprehension skills lessons to teach what's in the curriculum.

Other Times That Work

After a round of assessment analysis and you identify the need for students to master a specific skill.

COMPREHENSION SKILLS

WORKSHOP PREPARATION SHEET

Workshop Objectives
• Participants will identify and practice the actions and strategies that make each component of a Comprehension Skills lesson effective.

Running Time
• 1 hour

Materials

Materials on Disc

Video Clips

• 17–20

Reading Comprehension Skills PowerPoint Presentation

Handouts

• Printout of Reading Comprehension Skills PowerPoint
• Comprehension Skills handout
• Comprehension Skills Reflection Template: I Do, We Do, You Do
• Comprehension Skills Framework

Other Materials
• One name tent per participant. • One binder per participant. (To organize each binder, print out the handouts listed above and arrange handouts in the order they are listed.)

Setup

Of the materials listed above, you'll need the following to start the workshop:
• One name tent per participant
• One binder per participant
Here's how to set up the workshop:
• Tables

  ○ Seat participants so that they can easily both see the presenter and turn and talk in small groups of three or four.
  ○ Place a binder and a name tent at each participant's seat.

COMPREHENSION SKILLS

COMPLETE WORKSHOP OVERVIEW

Living the Learning Components Legend

AA = **Airtight activity** that leads participants to the right conclusion mostly on their own

R = **Reflection** during which participants quietly generate and record conclusions or takeaways

S = Small- or large-group **sharing**

F = **Framing** that gives participants a common vocabulary to use to describe what they learn

A = **Application** of learned principles

Section	Time	Activities	Type
1: Introduction	6 minutes	Introduction	AA, S
2: I Do	16 minutes	Video: Skill Review/I Do	AA, S, F, R
3: We Do	20 minutes	Video: We Do	AA, F
4: You Do	13 minutes	Video: You Do	AA, S, F
5: Reflection	5 minutes	Reflection	R, S
		Closing	S

Chapter 17

Guided Reading Planning Workshop

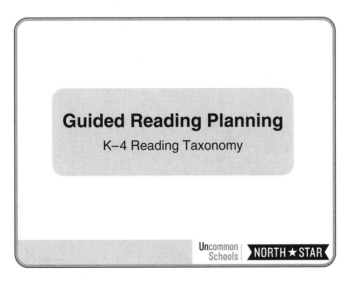

WHAT'S THE GOAL?

Plan effective guided reading lessons. By the end of the workshop, participants will know how to

- Structure an effective guided reading lesson.
- Select a text that matches students' needs as determined by data analysis.
- Script the key components of a guided reading lesson, differentiating each based on students' reading level.

WHO'S THE AUDIENCE?

Anyone who teaches K–4 reading. This could mean coaches or school leaders as well as teachers.

WHEN TO USE IT

Best Time

When teachers launch guided reading—often in the second month of school.

Other Times That Work

Every time teachers are about to teach a new reading level; this allows them to revisit the demands of planning at that level of reading complexity.

GUIDED READING PLANNING

WORKSHOP PREPARATION SHEET

Workshop Objectives
1. Identify the structure of an effective guided reading lesson. 2. Select a text for guided reading that matches students' needs based on data analysis. 3. Script the key components of a guided reading lesson, differentiating each based on students' reading level.

Running Time
• 3 hours, 52 minutes

Materials

Materials on Disc

Video Clips

• 27, 28, 30, 35, and 1

Guided Reading Planning PowerPoint Presentation

Handouts

• Printout of Guided Reading Planning PowerPoint
• Guided Reading Framework Handout
• Guided Reading Planning Reflection Template
• Guided Reading Text Selection
• Guided Reading Planning Part II Handout
• Exemplar lesson plans for up to 100L, 100L–300L, 300L–500L, and 700L+
• Guided Reading Blank Lesson Template
• Student profiles for up to 100L, 100L–300L, 300L–500L, and 700L+
• Guided Reading Lesson Planning

Other Materials
• One name tent per participant. • One binder per participant. (To organize each binder, print out the handouts listed above and arrange handouts in the order they are listed.) • Copies of *Minerva's Dream*, *The Subway Mouse*, and *Angel Child, Dragon Child*— one set for each group; you may substitute books so long as they fulfill the needs of the activity described in this plan. • For each group, three copies of a text at 150L or below, which your participants might read with students in a guided reading lesson. • For each group, three copies of a text between 450L–500L, which your participants might read with students in a guided reading lesson.

(continued)

(continued)

Setup

Of the materials listed above, you'll need the following to start the workshop:
• One name tent and binder (with handouts) per participant
Here's how to set up the workshop:
• Groups

- Divide participants into small groups of three or four. Ideally, all participants in each group will teach at about the same grade level.

• Tables

- Seat participants so that they can easily both see the presenter and partners.
- Place a binder and a name tent at each participant's seat.
- Place books at assorted reading levels where each small group will have easy access to them.

GUIDED READING PLANNING
COMPLETE WORKSHOP OVERVIEW

Living the Learning Components Legend

AA = **Airtight activity** that leads participants to the right conclusion mostly on their own

R = **Reflection** during which participants quietly generate and record conclusions or takeaways

S = Small- or large-group **sharing**

F = **Framing** that gives participants a common vocabulary to use to describe what they learn

A = **Application** of learned principles

Section	Time	Activities	Type
1: The Guided Reading Framework	1 hour, 10 minutes	Introduction and objectives	F
		Video: Before Reading —50L	AA, S
		Video: Before Reading —390L	AA, S, F, S, F
		Video: During Reading	AA, S, F
		Video: After Reading	AA, S, AA, S, F
		Reflection: one-pager markup	R, S
2: Guided Reading Text Selection	32 minutes	Activity: Level L data analysis	AA, S, F
		Reflection: key takeaways	R
3: Planning for Before Reading	56 minutes	Activity: Before Reading lesson plan study	AA, S, F
		Application: crafting book introductions	A, S, R
4: Planning for During & After Reading	1 hour, 9 minutes	Activity: retell lesson plan study	AA, S, F
		Application: crafting retell questions	A, R
		Activity: comprehension question lesson plan study	AA, S, F
		Application: crafting factual, inferential, and critical thinking questions	A, S
5: Conclusion	5 minutes	Reflection	R, S, F

Chapter **18**

Guided Reading Prompting Workshop

WHAT'S THE GOAL?

Prompt students effectively to increase the rigor of the classroom and allow teachers to see evidence of student learning. By the end of the workshop, participants will

- Diagnose student errors during a comprehension conversation.
- Plan and deliver prompts that will nudge students to the ideal response without doing the work for them.

WHO'S THE AUDIENCE?

Anyone who teaches K–4 reading. This could mean coaches or school leaders as well as teachers.

WHEN TO USE IT

Best Time

When teachers launch guided reading—often in the second month of school.

Other Times That Work

Every time teachers are about to teach a new reading level; this allows them to revisit the demands of planning at that level of reading complexity.

GUIDED READING PROMPTING

WORKSHOP PREPARATION SHEET

Workshop Objectives

1. Diagnose student errors during a comprehension conversation.
2. Plan and deliver prompts that will nudge students to the ideal response without doing the work for them.

Running Time

- 2 hours, 12 minutes

Materials

Materials on Disc

Video Clips

- 26, 30, 31, 34

Guided Reading Prompting PowerPoint Presentation

Handouts

- Printout of Guided Reading Prompting PowerPoint
- Guided Reading Prompting handout
- Guided Reading Narrative Prompting Guide
- Guided Reading Prompting Reflection Template
- Guided Reading Prompting Convo Role Play Cards

Other Materials

- One name tent per participant.
- One binder per participant. (To organize each binder, print out the handouts listed above and arrange handouts in the order they are listed.)

Setup

Of the materials listed above, you'll need the following to start the workshop:
- One name tent per participant
- One binder per participant
- One *Perfect Paper Planes* text per participant
- Three envelopes for every four participants, each containing a student role description for the role play

Here's how to set up the workshop:
- Groups

  ○ Seat participants so that everyone will easily be able to turn and talk with a partner and so that each partner pair will easily be able to team up with another pair for small-group work.

- Tables

  ○ Place a binder, a name tent, and a copy of *Perfect Paper Planes* at each participant's seat.

GUIDED READING PROMPTING

COMPLETE WORKSHOP OVERVIEW

Living the Learning Components Legend

AA = **Airtight activity** that leads participants to the right conclusion mostly on their own

R = **Reflection** during which participants quietly generate and record conclusions or takeaways

S = Small- or large-group **sharing**

F = **Framing** that gives participants a common vocabulary to use to describe what they learn

A = **Application** of learned principles

Section	Time	Activities	Type
1: Introduction to the Prompting Guide	38 minutes	Quick Read: data analysis	AA, S
		Video: introduction to prompting	AA, S, F
		Reflection: prompting guide markup	R, S
2: Guided Reading Prompting Deep Dives	30 minutes	Video: Level 380L–450L	AA, S
		Video: Level 450L–500L	AA, S
		Video: Level 600L–700L	AA, S, R
3: Application	57 minutes	Application, Part I: scripting prompts	A
		Application, Part II: prompting role play	A, S, A, S
4: Key Takeaways	7 minutes	Reflection: key takeaways handout	R, S

Appendix: Tools and Resources

LESSON TYPES IN THE READING-BY-HABIT MODEL

Lesson Type	Group Size	What to Teach?	Definition	Structure
Read-Aloud (Chapter 4)	Whole class	Skills from yearlong syllabus	**Read-aloud lessons** offer deep modeling and extended group practice with a text. Use these to introduce and demonstrate a skill that students will apply independently later on.	I Do, We Do, check for understanding
Comprehension Skills (Chapter 5)	Small group by reading level or whole class if necessary	Skills from yearlong syllabus	**Comprehension skills lessons** teach a skill through the traditional I Do, We Do, You Do instructional design. Use these lessons to give your students practice with a new reading skill or to reinforce a previously taught one.	I Do, We Do, You Do
Phonics (Chapter 6)	Small group or whole class if necessary	Skills from premade program	**Phonics lessons** teach children to understand the relationship between written letters and spoken sounds. Teach this skill separately to give it the necessary attention.	Scripted, pre-fabricated lesson
Guided Reading (Chapters 8 and 9)	Small group by reading level	Skills determined by assessment analysis (Chapter 7)	**Guided reading lessons** are flexible, small-group sessions that allow you to target the aspect of reading your students need support with most—even while they employ all the skills needed to make sense of a text. Use them to address specific student needs while providing greater (but not total) reading independence.	Before Reading, During Reading, After Reading
Independent Reading (Chapter 10)	Individual	Skills for all students	**Independent reading** time is a carefully designed, accountable moment for students to read a book without your support. Use this time to allow your students to use the skills you've already taught and to help them fall in love with reading.	You Do

KEYS TO EFFECTIVE HABITS OF THE CLASSROOM

Room Setup

Top Materials to Have at Hand

- **Extra pencils**—sharpened, please!
- **Copies of the text students are reading:** one for each student, plus a few extra
- **Copies of comprehension questions** students will be working on
- **Sound cards** (these aren't necessary for extended readers)
- **An extra chair or two**
- **All visual aids needed for the lesson**
- **Note-taking template** for recording student errors during instruction

Transitions

Keys to Effective Transitions

Teacher location: The teacher is in a place where he or she can see and access all students.

Instructional materials: Materials are on seats or tables, underneath seats, or with students.

Designated pathways: Students know where to walk during transition.

Economy of language: The teacher uses minimal narration and precise signals.

Immediate start: The lesson begins *immediately* after the transition is complete.

Chants (optional): Students can be engaged in a quick, upbeat transition chant.

How to Teach Routines

Best Practices for Training Classroom Habits

- **Teach the routine with guided practice:**
  - **I Do:** 10% (3–4 min)
  - **We Do:** 60% (first time: 15–20 min)
  - **You Do:** 30% (first time: 10–15 min)

- **Rinse and repeat:** Perfect the routine with each successive practice.
- **Use positive framing:** Narrate what goes well, not what goes wrong.
  - **Assume the best:** Narrate the best effort of the students; assume they're trying to comply.
- **Challenge:** Make even the driest transition something that is exciting: use cheers, team challenges, the tone of your voice, and so on.

SAMPLE LESSON PLAN ON TEACHING A SMALL GROUP-TO-GROUP TRANSITION

Sample Lesson Plan

HABITS:	Small-group transition with song; raise hands
KEY VOCABULARY	
n/a	

Key to abbreviations in table:

T: teacher; TW: teacher will; S: students; SW: students will

Before Reading/Preplanning	**OBJECTIVE(S)**
	SW be able to • Raise hand to ask and answer questions • Transition to and from the comprehension skills area • Sing the "Rockin' Readers" Chant
	COMPREHENSION STRATEGY (BOYLES)
	N/A
	GRAPHIC ORGANIZER(S)
	"Rockin' Readers" on chart paper
	ORAL DRILL QUESTIONS or DO NOW
	• Review basic information that is a prerequisite to day's objective • "Who are you?" (college name) • "What grade are you in?" (first grade)

Heart of the Lesson

HOOK and OPENING
- Engage students and capture their interest.
- Introduce objective using chants, poems, hand movements, images, or props.
- Introduce topic.
- Provide an explanation of objective.

- TW say, "Scholars, last year you did the 'Hey Readers!' chant all year. That was the kindergarten chant, and you did it well. This year, you will all be able to do the first-grade chant, 'Rockin' Readers!' I know some of you might remember it. But in order to be able to sing it, you have to show that you are now first-grade scholars! We are going to learn the 'Rockin' Readers!' chant, but first we have to learn the expectations for your reading group."
- TW tell S that they will be spending the next couple of weeks learning about their reading group and the expectations at the table in order to become a great reader. TW tell S that today they will practice sitting properly, listening attentively, and raising their hand to ask and answer questions, just as they did during the read-aloud. TW tell S that they will need to remember that if they work hard all day long, they are on their way to college.

MODELING (I DO)
- Keep in mind the objective as you complete the lesson—what do you want *all* students to be able to do at the end of the reading block for this skill?
- Model the objective, completing a think-aloud as you do so.
- Complete a check for understanding of the objective.

- TW say, "Scholars, you all just practiced answering questions raising a scholarly hand. Remember, a scholarly hand is a vertical hand [show students]. Is a what? [Vertical hand!] Yes, a vertical hand. Show me! [All students will raise a vertical hand. Repeat at least three times.] Great! Whenever I ask a question, I want to see sharp vertical hands. When I call on someone else, all hands go down. All hands go what? [Down!] Yes, all hands go down. This way everyone is paying attention to the scholar who is speaking. Then you track the speaker. Then you what? [Track the speaker!] Yes, you track the speaker with your laser eyes!"
- TW repeat having students raise a vertical hand, then put their hands down and track whomever T calls on. Do this several times until firm.
- TW say, "Great, scholars, now you are on your way to learning the 'Rockin' Readers!' chant! We still have some things to do before we begin singing it."
- TW tell S that they will practice transitioning to and from the reading table. (Reference individual management plan.) TW model the transitioning procedure at least three times.

- TW tell S that once they transition and sit down at the reading table, they will immediately sit in STAR [proper sitting position] and track the speaker. TW demonstrate transitioning to the table, sitting down, and sitting in STAR.
- TW tell S that now that they have practiced and learned how to sit and listen attentively (in STAR), they will also need to learn what to do once they start talking about reading. "When we are discussing a book or talking about what great readers do, we have to make sure that we are raising our hand to ask and answer questions and that we are listening and tracking the speaker. We never call out when we are talking about a book, and we are always listening to others' ideas."
- Once students have modeled transitioning to their seats several times, then review the "Rockin' Readers!" chant.
- TW show chart with song written. TW demonstrate singing the song. (Break it up by two or three lines at a time, gauging how much students already know.) Have students repeat after two to three lines at a time. Be sure to use the hand motions that are the expectation.

CHECK FOR UNDERSTANDING
- Complete a check for understanding of the objective. TW ask S, "What did you notice as I did a think-aloud of the objective? What am I doing as a reader?"

  ○ TW ask, "What do you do when I ask a question?" (Raise a vertical hand.) "Yes, and you just practiced that now." Be sure to praise those scholars who are continuously modeling a vertical hand. Demand 100 percent from all scholars. Make them repeat this process as many times as necessary.
  ○ "What happens to everyone's hands when I call on someone?" (They go down!)
  ○ "Where do we look after I call on someone?" (We track the speaker!)
  ○ After T models, TW have one student demonstrate to the rest of the group how to transition to and from the reading table.

GUIDED PRACTICE (WE DO)
- Keep in mind the objective as you complete the lesson—what do you want *all* students to be able to do at the end of the writing block for this skill?
- Integrate interactive ways for students to give and show you the objective.
- Think about the common misunderstandings with the skill and provide opportunities for mistakes and corrections.
- Complete a check for understanding of the objective.

- ○ TW have students practice transitioning to the RC table several times. Once students get there, have them begin singing "Rockin' Readers" right away. Then ask students questions like "Who are you?" "What is your group name?" "What kind of hand do we raise?" "Why is it important to raise our hands instead of calling out?" "What day is today?" "What is today's date?"
- ○ TW ask questions so that students can practice raising their hands and tracking the speaker.

More Possibilities:

- ○ T may also begin cold calling students to establish the culture of high accountability. Be clear to say the student's name or point to the student you want to have answer.
- ○ Some students may not realize that their hand is up when someone else is called on. Give them a quick nonverbal so that they know to put their hands down.

INDEPENDENT PRACTICE (YOU DO)

- Provide opportunity(ies) for the students to practice the same activity that was put through modeling and guided practice.
- Monitor student work, moving first to students who struggle.
- Take note of common tricky aspects of comprehension and/or questions (anticipate in the plan and note as students are working).

1. TW have S practice transitioning to and from the reading table using the phrase "transition to reading comprehension."
2. TW have S transition to the table, sit down in STAR.
3. TW have S sing the song on their own.

CLOSING

- Revisit tricky skills.
- Provide a reminder of the topic and objective.
- Use student work to revisit the objective and to complete final check for understanding.

- TW ask S why they practiced transitioning to the table and STAR behaviors. (They will help us focus on our reading.) TW praise S for following directions and tell them that she will pay attention tomorrow to see who has remembered how to transition and perform STAR behaviors.

Assessment

Reflection

HABITS OF DISCUSSION TRAINING AND PROMPTING GUIDE

In the following tables, you will find a list and trajectory of the habits of discussion most often used during reading discussion—these are directly aligned to CCSS for Speaking & Listening[1] and are listed in the order we recommend for teaching them.

LEARNING TO SHARE (START IN GRADES K–1)		
CORE HABIT OF DISCUSSION	**IDEAL STUDENT ACTIONS**	**TEACHER TRAINING OR PROMPTING** **to encourage these actions**
Listen and Talk Only in Turn SL.K.1.A, SL.1.1.A	• Track the speaker. • Keep hands down when someone is speaking. • Do not interrupt.	• Teacher models "hands down": when one student has been called on, all other students must put their hands down. • Teacher uses eye contact, hand movement. • Teacher prompts students to give peers a chance to think and talk.
Speak Audibly SL.K.6	• Use a voice others can hear.	• Teacher prompts: "Loud and proud."
Speak in Complete Sentences SL.1.6, SL.2.6	• Restate the question in the response; use no incomplete sentences.	• Teacher uses nonverbal prompt: fingers pursed together and then spread apart (like pulling gum apart).
Interact Peer to Peer: direct answers to the group SL.3.1.A	• Look at every group member when giving an answer, not just the teacher.	• Teacher uses nonverbal prompts: fingers pointing to eyes and then to the rest of the group. • Teacher prompts: "Tell him."

LEARNING TO BUILD (START IN GRADES 1–3)		
CORE HABIT OF DISCUSSION	**IDEAL STUDENT ACTIONS**	**TEACHER TRAINING OR PROMPTING** **to encourage these actions**
Elaborate on Your Answer SL.3.1.D, SL.4.1.D, SL.5.1.D	• When prompted, add relevant detail to an answer.	• Teacher prompts for a more developed answer: "Tell me more." • Teacher gestures for student to keep going.
Build Off Others' Answer SL.K.1.B, SL.1.1.B, SL.2.1.B	• Build off what the previous student said; comments are not in isolation.	• Teacher says, "Build off that." "Tell me more about what ____ said." "Can you tell me more about what ____ is thinking?"
Evaluate Others' Responses (agree, disagree, somewhat agree or disagree) SL.4.1.D, SL.5.1.D	• Use thumbs up, to the side, or down: agree, slightly agree or disagree, disagree. • Say, "I agree with what you said because…" or "I somewhat agree with what you said, but…"	• Teach the stems of agree, disagree, and somewhat agree or disagree: "I agree with what you said because…" and "I somewhat agree with what you said, but…" • Teacher prompts the group: "What do you think about that?" "Do you agree?"
Praise Your Peers	• Praise each other's work or thinking.	• Teacher prompts for praise: "What did you like about [student]'s answer?" "Could someone offer some praise for that answer?"
Prompt Peers with Universal Prompts SL.4.1.C, SL.5.1.C	• Say, "Tell me more." • Ask, "What in the story makes you think that?" "Why do you think that?" "Why is that important?" • Repeat the original question.	• Teacher trains: "So now we're at a point where if you don't agree, you need to prompt that student with a universal prompt."

LEARNING TO BUILD (START IN GRADES 1–3)		
CORE HABIT OF DISCUSSION	**IDEAL STUDENT ACTIONS**	**TEACHER TRAINING OR PROMPTING** to encourage these actions
Hint, Dont't Tell: cue peers to help them in their response SL.5.1.C	• Give a hint to another student to find the answer without telling him or her.	• Teacher could say, "I want you to help your neighbor" or "Instead of telling the answer, you could have prompted like this . . ." • Teacher could tie in another lesson: "Remember in read-aloud this morning what we did? How can you [tie that in, use that here]?"
No Hands: aid the conversation without raising your hand SL.4.1.B, SL.5.1.B	• Understand wait time, and know when to prompt a peer in the conversation.	• Teacher uses a nonverbal prompt: he backs away in his chair and reaches out his hands to the students to encourage them to continue the conversation.
Lead: facilitate the conversation from start to finish SL.4.1.B, SL.5.1.B	• Stay focused on the core question. • Identify when the sharing strays and redirect the conversation.	• Teacher takes no action (but gives signs of watchful oversight). • Teacher demonstrates how to redirect a literature circle that's off task. Once this has been demonstrated, teacher signals to students to redirect the conversation themselves. • Teacher intervenes: "What is our core question? Are you answering that question?"
Come Prepared in Writing: use written response to aid discussion SL.3.1.A, SL.4.1.A, SL.5.1.A	• Use written responses done during independent reading to guide the discussion.	• Teacher prompts: "As you were writing, I noticed that many of you wrote _____. What were you thinking?"

READ-ALOUD: KEY GUIDELINES TO REMEMBER

Preparation (Prework Before the Lesson Begins)

- Flag the text. (Premark book for stopping and thinking points.)
- Prepare anchor chart and post.

Lesson Introduction
Teacher explains exactly what the students will do
8 min (new skill); 6 min (review of skill)

- [Optional] Start with a vocabulary mini-lesson (Beck's Text Talk, or words from the text).
- Include a hook or catchy opening (skit, metaphor, real-world connection, choral review of previous skills and strategies).
- Introduce and define reading skill.
    - Precise and student-friendly
    - Check for understanding: choral response and student hand gestures
- Preview the text.
    - Adjusted to the reading level of the students (in other words, students do more of the previewing themselves as they progress in their reading levels)
    - Tied to the objective
- Summarize the previous day's reading (if a continuation of book).
    - Fast paced
    - Includes bridging from the teacher (if needed)
    - Includes questions that review plot

I Do
Teacher models exactly what the students will do
5 min

- Read the text while modeling fluency; remember to bring the drama!
- Conduct a think-aloud.

- Use precise, scripted language on targeted skill.
- Cue students in and out ("I'm realizing/thinking . . ." "Now back to the text").
- Chart thinking (as needed).
- Teach vocabulary (as it is encountered in the text).

We Do

Teacher continues to model; students begin to practice
12 min

- Continue to think aloud.
- Continue to teach vocabulary.
- Ask targeted questions that build to the objective. (Often the big question related to the skill might be the final question rather than repeated continuously, as would happen with "theme.")
  - Utilize Turn and Talk for inference and critical thinking questions.
  - Use strategic universal prompts to deepen understanding or address student confusion.

Check for Understanding

Teacher reviews and reinforces targeted skill
3 min

- Ask a critical thinking question that nails the targeted skill.
- Ensure that all students have an opportunity to answer.
  - Up to 300L: Turn and Talk
  - 300L–600L: Turn and Talk or written student response
  - 600L+: written student response
- All students answer recapping how they applied the skill to the reading.

COMPREHENSION SKILLS FRAMEWORK

Preparation (Prework Before the Lesson Begins)

- Flag the text (premark book for stopping and thinking points).
- Prepare an anchor chart and post.
- Prepare all materials (independent work, folders, pencils, crayons, and so on).

I Do

Teacher models exactly what the students will do
5–8 min

- State the objective with clear, precise language.
- Teach the skill or strategy with a preplanned think-aloud from a shared experience or text.
  - Break down the steps consistently.
  - Chart thinking.
  - Explain the rationale behind the strategy.
- Check for understanding: ask, "What did I just model for you?" (students articulate).

We Do

Teacher checks for understanding and gets the students to share the work
10–15 min

- We Do mirrors the I Do: students practice the same skill that the teacher modeled.
- Students and teacher work together.
  - Teacher starts a think-aloud; students take over.
  - Teacher questions and prompts strategically.
  - Turn and Talk is followed by discussion.
  - Quick-writes follow discussion.

- Evaluate skill implementation.
  - Teacher assesses quality of skill implementation.
  - Students assess the quality of their peers' skill implementation.
- Keep this tightly timed: make sure students end promptly to move to You Do.

You Do

Students do the work; teacher monitors
15–20 min

- Make a clear connection to the skill that was just presented and practiced.
- Give clear directions for independent practice: reading task (plus a writing task for grades 1–4).
- For grades 2–4, use a separate text for students to apply the skill (articles, texts, excerpts).
- Monitor to check for understanding (move around, observe work).

PHONICS INSTRUCTION FRAMEWORK

Purpose of Phonics Instruction

Give students the tools to accurately, fluently, and independently read a text, therefore allowing them to focus on the meaning of the story.

Introduction/Hook (3–4 min)

Opening chant

Conduct a quick review of a challenging skill (choose one or two of the following):

- **Sight word review (K and struggling grade 1)**
  - ○ Flashcard review examples:

    "This word is [teacher gives]. What word?" *(Students repeat)*

    "This word is [students give]. What word?" *(Students repeat again)*

    "[Student name], what word is this? What word?" *(All students repeat)*

- **Vowel Sounds**
  - ○ Vowel chant:

    "A, E, I, O, U, and sometimes Y. AGAIN!" *(A, E, I, O, U, and sometimes Y)*

    "Short A says its sound [students give]. Long A says its name [students give]. Short E says its sound [students give]. Long E says its name [students give]." *(Continue with all vowels.)*

- **Consonant sounds**
  - ○ Example: Blend flashcard review:

    "Sound check, sound check, 1-2-3. This sound is [students give]. What sound? [students give]."

    "What sound is this? [ch] What sound is this? [ch] What word is this? [check]"

- **Decoding rules—final e, double consonant, vowel pairs...**
  - ◦ Sample chant—silent "e":

    "Silent E. Say my name. [Students give.] Silent E. Say my name. [Students give.]"

    "An E at the end, makes the vowel say its— *NAME!*"
  - ◦ Sample chant— double consonant:

    "Two say the sound, one says the name."
- **Fluency strategies**

Scripted Lesson (18 min)

- Lesson is derived from the teacher's manual.
- Students practice decoding skills and word-solving strategies.
- Teacher identifies student errors and guides students to self-correct.
- Teacher models how to use decoding skills and strategies.

Oral Reading (10 min)

- Students have their own storybooks.
- Students read aloud to practice decoding skills and word-solving strategies.
- Teacher identifies student errors and guides students to self-correct.
- Teacher models how to fluently read and word-solve in context.

Independent Work (10 min)

- Students complete "take-home" sheets that coincide with the scripted lesson.
- Teacher and students go over the answers and review work.

PHONICS PROMPTING GUIDE

PHONICS PROMPTING GUIDE	

Identifying the Student
• Isolate the section of the group:
  ◦ "Back row get ready..."
  ◦ "Front row get ready..."
• Isolate boys and girls:
  ◦ "Boys get ready..."
  ◦ "Girls get ready..."
• Target specific student:
  ◦ "Nakai get ready..."
	Universal Prompts
	• You said ___. Try it again.
	• Read through the word.
	• Does that make sense?
	• Sound it out.
	• Does that sound right?
	• Chunk it.
	• Does that look right?
	• Skip it and come back.

Consonant Sound • The sound is ___. Watch my mouth. • This is ___. It makes the ___ sound. • You said ___. Try again. • What sound does this letter make? • What letter is this? What sound does it make? • This is ___. What sound does it make? • Think of the word ___. What sound did the ___ make?	**Vowel Sound** • Try another vowel sound. • Is this long or short? Is it wearing a hat? • What sound does ___ make when it is long? Short? • This is the [long, short] ___. What sound does it make? • Think of the word ___. What sound did the ___ make?

Letter Pairs
- You said ___. Try again.
- Get your mouth ready.
- What sound do these letters make when they are together?
- Together, the letters "ch" make /ch /. Try the word again.
- Together, the letters "ch" make /ch /, so this word is "check." What's the word?

Misunderstanding with Common "Rules"
- What rule does this word follow?
- What is the rule for [final "e" words]?
- Is there a resource you can use to help?
- In most words that end with "e," the middle vowel says its long sound. Try it again with the rule.
- In most words that end with "e," the middle vowel says its long sound. So the word must be ___.

PHONICS PROMPTING GUIDE

Fluency and Rate	Attending to Punctuation
• Read so it sounds like you are talking. • Can you make your voice sound like _____? • Read it so the words match the feelings. • *Model:* Can you read it like this? • Can you read it with your eyes? *(Level G on)*	• What do you do when you come to a _____? • Try it again and ○ Stop at the period. ○ Pause at the comma. ○ Make your voice go up at the question mark. • Look for punctuation.

Prompting Protocol

1. Teacher prompts when he or she hears the error.
2. Student responds (with correct answer).
3. Teacher signals the whole group to chorally respond with the correct answer.

If student does not respond with the correct answer after a prompt:

1. Teacher asks a higher-achieving student the same prompt. Higher-achieving student provides the answer.
2. Teacher returns to original student with the error. That student repeats answer.
3. Teacher signals the whole group to chorally respond with the correct answer.

NARRATIVE GUIDED READING PROMPTING GUIDE, BY LEXILE LEVEL

Up to 50L: Concepts Related to Print and Word Solving		
CORE ELEMENT and IDEAL STUDENT ACTIONS	**TYPICAL STUDENT ERRORS**	**TEACHER-TO-STUDENT PROMPTS to encourage these actions**
1-to-1: Following print with finger RF.K.1.A, RF.K.1.C	Does not move finger appropriately with the text Does not point to the text at all (e.g., points at picture)	• Point to the words as you read. • Were there enough words? • Did you run out of words?
PICTURE: Use pictures to solve unknown words	Cannot solve an unknown word (the picture will help)	• Can the picture help you figure out that word? • Does it match the picture?
PATTERN: Recognize or remember pattern of words in text	Cannot identify the pattern of words that repeat on each page	• Does this page start the same way?
1ˢᵗ LETTER ID: Recognize letter names and most letter sounds RF.K.1.D	Cannot solve an unknown word (the first letter can help)	• What word would make sense that starts with ___? • What letter is at the beginning of ___?
HIGH FREQ 2: Use a few high-frequency words to monitor reading RF.K.3.C	Cannot recognize a high-frequency word *in context*	• That's a sight word. • Find the word ___ and point to it. • Have you seen these words before?

Up to 50L: Comprehension		
CORE ELEMENT and IDEAL STUDENT ACTIONS	**TYPICAL STUDENT ERRORS**	**TEACHER-TO-STUDENT PROMPTS to encourage these actions**
SEQUENCE: Retell parts of the story accurately and in proper sequence RL.K.2	Cannot describe events in order	• *Ask children to retell parts of the story.* • What happened on page _____? • What happens [after, before] [event in story]? • Turn the page [forward, backward].

Uncommon Schools | **NORTH ★ STAR**

50L–100L: Word Solving and Fluency		
CORE ELEMENT and IDEAL STUDENT ACTIONS	**TYPICAL STUDENT ERRORS**	**TEACHER-TO-STUDENT PROMPTS to encourage these actions**
1st LETTER SOUND: Use first-letter sounds when attempting to problem-solve unknown words RF.K.3.A	Mistakes the first sound or mistakes the first blend	• Get your mouth ready. • Do you know a word that starts with those letters? • Check it. Does it look right? Does it sound right? • Do you think it looks like ____? • Do you know a word with those letters? • Does that make sense? • What was wrong? Try it again. Were you right?
HIGH FREQ 3: Use a core of high-frequency words automatically to support reading RF.K.3.C	Sounds out word but never puts sounds all together	• Can you read the whole word at once?
SUBTLE PICS: Use pictures to solve unknown words (subtle connection between picture and text)	Cannot solve an unknown word (the picture can help)	• Can the picture help you figure out that word?
NO MONOTONE: Reread familiar stories with some phrasing; use expression on familiar refrains	Reads story with a monotone or without expression Does not take on tone of character	• Read the story so it sounds as if you are talking. • *Model expressive reading and ask,* Can you read it like this? • Can you make your voice sound like [a character in the story]?

50L–100L: Comprehension		
CORE ELEMENT and IDEAL STUDENT ACTIONS	**TYPICAL STUDENT ERRORS**	**TEACHER-TO-STUDENT PROMPTS to encourage these actions**

FACT: Recall factual information and find it in the text
 	
RL.K.1, RL.1.1
	Incorrectly states events in the story	• *Ask children to talk about the story's plot and characters while referring to specific parts of the text— for example:*
		  ○ What does the child like to draw?
		  ○ What happened when ___?
		  ○ Turn to the page that told us about ___.

CROSS-CHECK: Put together details from pictures and text to make sense of a story RF.K.7	Struggles to make sense of the story	• Look at the picture. What moment in the story is this showing us? • What does the picture tell us about the story? • [After student response]: Why? • How do the pictures and the words in the text match?
STORY ELEMENTS I: Respond to questions around setting and characters	Student cannot state evidence for claims around setting and characters	• What pictures or words let us know the setting of the story? • Who are the characters? • What does the text tell us about the characters?

50L–100L: Comprehension		
CORE ELEMENT and IDEAL STUDENT ACTIONS	**TYPICAL STUDENT ERRORS**	**TEACHER-TO-STUDENT PROMPTS to encourage these actions**
CHARACTER FEELINGS: Can use personal experience along with text evidence to draw conclusions about character feelings	Struggles to use personal experience in a meaningful way; the student is either too reliant on the text evidence or uses personal experience unrelated to the text	• How does [character] feel at the end of the story? How do you know? • What are the character's actions? What does this reveal about the character's feelings? • Has something like what happened in the text ever happened to you? How can you use your experience to understand how [character] feels? • Which text evidence did you use to make your personal connection?

100L–150L: Word Solving and Fluency		
CORE ELEMENT and IDEAL STUDENT ACTIONS	**TYPICAL STUDENT ERRORS**	**TEACHER-TO-STUDENT PROMPTS** to encourage these actions
BLENDS AND ENDS: Attend to initial blends and inflectional endings: -ing, -ed, -s RF.K.3.A, RF.1.3.F	States initial blend but gets rest of the word wrong OR States correct root word but misses ending (e.g., *fish* vs. *fisher, run* vs., *runs*)	• Read through the word. • It could be ____, but look at ____. • Check the beginning and ending letters. • You made a mistake. Can you find it? • How does that word start? Try it again with the ending. • Read that again. • Try ____. Would that sound right? • Would that make sense?
MIDDLE VOWELS: Attending to middle vowel sounds RF.K.3.B	Does not pay attention to the middle of the word	• Ask student to quickly differentiate between words that have different short vowels—For example, *run* vs. *ran; then* vs. *thin* • What sound does [vowel] make?
HIGH FREQ 4: Recognize many high-frequency and other known words quickly and automatically RF.K.3.C	Does not recognize words that he or she has already read previously	• You've seen that word before. Do you think it looks like ____?
WORD FAMILIES: Use word families to figure out some new words RF.K.3.D	Does not make connections between words in the same family to comprehend	• Do you know a word like that? • What word family might help you figure it out? • It rhymes with ____. Can you change the first sound?

100L–150L: Word Solving and Fluency		
CORE ELEMENT and IDEAL STUDENT ACTIONS	TYPICAL STUDENT ERRORS	TEACHER-TO-STUDENT PROMPTS to encourage these actions
SELF-CORRECT: Begin to check one source of information against another to confirm, make another attempt, or self-correct RF.1.4.C, RF.2.4.C	Does not make self-corrections	• Do you remember reading that word before? • Does that make sense? What do you think is happening in the text?
PHRASE-READ: Move away from finger pointing and word-by-word reading; read with 2–3 word phrasing RF.K.4, RF.1.4	Reads word by word and does not connect in phrasing; points finger at text	• Put the words together so it sounds like you're talking. • Can you read it with your eyes?
REREAD: Reread to problem-solve and confirm new words and to maintain meaning	Does not reread to confirm meaning	• Now read that again all together.

100L–150L: Comprehension		
CORE ELEMENT and IDEAL STUDENT ACTIONS	**TYPICAL STUDENT ERRORS**	**TEACHER-TO-STUDENT PROMPTS to encourage these actions**
CITING EVIDENCE I —DETAIL: Remember details from pictures and text and use them to clarify meaning RL.K.2	Does not go back to the text or pictures to search for specific facts and information	• Look back to find where the writer tells about ____. • What is your evidence for that? • On what page did you find evidence about ____? • Reread page ____. What did you learn about ____?
STORY ELEMENTS II: Identify primary problem and solution in a story RF.K.3	Does not identify the traditional structure of a story when trying to comprehend	• What is the problem in this story? • What are they trying to solve? • How do the characters work to solve the problem?

150L–250L: Word Solving and Fluency		
CORE ELEMENT and IDEAL STUDENT ACTIONS	**TYPICAL STUDENT ERRORS**	**TEACHER-TO-STUDENT PROMPTS to encourage these actions**
PUNCTUATE: Begin to use punctuation to assist smooth reading RF.1.1.A	Reads straight through punctuation	• Try it again and [stop at the period, pause at the comma, make your voice go up at the question mark].

CHUNK LETTERS: Use letter-sound relationships and letter chunks to decode many new words; blend consonants and vowels to problem-solve new words
 	
RF.1.3.B
	Incorrectly reads a word
	
	Says a long vowel sound when it should be short vowel
		• *Prompt children to use the phonetic patterns they know—for example:*
		  ◦ Could it be a blend?
		  ◦ Do you think it looks like a "silent e" word?

READ WITH EXPRESSION: Read embodying a character's emotions RF.2.4.B, RL.2.6	Reads with inflection but no recognition of a character's feelings	• Can you read it so that the words match the feelings? • How would this character be speaking right now? With what tone?
SPEED: Move quickly through the text: 40 words per minute RF.2.4.B	Reads very slowly	• Try that again. • Can you read this quickly?
CHECK NEW WORDS: Check new words using multiple sources of information (visual, syntax, and meaning) RL.2.4.C	Does not use all strategies to understand new words; relies heavily on only one or two strategies (visual, syntax, meaning)	• You said ___. Does that make sense? • Does that sound right? • Does that look right? • You said ___. Can we say it that way?
SILENT: Begin to silently read some of the time	Is not able to read silently	• Can you read it in your head?

150L–250L: Comprehension		
CORE ELEMENT and IDEAL STUDENT ACTIONS	**TYPICAL STUDENT ERRORS**	**TEACHER-TO-STUDENT PROMPTS to encourage these actions**
CHARACTER MENTAL STATE AND TRAITS: Draw on personal experiences to respond to questions on character's mental state RL.K.3	Cannot identify what character is thinking as support for character actions	• What does the text say about the character's thinking? • What does the character's dialogue reveal about the character's thinking? • What happened in the story to cause the character to think this way? • What is the character like [personality traits]? • What words or phrases reveal the character's personality trait?
CAUSE AND EFFECT: Describe the cause and effect of specific events RL.2.5	Struggles to identify the cause or effect of an action	• What caused [event] to happen in the story? • How is [earlier action] related to [later action]?
CHARACTER CHANGE: Describe the cause and effect of specific events that led to a change in a character's mental state RL.2.3	Struggles to identify the moment the character changed or the reason why	• How did [character] change from the beginning to the end of the story? • What was the character thinking at the [beginning, end] of the story? How was this different from [or the same as] the ending of the story?

250L–320L: Word Solving and Fluency		
CORE ELEMENT and IDEAL STUDENT ACTIONS	**TYPICAL STUDENT ERRORS**	**TEACHER-TO-STUDENT PROMPTS to encourage these actions**
CHUNK SYLLABLES: Figure out some longer words by breaking them into syllables or chunks RF.1.3.E	Gets stuck after the first syllable with a difficult word	• Can you take the word apart? • Look for the root word.
NO STOP AND START: Self-correct at the point of error with fewer returns to the beginning of sentences or phrases RF.1.4.C	Reads through passage with stumbles, so rereads the whole sentence again	• Where's the tricky word? • Why did you stop? • Were you right? Keep going.
VOWEL PATTERNS: Use some complex letter patterns (long vowel patterns, complex blends) to problem-solve while reading RF.2.3.B, RF.2.3.C	Does not look for vowel patterns when deciphering a word	• *Prompt children to use the phonetic patterns they know—for example:* ○ Do you think it looks like a vowel team? ○ Try it again with a long "o."
PERSEVERE: Sustain problem solving of words and development of meaning through a longer text	Stops correcting words as the passage goes along	• Keep using your word-solving strategies.

250L–320L: Comprehension		
CORE ELEMENT and IDEAL STUDENT ACTIONS	**TYPICAL STUDENT ERRORS**	**TEACHER-TO-STUDENT PROMPTS to encourage these actions**
STORY ELEMENTS III: Apply the narrative story elements (S-T-O-R-Y) to support comprehension: main idea, primary and secondary characters, problem, attempts to solve, resolution RL.K.6, RL.1.3, R.L.2.1, RL.2.5	Student does not apply the literary elements to comprehend the story	• Who were the important characters in the story? • What does the text say about the main characters and their personality? • Who are the secondary characters? • What impact does [main character]'s actions have on [secondary character]? • What is the problem? Why is this a problem? • How was the problem solved? • How is the setting important?
CITING EVIDENCE II: Recall details from the story to support answers to inferential and critical thinking questions, with some support RL.2.1, RL.3.1, RL.4.1	Can state inference but without support from text Does not use background information to interpret actions in a text	• Can you explain why you think that? What in the story gives you that idea? • How does [character] feel after [event]? • Look at page ___. Where is there evidence to support your inference? • *For critical thinking questions:* Give me at least two pieces of evidence that tell why [character] did [character action].
CLARIFY IDEAS I: Talk about reasons for an answer and attempt to explain why inferences about an idea are valid RL.4.1	Primarily uses text evidence, but does not support with inference	• Why do you think [character] did [action]? • That's what the author said. What do you think he/she means? • Why did [event] happen?

320L–380L: Word Solving and Fluency		
CORE ELEMENT and IDEAL STUDENT ACTIONS	**TYPICAL STUDENT ERRORS**	**TEACHER-TO-STUDENT PROMPTS to encourage these actions**

LETTER PATTERNS: Use knowledge of common letter patterns and long vowel patterns to problem-solve and decode new words
 	
RF.1.3.C
	Does not try another sound for irregular words (soft "c" and "g" rules)
	
	Has difficulty decoding complex vowel patterns
		• *Encourage flexibility—for example:*
		  ◦ What other sound does the letter "g" make?
		  ◦ What could you try?
		• Have you seen that vowel combination before?

BIG WORD CHUNK: Use syllables and letter chunks consistently for problem-solving longer two-syllable words
 	
RF.1.3.E, RF.2.3.D
	Does not say each chunk in a word; omits part of the word (including middle and ending blends)	• *Prompt children to use the syllable patterns they know—for example:*
		  ◦ What is the first syllable?
		  ◦ Do you think it looks like a closed syllable?
		  ◦ Do you recognize a prefix? A suffix?

SILENT SPEED: Read most texts fluently, slowing down to figure out new words and then resuming speed Read silently most of the time	Not able to resume speed after slowing down for a new word Reads aloud (or in a whisper)	• Put the words together so that it sounds like talking. • Can you read it in your head?

320L–380L: Comprehension		
CORE ELEMENT and IDEAL STUDENT ACTIONS	**TYPICAL STUDENT ERRORS**	**TEACHER-TO-STUDENT PROMPTS to encourage these actions**

CHARACTER MOTIVE: Generate questions about characters' actions, motives, and feelings
 	
RL.3.3
	Not able to see the character as more rounded, with wants and needs	• *Encourage children to ask their own questions—for example:*
		  ◦ What questions do you have for [classmate]?
		  ◦ What is the character's motivation?
		  ◦ How do you know from the text that [character] wants or needs ___?
		• Why do you think [character] is ___? What in the story makes you think so?
		• What did [character]'s dialogue reveal about his/her motivation?

CITING EVIDENCE III: Use details and events in a story to support answers to inferential and critical thinking questions RL.2.7, RL.4.1	Does not go back into the text to find information that supports ideas and thinking Relies primarily on factual information to respond to questions Doesn't know how to provide evidence	• What in the book makes you think that? • Try looking back for the information you need. • Look back to find where the writer tells about ___. • What is your evidence? • How does that [word, phrase] help you think about this ___? • How does this part of the text help you understand this character? • That's what the character said. What did he/she mean? • Using information in the story, tell about how [character] felt when [event occurred]. • On what page did you find information about ___?

380L–450L: Word Solving and Fluency

CORE ELEMENT and IDEAL STUDENT ACTIONS	TYPICAL STUDENT ERRORS	TEACHER-TO-STUDENT PROMPTS to encourage these actions
AUTO-PILOT: Read most regularly spelled two-syllable words automatically RF.2.3.C	Does not try another sound for irregular words (soft "c" and "g" rules)	• Look at the whole word. • *For the child who overly relies on decoding, ask:* ○ Do you know the word by sight?
IRREGULAR WORDS: Figure out many irregularly spelled words—e.g., with diphthongs or special vowel spellings RF.2.3.E, RF.2.3.F	Cannot decipher diphthongs or special vowel spellings	• Do you know any words like that? What could you try?
PUNCTUATE: Read new text in 3–4 word phrases with attention to punctuation RF.2.4.B	Does not use dialogue tags to read with meaning	• Read it with expression. • Look for the punctuation.

380L–450L: Comprehension		
CORE ELEMENT and IDEAL STUDENT ACTIONS	**TYPICAL STUDENT ERRORS**	**TEACHER-TO-STUDENT PROMPTS to encourage these actions**
THEME: Discuss themes of a book—what the "message" or "big picture" might be RL.2.2	Relies on specific events but does not see the "big picture" or theme in the text	• What lesson does [character] learn in this story? • What is the theme in this text? • What is the author trying to teach us in this story? • What specific lines or phrases from the text help to reveal the theme?

SUSTAIN: Sustain attention to the meaning of a longer text over several days
 	
RL.3.5
	Is unable to recall details from previous reading	• *Help children connect related parts of a text—for example:*
		  ◦ What happened in the [beginning, middle, end] of the story?
		  ◦ What did we read about yesterday?
		  ◦ What new information did you learn about ___?

CHARACTER CONTRAST: Compare different characters' points of view and discuss why they might see things differently RL.3.3, RL.4.3, RL.5.3	Has difficulty holding on to multiple characters	• Is there something that you know about this character that can help you understand him/her now? • Why don't these characters agree with each other? Does it matter that one character is older than the other? • What is [character]'s main problem in the story? • Compare these characters: [character] and [character]. • And what did [character] say? • Who were the important characters in the story? • Who is telling the story?

380L–450L: Comprehension

CORE ELEMENT and IDEAL STUDENT ACTIONS	TYPICAL STUDENT ERRORS	TEACHER-TO-STUDENT PROMPTS to encourage these actions
CITING EVIDENCE IV: Cite the best evidence from a story to support answers to inferential and critical thinking questions RL 2.7, RL.4.1	Does not weigh the value of two pieces of evidence to determine which is stronger Relies primarily on the first evidence found	• Is there another piece of evidence that can be used to support your argument? • Compare your evidence to [another passage.] Which is stronger evidence? • How does that [word, phrase] make your evidence strong?

450L–500L: Word Solving

CORE ELEMENT and IDEAL STUDENT ACTIONS	TYPICAL STUDENT ERRORS	TEACHER-TO-STUDENT PROMPTS to encourage these actions
WORD MASTERY: Flexibly apply word-solving strategies to complex multisyllable words RF.3.3.C	Slows down to word-solve using only one strategy	• What can you do to figure it out? • What do you already know that might help you?

450L–500L: Comprehension		
CORE ELEMENT and IDEAL STUDENT ACTIONS	**TYPICAL STUDENT ERRORS**	**TEACHER-TO-STUDENT PROMPTS to encourage these actions**
MULTIPLE PLOTS, EVENTS: Trace characters across multiple episodes, elaborating own understanding as the story progresses Relate earlier and later parts of a text, figuring out how they make sense together RL.3.6	Focuses on one character and plot throughout story	• What have you learned about the character here? • Why are you [not] surprised about what the character does here? • How did ___ affect ___? Tell about the relationship between ___ and ___. • What did you find out? • Does reading this section make you rethink your earlier idea? • How does this section help you to understand ___? • What's going on? • We need to connect different parts. It's important for us to connect what happened earlier in the text to what is going on later in the text.
CROSS-BOOK THEMES: Connect general themes among books, discussing some similarities and differences RL.1.9, RL.2.9, RL.3.9, RL.4.9	Does not connect multiple parts of the text OR Does not extend and relate background knowledge to reading	• What other books have we read about [theme]? What are the similarities or differences? • Could we make a connection to another book that we have read? What were the perceptions in that book? • This book reminds me of ___. Can you think why? • Think of another book you read that is like this. • Have you ever read about other characters like this? How did they approach ___? • Do you know anyone who is like a character in this book? • How does that help you think about this ___?

450L–500L: Comprehension		
CORE ELEMENT and IDEAL STUDENT ACTIONS	**TYPICAL STUDENT ERRORS**	**TEACHER-TO-STUDENT PROMPTS to encourage these actions**
DEEP RETELL: Retell stories using some synthesis and interpretation of events—going beyond factual recall and sequencing and including character motivation, feelings, actions, thoughts RL.3.2, RL.4.2	Uses factual information to retell, excluding important details Is unable to synthesize information Does not include character motive in retell	• Using the events from the story, tell me the big ideas in this section. • You've given me the text evidence: now how can you give a big idea of what happened in the very beginning of the story? • Let's dig a little deeper about the part between ___ and ___; what's going on? • Why [does, doesn't] a character do an action? • What were the most important things this writer had to say? • Summarize the main events in this story. • What are you missing in your retell? [character development: motivation, feelings, actions, thoughts; setting; problem; solution] • How can you make that retell more concise? • When you retell, you need to include ___. You're missing ___ in your retell. • How can we make this important part of the text a big idea? • So let's stop . . . that's the fact in the text, we know that happens, those are the character's actions; why did they do that? We need to understand the why. (What are their motivations? How do we better understand this? What are they doing?)

450L–500L: Comprehension		
CORE ELEMENT and IDEAL STUDENT ACTIONS	**TYPICAL STUDENT ERRORS**	**TEACHER-TO-STUDENT PROMPTS to encourage these actions**
TYPES OF CONFLICT: Recognize the difference between internal and external conflict, and can identify types of conflict (person vs. person, person vs. nature, person vs. self) RL.4.6	Struggles to recognize the difference between internal and external conflict Assumes conflict is external	• What is the [problem, conflict]? • Is the problem caused by an internal or external force? How do you know? • Tell me about the character's personality or experiences. How are these contributing to this conflict?

500L–550L: Word Solving		
CORE ELEMENT and IDEAL STUDENT ACTIONS	**TYPICAL STUDENT ERRORS**	**TEACHER-TO-STUDENT PROMPTS to encourage these actions**
WORDS IN CONTEXT: Use context clues to figure out meaning of words and ideas RL.3.4	Does not slow down to clear up confusion around the meaning of a word	• Keep reading to figure it out. • What do you think the paragraph is about? Now can you predict what the word means?

500L–550L: Comprehension		
CORE ELEMENT and IDEAL STUDENT ACTIONS	**TYPICAL STUDENT ERRORS**	**TEACHER-TO-STUDENT PROMPTS** to encourage these actions
GENRE I: Use knowledge of literary genre and text structure to support comprehension RL.2.5	Does not use predictable genre structures to support comprehension	• How do you know that this is a [poem, mystery, biography]? • What [key words, phrases, sentences] reveal the genre of this book? • Think about what you know about ____ [genre]. What kind of book is this? How does knowing that help you understand this [character, event]? • What did the writer do to make the characters (animals or human) seem as though they were real? • What makes this a good ____ [genre]?
SEARCH TEXT: Identify pertinent information in a text when searching for answers RL.3.1	Gives a response but without textual support, or does not recall detail to provide answer	• Can you find the place in the book that gave you the answer? • How does this support your answer? • Go back in the text. Look for ____.
CONNECT WITHIN TEXT: Connect different parts of a text to build understanding of overall meaning RI.3.5	Does not build on previous understanding of characters and plot over time; comprehension is limited to part of text currently being read	• Does this earlier section help you understand what is happening here? • How can you explain this change in the character? What was he/she like before? • How did your thinking change? • How do you know [character] changed?

500L–550L: Comprehension		
CORE ELEMENT and IDEAL STUDENT ACTIONS	**TYPICAL STUDENT ERRORS**	**TEACHER-TO-STUDENT PROMPTS to encourage these actions**
CHARACTER PERSPECTIVE: Understand that characters and perspectives are revealed by what they say, think, and do and what others say and think; characters change over time RL.4.3	Does not connect character's words, thoughts, or actions to character's perspective Struggles to see character changing over time	• Notice what a character does or says or thinks to provide clues to what is important to him/her. • Notice the actions, motives, and feelings of a character. • Choose one word that best describes the way other characters see this character. • How did [character, character perspective, the way others see the character] change from the beginning to the end? • What specific moments from the text show what is important to [character]?
CITING EVIDENCE V: Evaluate the use of evidence by another reader in order to push inferential and critical thinking	Has difficulty determining the best evidence from the text to support inferential or critical thinking Does not understand how another reader drew a conclusion from the text	• How could you push your peer to make a better inference? What text would he/she need to cite? • How did your thinking change after rereading this evidence? • Who has stronger evidence to support this thinking? • What do you think about [other reader]'s evidence? Is it the right evidence? Why or why not?

550L–600L: Comprehension		
CORE ELEMENT and IDEAL STUDENT ACTIONS	**TYPICAL STUDENT ERRORS**	**TEACHER-TO-STUDENT PROMPTS to encourage these actions**
NEW INFORMATION: Incorporate new information into own understanding of narrative topic RL.3.2, RI.3.2	Does not build on or adjust previous understanding of the text	• *Create reading logs that ask students to record new ideas learned from the text.* • *Give students practice in note-taking.* • What's going on right now? • Which lines reveal information about the [character, plot]?
FIGURATIVE: Recognize some figurative language and make attempts to understand beyond a literal interpretation RL.3.4, RL.5.4	Relies on literal interpretation; gives very factual response	• *Prompt children to notice similes and metaphors.* • What associations do you have with ___? How do these associations help you understand what the author is saying? • I noticed this language. *(Read.)* What did the writer mean by that? [figurative, language, metaphor, idiom] • Take a look again at [figurative language]. What is happening here? • Tell me more about the [figurative language]. • Why did the author use [figurative language] here?
SKIM: Skim text independently to find information and clarify meaning	Reads entire section during a comprehension discussion	• Read just enough to remember what the paragraph is saying. • Skim this page. Does reviewing this section make you rethink your earlier comment?

550L–600L: Comprehension		
CORE ELEMENT and IDEAL STUDENT ACTIONS	**TYPICAL STUDENT ERRORS**	**TEACHER-TO-STUDENT PROMPTS** to encourage these actions
REVISE PREDICTIONS: Revise understanding of a text while reading when initial ideas no longer fit the story	Refuses to entertain differing ideas or opinions even when presented with textual evidence	• What do you think of the character now? • What did [character] say or do to change your thinking? Which event from the story changed your thinking about ___? • Has this changed your mind about your earlier prediction?
PARAPHRASE: Test own understanding of a text by summarizing, paraphrasing, or self-questioning	Has difficulty synthesizing a dense amount of information	• Can you say in your own words what the author is saying? Do you have questions about this section? • Based on what you know about [character, story], are you wondering what will happen? • Think about what you know from the text. What do you think will happen?

600L–700L: Word Solving		
CORE ELEMENT and IDEAL STUDENT ACTIONS	**TYPICAL STUDENT ERRORS**	**TEACHER-TO-STUDENT PROMPTS** to encourage these actions
SHADES OF MEANING: Discuss the shades of meaning of particular words in understanding a text RL.3.4	Cannot distinguish between meanings of similar words	• Why do you think the author chose this particular word? • How does that word help you understand ___?
DICTIONARY: Use a dictionary for highly sophisticated words	Has trouble locating words in dictionary Cannot determine the right definition when presented with multiple definitions	• *Teach children how to look up words in the dictionary and thesaurus.* • Look at [vocabulary word]; which definition applies to how the author used this word?

600L–700L: Comprehension		
CORE ELEMENT and IDEAL STUDENT ACTIONS	**TYPICAL STUDENT ERRORS**	**TEACHER-TO-STUDENT PROMPTS** to encourage these actions
GENRE II: Use knowledge of literary genre and text structure (chapter, scene, stanza) to support comprehension RL.3.5 Engage in reading different genres RL.3.10	Does not use text structures of a particular genre to support comprehension	• In this poem, how does the third stanza build off the second one? • What are the different scenes of this play? How does the setting change in each scene? • Think about what you know about [genre, e.g., fantasy] books as you read. What kind of book is this? How does knowing that help you? • What did the writer do to make the characters (animals or human) seem as though they were real? • How does this genre help you to understand ___?
EVALUATE INTERPRETATIONS: Entertain and evaluate differing interpretations of a story Use comparison and analogy to explain ideas SL.4.3	Does not entertain others' interpretations and evaluate responses	• Does anyone else have a different interpretation? • You've heard several answers and reasons. Which answer makes more sense to you? • What have you [read, heard, seen] that can help explain this passage? • Let's consider this: you think the reason the character did ___ is because of [restate student answer]. So what does that tell you? • *Restate student's interpretation for other students to evaluate.* • *Prompt other students to build off another's answer.*

600L–700L: Comprehension

CORE ELEMENT and IDEAL STUDENT ACTIONS	TYPICAL STUDENT ERRORS	TEACHER-TO-STUDENT PROMPTS to encourage these actions
APPLY PRIOR KNOWLEDGE: Apply knowledge from other sources (personal experience, media) to examine ideas in nonfiction texts RI.4.6		• Do you remember when you learned to ride a bike? What was it like? • Does thinking about that experience help you to understand what the character is going through here?

700L–800L: Vocabulary

CORE ELEMENT and IDEAL STUDENT ACTIONS	TYPICAL STUDENT ERRORS	TEACHER-TO-STUDENT PROMPTS to encourage these actions
VOCABULARY IN CONTEXT: Define words in text using context clues and use these words to speak about themes of the text	Has difficulty defining words in context Is unable to recognize other key words or phrases that reveal the meaning of a word Has difficulty identifying *why* an author used a specific word or phrase	• What does [unknown word] mean? • What other [words, phrases] helped you determine the meaning of [unknown word]? • Why did the author choose this [unknown word] to describe [setting, character, plot]? • What did the author mean when he/she said [excerpt from text with unknown word]? • How does the author's use of [unknown word] help you better understand the main idea of the story?

700L–800L: Comprehension		
CORE ELEMENT and IDEAL STUDENT ACTIONS	**TYPICAL STUDENT ERRORS**	**TEACHER-TO-STUDENT PROMPTS to encourage these actions**
CONNECT BETWEEN TEXTS: Connect different texts to build understanding of common themes about a topic	Has difficulty comparing and contrasting themes across texts Has difficulty applying knowledge of one theme to another text	• What [ideas, themes] are found in both texts? • How do these [ideas, themes] help us better understand these texts?
SUSPENSE: Recognize how the author built suspense throughout the story	Has difficulty recognizing events and clues in a text that can foreshadow a later event	• Which [words, phrases, sentences] give you a hint about what could happen next? • When does the author leave you "on the edge of your seat"? • At which point in the story did you feel you had to keep reading to find out what was going to happen? • What made you gasp?

800L–900L: Vocabulary		
CORE ELEMENT and IDEAL STUDENT ACTIONS	**TYPICAL STUDENT ERRORS**	**TEACHER-TO-STUDENT PROMPTS** to encourage these actions
CONTENT SPECIFIC: Solve content-specific words and technical words using graphics and definitions embedded in the text RI.3.4, RI.4.4	Does not pay attention to the context clues that define content-specific words	• Why is this word in bold? • What clues can you use to figure out the word? • What does the text tell us this word means? • How does this word describe ___ in the text?

800L–900L: Comprehension		
CORE ELEMENT and IDEAL STUDENT ACTIONS	**TYPICAL STUDENT ERRORS**	**TEACHER-TO-STUDENT PROMPTS** to encourage these actions
MULTIPLE EVENTS: Keep track of multiple events happening simultaneously RL.3.1, RL,4.1	Cannot make inferences that connect what is happening simultaneously or in two different sections of story	• What happened in the previous chapter? How was that connected to what's happening right now? • What was happening while ___ happened? How do you know? • What did [character] do when ___? • Tell me about [multiple events].
NEW PERSPECTIVES: Demonstrate learning new content and perspectives from reading Distinguish their own perspective from the character's RI.3.6	Does not recognize the different perspectives about the same event or theme Focuses on problem from own perspective	• How does the [time period, societal characteristic] affect the perspective of the character? Is this [similar to, different from] how people feel today? • How would you describe this character's feelings toward ___? • Characters have a perspective. What is this character's perspective? • How does this character see the problem? Compare with [other character or your own]. How are they the same or different?

800L–900L: Comprehension		
CORE ELEMENT and IDEAL STUDENT ACTIONS	**TYPICAL STUDENT ERRORS**	**TEACHER-TO-STUDENT PROMPTS to encourage these actions**
APPLY NEW CONTENT KNOWLEDGE: Build background knowledge to connect multiple texts RI.3.9	Has difficulty extending information learned from a nonfiction text to understand a narrative text	• What information did you learn from this [informational text] that helps you understand this story? • Which part of this [informational text] helped you better understand what the character is thinking? • What do you know about this subject from what you've read? • Use what you read to help you understand what is happening now in this story. • So I'm going to challenge you. I hear you talking about ____, but I think we have another way to talk about ____ based on another text we read.
SETTING: Understand and talk about the role of the setting in realistic fiction and historical fiction RL.4.3	Has difficulty describing how the setting impacts the characters or plot	• How are the characters reacting to this time period? • Would this story have been different if it had taken place in another [area, country, time period]? How so?

900+: Vocabulary		
CORE ELEMENT and IDEAL STUDENT ACTIONS	**TYPICAL STUDENT ERRORS**	**TEACHER-TO-STUDENT PROMPTS** to encourage these actions
CONNOTATIVE MEANING: Recognizes connotative meanings and their impact on the characters or plot RI.3.9	Only recognizes the literal meaning Does not have enough schema to understand the connotative meaning	• What does the word *home* mean in this text? [warmth, love, comfort] • The author wrote the word ___ to describe ___.? What did he/she really mean? • Have you heard this phrase before? Where have you heard it? How was it used? Do you think it is being used the same way here?

900+: Comprehension		
CORE ELEMENT and IDEAL STUDENT ACTIONS	**TYPICAL STUDENT ERRORS**	**TEACHER-TO-STUDENT PROMPTS** to encourage these actions
SYMBOLISM: Notice the writer's use of symbolism RL.4.4	Relies too heavily on the literal meaning of an object, setting, or person	• When you think of ____, what do you think of? • What does the ____ represent? • The author mentions ____ in the story.? What is the meaning of this ____? • If ____ were not mentioned in the story, how would this story be different? • Have you seen or read about this symbol in any other works of art? How was it used? • I want you to bring it back to the symbolism of ____; how does that relate to themes in the story? • How does ____ help you better understand ____?
GENRE III: Use knowledge genre's structural elements (verse, rhythm, meter) to support comprehension RL.4.5	Does not use structural elements to support comprehension	• Why did the author use this meter? • What would the stage look like in this performance? • What was the role of the joker in this play?
KEEPING TRACK OF DIALOGUE: Keep track of assigned and unassigned dialogue RL.5.3	Occasionally gets lost in which characters are speaking	• There was a line switch [return sweep]. Who is speaking now? • Which character said ____? How do you know?

INFORMATIONAL GUIDED READING PROMPTING GUIDE, BY LEXILE LEVEL

Up to 50L: Concepts Related to Print and Word Solving		
CORE ELEMENT and IDEAL STUDENT ACTIONS	**TYPICAL STUDENT ERRORS**	**TEACHER-TO-STUDENT PROMPTS to encourage these actions**
1-to-1: Following print with finger RF.K.1.A, RF.K.1.C	Does not point to the text at all (e.g., points at picture)	• Point to the words as you read. • Were there enough words? • Did you run out of words?
PATTERN: Recognize or remember pattern of words in text	Cannot identify the pattern of words that repeat on each page	• Does this page start the same way?
1st LETTER ID: Recognize letter names and most letter sounds RF.K.1.D	Cannot solve an unknown word (the first letter can help)	• What word would make sense that starts with ___? • What letter is at the beginning of ___?
HIGH FREQ 2: Use a few high-frequency words to monitor reading RF.K.3.C	Cannot recognize a high-frequency word *in context*	• That's a sight word. • Find the word ___ and point to it. • Have you seen these words before?

50L–100L: Word Solving and Fluency		
CORE ELEMENT and IDEAL STUDENT ACTIONS	**TYPICAL STUDENT ERRORS**	**TEACHER-TO-STUDENT PROMPTS to encourage these actions**
1st LETTER SOUND: Use first-letter sounds when attempting to problem-solve unknown words RF.K.3.A	Mistakes the first sound or mistakes the first blend	• Get your mouth ready. • Do you know a word that starts with those letters? • Check it. Does it look right? Does it sound right? • Do you think it looks like ____? • Do you know a word with those letters? • Does that make sense? • What was wrong? Try it again. Were you right?
HIGH FREQ 3: Use a core of high-frequency words automatically to support reading RF.K.3.C	Sounds out word but never puts sounds all together	• Can you read the whole word at once?
SUBTLE PICS: Use pictures to solve unknown words (subtle connection between picture and text)	Cannot solve an unknown word (the picture can help)	• Can the picture help you figure out that word?

Up to 100L: Comprehension		
CORE ELEMENT and IDEAL STUDENT ACTIONS	**TYPICAL STUDENT ERRORS**	**TEACHER-TO-STUDENT PROMPTS to encourage these actions**
BASIC STRUCTURE: Identify front and back covers, title, and author RI.K.5, RI.K.6	Cannot identify front and back covers, title, or author	• Can you point to the [front cover, back cover]? • Who is the author? Who is the illustrator? Where did you find this information? • What is the title of the story? How did you know this was the title?

FACT: Recall factual information and find it in a text
 	
RI.K.5, RI.K.8
	Incorrectly finds examples from the text
	
	Cannot explain what examples in the text demonstrate
		• *Ask children to talk about the text's basic examples. For instance:*
		  ○ What were some of the examples in the text?
		  ○ What does the text say about ___?
		  ○ What is the example on page ___ telling us?
		• What are the key aspects about this passage that you understand?

TEXT FEATURES I —PICTURES: Put together details from pictures to make sense of a story RI.K.2, RI.K.7, RI.1.6	Struggles to make sense of the story	• Look at the picture. What is this showing us? • What does the picture tell us about the [topic of the text]? • [After student response]: Why did the author include this image?

Up to 100L: Comprehension		
CORE ELEMENT and IDEAL STUDENT ACTIONS	**TYPICAL STUDENT ERRORS**	**TEACHER-TO-STUDENT PROMPTS to encourage these actions**
BACKGROUND KNOWLEDGE I —PERSONAL EXPERIENCE: Draw on personal experiences to support understanding of the text	Has difficulty connecting to background knowledge to make simple inferences about the text	• What do you know about ___? So based on that knowledge, what is happening in the text? Why ___? • What in the text sparked you to make a connection? How does that help you understand ___? • Reread the page. What does that make you think of?

100L–150L: Word Solving and Fluency		
CORE ELEMENT and IDEAL STUDENT ACTIONS	**TYPICAL STUDENT ERRORS**	**TEACHER-TO-STUDENT PROMPTS to encourage these actions**
BLENDS AND ENDS: Attend to initial blends and inflectional endings: *-ing, -ed, -s* RF.K.3.A, RF.1.3.F	States initial blend but gets rest of the word wrong OR States correct root word but misses ending (e.g., *fish* vs. *fisher, run* vs., *runs*)	• Read through the word. • It could be ____, but look at ____. • Check the beginning and ending letters. • You made a mistake. Can you find it? • How does that word start? Try it again with the ending. • Read that again. • Try ____. Would that sound right? • Would that make sense?
MIDDLE VOWELS: Attend to middle vowel sounds RF.K.3.B	Does not pay attention to the middle of the word	• What sound does [vowel] make?
HIGH FREQ 4: Recognize many high-frequency and other known words quickly and automatically RF.K.3.C		• You've seen that word before. Do you think it looks like ____?
WORD FAMILIES: Use word families to figure out some new words RF.K.3.D		• Do you know a word like that? • What word family might help you figure it out? • It rhymes with ____. Can you change the first sound?

100L–150L: Word Solving and Fluency

CORE ELEMENT and IDEAL STUDENT ACTIONS	TYPICAL STUDENT ERRORS	TEACHER-TO-STUDENT PROMPTS to encourage these actions
SELF-CORRECT: Begin to check one source of information against another to confirm, make another attempt, or self-correct RF.1.4.C, RF.2.4.C		• Do you remember reading that word before? • Does that make sense? What do you think is happening in the text?
PHRASE-READ: Move away from finger pointing and word-by-word reading; read with 2–3 word phrasing RF.K.4, RF.1.4	Reads word-by-word and doesn't connect in phrasing; points finger at text	• Put the words together so it sounds like you're talking. • Can you read it with your eyes?
REREAD: Reread to problem-solve and confirm new words and to maintain meaning	Doesn't reread to confirm meaning	• Now read that again all together.

100L–150L: Comprehension		
CORE ELEMENT and IDEAL STUDENT ACTIONS	**TYPICAL STUDENT ERRORS**	**TEACHER-TO-STUDENT PROMPTS to encourage these actions**
MAIN IDEA I—TOPIC: State the topic of a descriptive text RI.K.2	Has difficulty identifying the main topic of the book and can only state small supporting details	• What is the main topic of this text? • What did the author want us to know about [topic]? • Give at least three pieces of evidence from the text that support the main topic. • How did the organization of this information support the main topic?
CITING EVIDENCE I —DETAIL: Recall text details and use them to clarify meaning RI.K.2	Does not go back to the text to search for specific facts and information	• Look back to find where the writer discusses ____. • What is your evidence for that? • What details help you understand this idea? How? • On what page did you find evidence about ____? • Reread page ____. What did you learn about ____?

100L–150L: Comprehension		
CORE ELEMENT and IDEAL STUDENT ACTIONS	**TYPICAL STUDENT ERRORS**	**TEACHER-TO-STUDENT PROMPTS to encourage these actions**
COMPARE AND CONTRAST I —CONNECTIONS WITHIN A TEXT: Describe the connection between two individuals, events, ideas, or pieces of information in a text	Is unable to compare and contrast two different individuals, events, ideas, or pieces of information in order within a topic	• Where in the text did we learn about [individual, event, idea, piece of information]? • What do you know about [individual, event, idea, piece of information]? • What aspects of [individual, event, idea, piece of information A] and [individual, event, idea, piece of information B] are similar?

150L–250L: Word Solving and Fluency		
CORE ELEMENT and IDEAL STUDENT ACTIONS	**TYPICAL STUDENT ERRORS**	**TEACHER-TO-STUDENT PROMPTS to encourage these actions**
PUNCTUATE: Begin to use punctuation to assist smooth reading RF.1.1.A	Reads straight through punctuation	• Try it again and [stop at the period, pause at the comma, make your voice go up at the question mark].

CHUNK LETTERS: Use letter-sound relationships and letter chunks to decode many new words; blend consonants and vowels to problem-solve new words
 	
RF.1.3.B
	Incorrectly reads a word
	
	Says a long vowel sound when it should be a short vowel
		• *Prompt children to use the phonetic patterns they know—for example:*
		  ○ Could it be a blend?
		  ○ Do you think it looks like a "silent e" word?

SPEED: Move quickly through the text: 40 words per minute RF.2.4.B	Reads very slowly	• Try that again. • Can you read this quickly?
CHECK NEW WORDS: Check new words using multiple sources of information (visual, syntax, and meaning) RF.2.4.C, RI.K.4		• You said ___. Does that make sense? • Does that sound right? • Does that look right? • You said ___. Can we say it that way?

150L–250L: Comprehension		
CORE ELEMENT and IDEAL STUDENT ACTIONS	**TYPICAL STUDENT ERRORS**	**TEACHER-TO-STUDENT PROMPTS to encourage these actions**
COMPARE AND CONTRAST II —CROSS-TEXT: Identify basic similarities and differences between two texts on the same topic (e.g., in illustrations, descriptions, or procedures) RI.K.9, RI.1.9	Is unable to identify basic similarities or differences between two texts on the same topic: illustrations, descriptions, procedures	• How did [text A/B] use [illustrations, descriptions, procedures, etc.] to explain [topic]? • How did the author in [text A] provide information about [topic]? How did the author in [text B] provide information about [topic]? • What were the similarities/differences about the way the information about [topic] was presented?

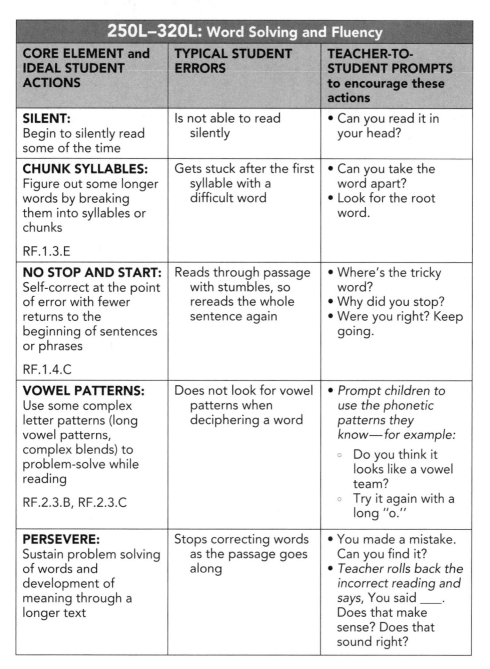

250L–320L: Word Solving and Fluency

CORE ELEMENT and IDEAL STUDENT ACTIONS	TYPICAL STUDENT ERRORS	TEACHER-TO-STUDENT PROMPTS to encourage these actions
SILENT: Begin to silently read some of the time	Is not able to read silently	• Can you read it in your head?
CHUNK SYLLABLES: Figure out some longer words by breaking them into syllables or chunks RF.1.3.E	Gets stuck after the first syllable with a difficult word	• Can you take the word apart? • Look for the root word.
NO STOP AND START: Self-correct at the point of error with fewer returns to the beginning of sentences or phrases RF.1.4.C	Reads through passage with stumbles, so rereads the whole sentence again	• Where's the tricky word? • Why did you stop? • Were you right? Keep going.

VOWEL PATTERNS: Use some complex letter patterns (long vowel patterns, complex blends) to problem-solve while reading
 	
RF.2.3.B, RF.2.3.C
	Does not look for vowel patterns when deciphering a word	• *Prompt children to use the phonetic patterns they know—for example:*
		  ◦ Do you think it looks like a vowel team?
		  ◦ Try it again with a long "o."

PERSEVERE: Sustain problem solving of words and development of meaning through a longer text	Stops correcting words as the passage goes along	• You made a mistake. Can you find it? • *Teacher rolls back the incorrect reading and says,* You said ___. Does that make sense? Does that sound right?

250L–320L: Comprehension		
CORE ELEMENT and IDEAL STUDENT ACTIONS	TYPICAL STUDENT ERRORS	TEACHER-TO-STUDENT PROMPTS to encourage these actions
CAUSE AND EFFECT: Describe the cause and effect of specific events RI.K.3, RI.1.3	Struggles to identify the cause or effect of an action	• Does this connect to another part of the text? How? • According to the text, what caused ____ to happen? • What was the effect of ____?
CITING EVIDENCE II: Recall details from the text to support answers to inferential and critical thinking questions, with some support RI.1.1, RI.2.1, RI.3.1, RI.4.1	Can state inference but without support from text Primarily uses text evidence but does not support with inference	• What makes you think that? What in the text gives you that idea? • Look at this section of the text. How can you use it to come to that conclusion? • Look at page ____. Where is there evidence to support your inference? • Where might we find evidence for that idea? • Based on what you know about [topic], what can you infer about this section?
DEFINITIONS I —GLOSSARY: Use a glossary to understand the definition of key or bolded words in the text RI.1.4, RI.1.5	Is unable to use the glossary to define a term from the text	• Where in the text does the author discuss [key domain-specific term]? • What information does the author give us about [key domain-specific term]?

320L–380L: Word Solving and Fluency

CORE ELEMENT and IDEAL STUDENT ACTIONS	TYPICAL STUDENT ERRORS	TEACHER-TO-STUDENT PROMPTS to encourage these actions

LETTER PATTERNS: Use knowledge of common letter patterns and long vowel patterns to problem-solve and decode new words
 	
RF.1.3.C
	Does not try another sound for irregular words (soft "c" and "g" rules)
	
	Has difficulty decoding complex vowel patterns
		• *Encourage flexibility—for example:*
		  ◦ What other sound does the letter "g" make?
		  ◦ What could you try?
		  ◦ Have you seen that vowel combination before?

BIG WORD CHUNK: Use syllables and letter chunks consistently for problem-solving longer two-syllable words
 	
RF.1.3.E, RF.2.3.D
	Does not say each chunk in a word; omits part of the word (including middle and ending blends)	• *Prompt children to use the syllable patterns they know—for example:*
		  ◦ What is the first syllable?
		  ◦ Do you think it looks like a closed syllable?
		  ◦ Do you recognize a prefix? A suffix?

SILENT SPEED: Read most texts fluently, slowing down to figure out new words and then resuming speed Read silently most of the time	Not able to resume speed after slowing down for a new word Reads aloud (or in a whisper)	• Put the words together so it sounds like talking. • Can you read it in your head?
AUTOPILOT: Read most regularly spelled two-syllable words automatically RF.2.3.C	Does not try another sound for irregular words (soft "c" and "g" rules)	• Look at the whole word. • *For the child who overly relies on decoding, ask:* Do you know the word by sight?

320L–380L: Word Solving and Fluency		
CORE ELEMENT and IDEAL STUDENT ACTIONS	**TYPICAL STUDENT ERRORS**	**TEACHER-TO-STUDENT PROMPTS to encourage these actions**
IRREGULAR WORDS: Figure out many irregularly spelled words: e.g., with diphthongs or special vowel spellings RF.2.3.E, RF.2.3.F		• Do you know any words like that? What could you try?
PUNCTUATE: Read new text in 3–4 word phrases with attention to punctuation in most texts RF.2.4.B	Does not use dialogue tags to read with meaning	• Read it with expression. • Look for the punctuation.

320L–380L: Comprehension		
CORE ELEMENT and IDEAL STUDENT ACTIONS	**TYPICAL STUDENT ERRORS**	**TEACHER-TO-STUDENT PROMPTS to encourage these actions**
AUTHOR'S PURPOSE I —DESCRIBE REASONS: Describe how reasons support specific points the author makes in a text RI.1.8, RI.2.6	Is unable to identify how reasons support specific points made by the author	• Why did the author write this text? • What does the author want us to know about [topic]? • Why is [reason] important to this point? • What would happen if the author did not include [reason] to support this point?
COMPARE AND CONTRAST III —IMPORTANT DETAILS: Compare and contrast the most important points presented by two texts on the same topic RI.2.9	Is unable to compare and contrast key points across two texts	• Look back to [paragraph, heading, section]. What is the author's point in this [paragraph, heading, section]? • Based on the points that the author makes, which is the most important? • What would happen if the author did not include [point] about [topic]? • How is [point] from [text A] the same as or different from [point] from [text B]?

380L–500L: Word Solving		
CORE ELEMENT and IDEAL STUDENT ACTIONS	**TYPICAL STUDENT ERRORS**	**TEACHER-TO-STUDENT PROMPTS to encourage these actions**
WORD MASTERY: Flexibly apply word-solving strategies to complex multisyllable words RF.3.3.C	Slows down to word-solve using only one strategy	• What can you do to figure it out? • What do you already know that might help you?
CONTENT SPECIFIC: Solve content-specific words and technical words using graphics and definitions embedded in the text RI.2.4, RI.3.4	Does not pay attention to the context clues that define content-specific words	• Why is this word in bold? • What clues can you use to figure out the word? • What does the text tell us this word means? • How does this word describe _____ in the text?

380L–500L: Comprehension		
CORE ELEMENT and IDEAL STUDENT ACTIONS	**TYPICAL STUDENT ERRORS**	**TEACHER-TO-STUDENT PROMPTS to encourage these actions**
DEFINITIONS II —SINGLE SECTION: Define the characteristics and behavior of a topic that appears in a single section but is not explicitly stated in the text RI.1.4, RI.1.5	Is unable to define a term from the text	• Where in the text does the author discuss [key domain-specific term]? • What information does the author give us about [key domain-specific term]?
ORGANIZING INFORMATION: Organize information in a text on a given topic in a logical order based on size, time, distance, etc. RI.2.3, RI.3.3, RI.3.8	Does not order information accurately based on size, time, distance, etc. Does not identify the basis for ordering that the author used	• What information is the author giving us that could help us order this information? • If we are ordering our information by [size, time, distance, etc.], then what would come first? What would come second? Why? • How did the author order this information? How does that ordering help us to better understand the information? • Did the author order this information from the [largest] to the [smallest] or from the [smallest] to the [largest]?

380L–500L: Comprehension		
CORE ELEMENT and IDEAL STUDENT ACTIONS	**TYPICAL STUDENT ERRORS**	**TEACHER-TO-STUDENT PROMPTS** to encourage these actions
CITING EVIDENCE III: Use details and events in a story to support answers to inferential and critical thinking questions RI.1.1, RI.2.1	Can state inference but without support from text Primarily uses text evidence but does not support with inference	• What makes you think that? What in the text gives you that idea? • Look at this section of the text. How can you use it to come to that conclusion? • Where might we find evidence for that idea? • Based on what you know about [topic], what can you infer about this section?
COMPARE AND CONTRAST IV —IDEAS ACROSS TEXT: Be able to compare and contrast the most important key details for a key point presented in two texts on the same topic RI.3.9	Is able to note the key points in two texts, but unable to cite the details that support each of these points Describes key points vaguely without using key details to sharpen their description of the difference between the two	• What information presented in [text A] and [text B] is similar/different? What does this mean for our understanding? • Look back to [paragraph, heading, section]. What details does the author include to support this point? • Based on the details that both authors included, what are the most important details? • Why is this detail important for this [point]? • What would happen if the author did not include [detail] about [point]?

500L–550L: Comprehension		
CORE ELEMENT and IDEAL STUDENT ACTIONS	**TYPICAL STUDENT ERRORS**	**TEACHER-TO-STUDENT PROMPTS to encourage these actions**
MAIN IDEA II —OVERALL TEXT: Identify the primary idea of an informational text that has one main idea and sections that follow a logical order RI.2.5, RI.3.2	Is unable to add up key details across sections of the text to defend a main idea	• What is the most important thing to know about the passage as a whole? What is the author's purpose in writing this text? • What are the main ideas of each subsection? • How does [section A] help us to understand [section B?] • How can you connect these ideas to generate the overall main idea of the text? • Why did the author include each of these sections? How does that help you understand the main idea? • What do you notice about the heading of each section? How do the headings help us understand the main idea?

500L–550L: Comprehension		
CORE ELEMENT and IDEAL STUDENT ACTIONS	**TYPICAL STUDENT ERRORS**	**TEACHER-TO-STUDENT PROMPTS to encourage these actions**
AUTHOR'S PURPOSE II —POINT OF VIEW: Be able to distinguish their own point of view from that of the author of a text RI.3.6	Is unable to identify the author's point view	• What is the author's point of view? • What facts did the author choose that revealed his/her point of view? • What reasons does the author provide to support his/her point of view? • Do you have the same point of view as the author? A different point of view? What points support your point of view? • What are the facts the author may have purposely left out of the book?
CITING EVIDENCE IV: Cite the best evidence from a story to support answers to inferential and critical thinking questions RL.2.7, RL.4.1	Does not weigh the value of two pieces of evidence to determine which is stronger Relies primarily on the first evidence found	• Is there another piece of evidence that can be used to support your argument? • Compare your evidence to [another passage]. Which is stronger evidence? • How does that [word, phrase] make your evidence strong?
BACKGROUND KNOWLEDGE II —OTHER SOURCES: Acquire background knowledge from other sources to support comprehension of new concepts	Does not acquire background knowledge from other texts or sources to draw connections to the text	• What do you know about [person, place, thing, idea] from the other text we just read? • How does your understanding of [other source] help you understand this text?

500L–550L: Comprehension		
CORE ELEMENT and IDEAL STUDENT ACTIONS	**TYPICAL STUDENT ERRORS**	**TEACHER-TO-STUDENT PROMPTS to encourage these actions**
EXPLAIN PROCESSES: Explain processes by defining sequential steps and their relationship to one another RI.3.3, RI.3.8	Is unable to identify all steps in a process Is unable to explain an individual step in a process Is unable to identify the relationship between two steps in a process	• What happened first in the process? What happened next? • Before [step] can happen, what has to happen first? • Why is [step] important in this process? • What would happen if you did not include [step] in this process?
TEXT FEATURES II —SUBSECTIONS: Use headings and tables of contents to find the right subsection to answer a specific question RI.2.5	Is unable to understand the question well enough to determine where to gather information Is unable to locate the right subsection to answer questions about the text	• What is the question asking for in your own words? • What key concept(s) comes up in the question that you recognize from your reading? • Which heading connects with the concept in the question? • Are there any diagrams or pictures that connect to the concept in the question?

550L–600L: Comprehension		
CORE ELEMENT and IDEAL STUDENT ACTIONS	**TYPICAL STUDENT ERRORS**	**TEACHER-TO-STUDENT PROMPTS** to encourage these actions
MAIN IDEA III —SUBSECTIONS: Identify the primary idea of a section of informational text with one main idea	Is unable to add up key details from a section of the text to defend that subsection's main idea	• Reread [section X]. What is the main idea of this section? • I see that you've pulled information from the [beginning, middle, end] of this section. Is there any additional information you could pull from the other parts that would inform your answer? • What are three of the most important facts the writer includes in this section? How do these facts connect to each other? • How do these details add up to a main idea? • What do you notice about the title? Why is this useful?
TEXT FEATURES III —CAPTIONS: Use captions and their corresponding images to understand a core detail or concept from the text RI.2.5	Does not use images and their captions to contribute to understanding the text Is unable to connect the caption to the topic of the text	• What is the question asking for in your own words? • What key concept(s) come up in the question that you recognize from your reading? • Which heading connects with the concept in the question? • Are there any diagrams or pictures that connect to the concept in the question?

550L–600L: Comprehension		
CORE ELEMENT and IDEAL STUDENT ACTIONS	**TYPICAL STUDENT ERRORS**	**TEACHER-TO-STUDENT PROMPTS to encourage these actions**
CITING EVIDENCE V: Evaluate the use of evidence by another reader in order to push inferential and critical thinking	Has difficulty determining the best evidence from the text to support inferential or critical thinking Does not understand how another reader drew a conclusion from the text	• How could you push your peer to make a better inference? What text would he/she need to cite? • How did your thinking change after rereading this evidence? • Who has stronger evidence to support this thinking? • What do you think about [other reader]'s evidence? Is it the right evidence? Why or why not?

600L–700L: Comprehension		
CORE ELEMENT and IDEAL STUDENT ACTIONS	**TYPICAL STUDENT ERRORS**	**TEACHER-TO-STUDENT PROMPTS to encourage these actions**
MAIN IDEA IV —OVERALL TEXT: Identify the primary idea of an informational text for which they have to deduce the connections between multiple sections RI.3.4, RI.4.2	Is unable to add up key details across sections of a text to defend a main idea	• What is the most important thing to know about the passage as a whole? • What are the main ideas of each subsection? • How does [section A] help us understand [section B]? • How can you connect these ideas to generate the overall main idea of the text? • Why did the author include each of these sections? How does that help you understand the main idea? • What do you notice about the heading of each section? How do they help us understand the main idea?

600L–700L: Comprehension		
CORE ELEMENT and IDEAL STUDENT ACTIONS	**TYPICAL STUDENT ERRORS**	**TEACHER-TO-STUDENT PROMPTS to encourage these actions**
RETELL: Retell informational texts using main ideas, text features, and key vocabulary RI.2.5	Uses factual information in retell that is not the subsection's main ideas Is unable to synthesize information Does not include text features or domain-specific vocabulary	• You included too many facts. Tell me the main ideas of each subsection. • What were the most important things this writer had to say? Summarize the main ideas in the text. • How could you make your retell more concise? • What are you missing in your retell? • What are the key vocabulary from this text? • How could you enhance your retell by using key vocabulary from the text? How could you include [domain vocabulary] in your answer?

600L–700L: Comprehension		
CORE ELEMENT and IDEAL STUDENT ACTIONS	**TYPICAL STUDENT ERRORS**	**TEACHER-TO-STUDENT PROMPTS to encourage these actions**
DEFINITIONS III —CROSS-SECTION: Define the characteristics or behavior of the key topic that gets defined across multiple sections RI.3.4, RI.3.5, RI.4.3	Is unable to define the characteristics or behavior of a key concept that appears across multiple subsections Gives definitions that are partial or limited to information from one section	• What are the key characteristics or behaviors of [key domain-specific vocabulary]? • I want more than just the simple definition [on p. X]. What are the additional characteristics you gather from other parts of the text? • How does [section X] add to the definition you've provided? • What else does this definition need to have to be complete?
TEXT FEATURES IV —STAND-ALONE VISUALS: Utilize stand-alone (don't require text to be understood) charts, diagrams, or pictures to understand text RI.1.7, RI.2.7, RI.3.7	Is unable to interpret a chart or diagram Does not integrate understanding of stand-alone visuals into comprehension of concept	• Why did the author include this [chart, diagram, model, etc.]? • How does this [chart, diagram, model, etc.] add to our understanding? • If the author removed this [chart, diagram, model, etc.], what information would we lose?

700L–800L: Comprehension		
CORE ELEMENT and IDEAL STUDENT ACTIONS	**TYPICAL STUDENT ERRORS**	**TEACHER-TO-STUDENT PROMPTS to encourage these actions**
DEFINITIONS IV —DEPENDENT CONCEPTS: Understand abstract conceptual ideas that depend on understanding other previously unknown concepts from a text	Makes literal, partial understandings of key abstract concepts in the text Confuses a concrete example as the complete definition of an abstract idea Doesn't understand preliminary abstract concept to contribute to understanding of the key abstract concept of the text	• Let's go back to [abstract concept A from one section of the text]. How do you define or describe it? • How does [abstract concept A] help you understand [abstract concept B]? • That's a concrete example but not the definition of the concept. What are other concrete examples? [Student or teacher gives more examples.] So what would be a general definition of the concept you could draw from these examples? • If we want to understand [abstract concept B], what do we first need to understand?

700L–800L: Comprehension		
CORE ELEMENT and IDEAL STUDENT ACTIONS	TYPICAL STUDENT ERRORS	TEACHER-TO-STUDENT PROMPTS to encourage these actions
TEXT FEATURES V —DEPENDENT VISUALS: Understand charts, diagrams, or pictures that require the text to be understood; use those visuals to deepen understanding of the text	Tries to understand charts without referring to the text Doesn't enhance his/her understanding with the visuals	• What is this [example, experiment, chart, diagram] trying to tell us? • What evidence in the text can you find to support your interpretation? • Put this [example, experiment, chart, diagram] into your own words. • Did you [try the experiment, look at the diagram]? How does that help you better understand the text? • How does this [example, experiment, chart, diagram] support what the text is saying?

800L–900L: Comprehension		
CORE ELEMENT and IDEAL STUDENT ACTIONS	TYPICAL STUDENT ERRORS	TEACHER-TO-STUDENT PROMPTS to encourage these actions
MAIN IDEA V —MULTIPLE MAIN IDEAS: Identify the overarching explicit main idea and additional implicit main ideas that occur across the text	Is unable to prioritize the explicit main idea Is unable to identify additional implicit main ideas that need to be inferred from the text	• You've mentioned one main idea of this text. But if you had to state the author's number-one purpose, what would it be? Does your main idea capture that purpose? • You've correctly identified the key main idea. What other main ideas are implicit in this text? • Look at the different sections. Where do you see new ideas forming that go beyond the central idea of the text? • Are there additional reasons why the author would write this text? • How does the author organize this text? How does this help us understand other ways the text could be used?

800L–900L: Comprehension		
CORE ELEMENT and IDEAL STUDENT ACTIONS	**TYPICAL STUDENT ERRORS**	**TEACHER-TO-STUDENT PROMPTS to encourage these actions**
AUTHOR'S PURPOSE III—EXPLAIN REASONING: Explain how an author uses reasoning or evidence to support particular points in a text. RI.2.8, RI.4.8	Is unable to explain how the author's evidence supports his/her argument Is unable to explain how the author's reasoning supports his/her argument	• How does the author's use of [evidence] help us understand [reason]? • How does the author's use of [reasoning] help us understand [point]? • What would happen if the author did not include [evidence, reason]? Would the author's point of view be as well supported? Why or why not? • Why do you think the author chose to include [evidence, reason]? What impact does it have on the reader?
TEXT FEATURE VI —HEADING FREE: Search for key information in a text without headings or where headings do not illuminate understanding	Is unable to identify section content in the absence of explicit headings Does not infer the organization of the text when it is not explicitly provided	• What does this section address? Make a note of it in the margin. • What can you do to remember what this section is about? • What is the organization of this text? [Chronological, steps, and the like] • If we wanted to make things clearer, how might we rename this section?

900L+: Comprehension		
CORE ELEMENT and IDEAL STUDENT ACTIONS	**TYPICAL STUDENT ERRORS**	**TEACHER-TO-STUDENT PROMPTS to encourage these actions**
DEFINITIONS V —ABSTRACT CONCEPTS: Combine text features, structures, and previously unknown concepts to understand abstract conceptual ideas that depend on understanding other previously unknown concepts from a text RI.4.4, RI.5.3	Is unable to synthesize new ideas from multiple concepts in the text	• How does what we know about [concept A] and what we know about [concept B] help us understand [concept C]? • If we want to understand [concept C], what else do we need to know about? • Let's add up what we know. If I know about [concept A] and [concept B], what are some things we can infer about [concept C]?

900L+: Comprehension		
CORE ELEMENT and IDEAL STUDENT ACTIONS	**TYPICAL STUDENT ERRORS**	**TEACHER-TO-STUDENT PROMPTS to encourage these actions**
COMPARE AND CONTRAST V —MULTIPLE MAIN IDEAS: Be able to describe the differences in focus and the information provided in multiple texts Be able to compare and contrast firsthand and secondhand accounts of the same event or topic in order to draw conclusions about that topic Be able to integrate information from two or more texts on the same topic in order to write or speak about the subject knowledgeably RI.4.6, RI.4.9	Is unable to compare and contrast information about the same topic, presented with different main ideas Has difficulty defining firsthand or secondhand accounts of the same event or topic Is unable to accurately pair information from two texts to support a single idea Does not integrate knowledge from a lower Lexile text to a higher Lexile text to develop meaning	• What are the [main ideas, key supporting details] in [text A] that help me to understand [topic]? What are the [main ideas, key supporting details] in [text B]? • How does [main idea, key supporting detail] from [text A] connect to [main idea, key supporting detail] from [text B]? How does this connection build my understanding of [topic]? • Is this a firsthand or secondhand account of [topic]? • What [concepts, ideas, evidence] from [lower Lexile text] helped me understand [higher Lexile text]? How did [lower Lexile text] help me understand [higher Lexile text]? • What are the larger conclusions we can draw about this topic based on all that we've read? • Which author presented the most compelling argument? • Which text gave you the most knowledge about [topic]? Why?

TOP TWELVE ACTION STEPS FOR GUIDED READING

Highest-Leverage Action Steps for Reading Results

Text Selection and Prework/Planning

1. Early reader— selecting text
   - Select a text that allows the student to practice the identified word-solving focus at least once per page.

2. Aligning the text to the data
   - Select the reading skill or standard based on the struggles revealed in the student learning data.
   - Select a text where students must use that skill or standard to get to the big idea of the text.
     - Example: If your students are struggling with character contrast, there should be two strong characters evident in the text.

3. Early reader— designing word-solving questions
   - Pre-identify and plan for words that may be unfamiliar to students during the reading, and script the appropriate prompt from the guided reading prompting guide into your lesson.
     - Example: If your student struggles with vowel rules, ask, "What vowel pattern can you use?" (*not* "Use the long 'a'")

4. Designing comprehension questions
   - Design factual, inference, and critical thinking comprehension questions that align to the guided reading prompting guides and the data for that group of students.
   - Anticipate wrong responses to inference and critical thinking questions and script into your lesson plan two to three prompts to address these wrong responses. (Use the guided reading prompting guides as your starting point.)
   - Ensure that the questions align to the reading focus you selected from the data.

(continued)

(*continued*)

Before Reading (Book Introduction)

5. Reading focus
   During the book introduction . . .

   - Use clear and concise language to state the reading focus and how you apply it.

   - Ask students to state their purpose for reading: "As I'm reading, I am thinking about [character motivation]."

6. Early reader word-solving
   When dealing with early readers with word-solving struggles . . .

   - Prior to reading the text, model the word-solving strategies that students will need the most.

7. Text preview
   When introducing the text . . .

   - For early readers: lead guided preview using the front cover and title.

   - For first grade and beyond: have students own the text preview— let them generate the preview themselves (using the front cover, back cover, title, first pages).

During Reading

8. Word-solving challenges
   When a student stumbles on an unfamiliar word . . .

   - Use a universal word-solving prompt that allows the student to do the majority of the work:

     - Roll back the response: "You said ___."

     - "Read through the word."

     - "Does that make sense?"

     - "Get your mouth ready."

- Have the guided reading prompting guide open on your desk or clipboard to the level of the students, and choose the appropriate prompt from the prompting guide.
  - Example: If your student struggles with vowel rules, ask, "What vowel pattern can you use?" (*not* "Use the long 'a'")
- Lean in to prompt one student's word-solving struggles, then lean back out to listen to errors in the whole group, then lean in again with the next student who is struggling.
- Have note-taking binder open and take notes on whether students are self-correcting without being prompted.

After Reading (Comprehension Conversation)

9. Retell (100L–500L)

- Start the comprehension discussion with a retell:
  - "Tell me what happened in the [story, chapter] as if I've never read it before."
- When the student reaches a natural break in the retell, call on another student to continue; repeat this process to include as many students as possible.
- Refrain from making such comments as "My next question is . . ."— that's not a conversation or discussion.
- Prompt the students to include the key reading focus within their retell.
  - Example: If the reading focus is character motivation, say, "Remember to include the characters' motivation in your retell."
- Infuse inference and critical thinking questions within the retell.

When the students are struggling with the retell . . .

- Factual: If total understanding has broken down, use a factual question— get back to the basics of the story:
  - "What did Tommy ask the teacher?" "What did Tommy want to be when he grows up?"

(*continued*)

(*continued*)

- Inference: If there is confusion about the key action in part of the story (if, for example, there are parts of the story where students don't understand Tommy's motivation), focus on a more specific chunk of the text and ask students to make an inference:

  ○ "Why did Tommy ask his teacher if he could skip math time?"

- Critical thinking: If students have a general understanding of the story (if, for example, the skill focus is motivation and they can identify Tommy's motivation throughout each part of the text), start with a critical thinking question:

  ○ "How did Tommy's motivation change throughout the text?"

10. Written response to text (500L+)

    - Review all written responses before beginning conversation: start the conversation with the error that you found in the written responses.

11. Increasing students' ownership of their own comprehension

    - Prompt students to use the habits of discussion (see prompts in Habits of Discussion Teacher Training and Prompting Guide)

      ○ Build off each other: "Who has a different point?" "Who can add to what [student] just said?"

      ○ Have students talk to members of their group instead of to the teacher (hand gesture)

    - Implement Turn and Talk.

    - Prompt students to give complete responses: don't assume what the student means or finish his or her thought.

    - Have students name the comprehension strategy they used to help them understand the text.

12. Student misunderstanding

    - Using the guided reading prompting guide, select the prompt that matches the student error.

    - Roll back the student misunderstanding to give you time to look at your preplanned prompts in your lesson plan or those in the guided reading prompting guide.

- If you had to prompt more than twice to guide them to the right answer, ask the original question again so that students can practice putting it all together without prompting.
- If 100 percent of the students are confused and no student is on the right track, do a think-aloud to model the thinking.
- Narrate the positive of strategies students are using: "I like the way Jimmy went back into the text."

Great Habits, Great Readers
Discussion Guide

School communities learn in lots of ways: through coaching, professional development, or collegial inquiry. We've constructed this chapter-by-chapter guide in hopes that it can be useful to a professional learning community (PLC) or grade-level team seeking to adopt some of the practices we've outlined. For each chapter, you'll find questions to help focus your discussion and lead you to some concrete action steps.

CHAPTER 1: HABITS OF THE CLASSROOM

Questions for Discussion

1. The parable of John Wooden and his players' socks has implications for how we view our classes. Can you think of an experience you've had as a teacher that links to Wooden's point?

2. Consider one of the core ideas for this chapter: the best classrooms don't just encourage student learning; they're designed for it. In what ways are classrooms at your school physically set up for reading instruction? In what places might your team push even further? Some aspects to consider include having

   - A discussion table where students can face each other to talk

   - A phonics instruction area with appropriate teaching posters

   - A reading comprehension area with space to display and use appropriate teaching posters

- A place where materials are organized and ready for student use (for example, pencils, erasers, dry-erase boards, markers, notebooks)
- An easy-to-use classroom library
- Pathways from one area to another that are clear and direct

3. Notice the amount of detail and care put into the most successful transitions. What transitions would be most powerful to teach and practice with students? Should these be consistent between classrooms? Possibilities include the following:

- Whole class entering or leaving the room
- Whole class putting away materials for one lesson and taking out materials for the next lesson
- Transition into or out of a new lesson segment
- Small groups moving between in-class stations
- Transition to and from independent reading time
- Choosing books
- Organizing materials for the next class segment

Question for Application

4. Choose one of the transitions you identified in question 3 and, with your team, develop a script for teaching it.

- What is the floor plan for how your students will move during the transition?
- What verbal or nonverbal cues will you use to let students know it's time to transition?

CHAPTER 2: HABITS OF DISCUSSION

Questions for Discussion

1. The chapter opens with two different case studies, depicting what is often described as the difference between a "Ping-Pong" and "volleyball" conversation. What makes the volleyball conversation so powerful for student learning?

2. The habits for sharing ideas in this chapter are linked to CCSS for Speaking & Listening for various grade levels. Which ones are most important for the grade level you teach? Which do you think your students are already doing?

- Listen and talk only in turn
- Speak audibly
- Speak in complete sentences
- Speak to the group, not the teacher

3. The habits for building ideas in this chapter are linked to CCSS for Speaking & Listening for various grade levels. Which ones are most important for the grade level you teach? Which do you think your students are already doing?

- Elaborate on your answer
- Build off other students' answers
- Evaluate others' answers
- Peer praise
- Prompt peers with universal prompts
- Hint, don't tell
- No hands
- Lead
- Come prepared in writing

4. This chapter closes by likening student discussions to Brazilian futsal. In what ways do you want your own class's discussions to match this analogy?

Questions for Application

5. Think about the habits for sharing ideas. How would you train students to meet the expectations for this standard? What phrases would you use to correct students? Can you think of any nonverbal gestures you might use?

6. Now consider the habits for building ideas. How will you train students to meet the expectations for the standards that you feel are most critical? What phrases or nonverbal gestures will you use to correct students?

CHAPTER 3: WHAT TO TEACH

Questions for Discussion

1. Review your current reading assessment. Do you have a test already available that

   - Assesses students over time, using texts of ever-increasing difficulty?
   - Assesses phonics, fluency, and accuracy?
   - Assesses comprehension skills that grow in complexity to match the increasing rigor of the passages?
   - Assesses comprehension with both narrative and informational texts?

Question for Application

2. Looking at the assessment you'll use, are there any places you'll need to supplement the information it provides?

CHAPTER 4: READ-ALOUD LESSONS

Questions for Discussion

1. The chapter opened with a case study from Ms. Indra. What are two concrete steps you think would best improve her read-aloud time overall?

2. Do you have ideas for read-aloud books that

   - Are of sufficient complexity (about a grade level above the grade you teach)?
   - Are of interest to students?
   - Easily and naturally support the teaching of one or more of the Common Core reading standards?
   - Provide a balance of fiction and nonfiction practice with the standards?

   If not, begin developing this list for your grade. You might consult Appendix B of the CCSS for ideas.

3. The point of this chapter isn't to abolish rocking chairs, just the rocking-chair mentality. What does that mean to you?

Questions for Application

4. It's one thing to think about creating stopping points in a text, but the best way to make that happen is to actually try it out. In your PLC, choose a book and a reading skill on which to focus. Then decide as a team where you think the stopping points should be, and label these with sticky notes.

5. Which of the read-aloud practices described will have the biggest impact on student learning in your class?

   - Hook the reader
   - Identify the skill
   - Preview the text
   - I Do (modeling the skill)
   - We Do (practicing the skill)
   - Check for understanding

CHAPTER 5: TEACHING COMPREHENSION SKILLS

Questions for Discussion

1. Consider the example of Meadowmount. How does slowing things down relate to the way you want your students to learn reading skills?

2. In your view, what are the advantages of teaching both the reader *and* the text? One activity to try in your PLC would be to create a master set of "teach the reader meets teach the text" questions for a certain book.

3. One of the biggest differences between a comprehension skills lesson and a read-aloud lesson is the inclusion of independent practice time. Why is this addition important enough to entail a whole new instruction type? What implications does it have for the kind of things you might teach in a comprehension lesson?

Question for Application

4. Which aspect of the comprehension skills lesson will you focus on first?

   - I Do
   - We Do
   - You Do

CHAPTER 6: TEACHING PHONICS

Questions for Discussion

1. Evaluate your phonics program. Do you have one that

   - Yields provable results for students?
   - Is focused on patterns and exceptions?
   - Provides frequent opportunities for students to practice?
   - Offers scripted lessons?

2. Besides what's scripted in your phonics program, there are plenty of ways to increase student practice during your lesson. Which of the following techniques feel most natural for you to try? Which have you had success with already?

   - Choral response
   - Whiteboard work
   - Individual turns
   - Smaller groups
   - Independent practice

Questions for Application

3. Once you've made sure that your students are getting enough practice, you can supercharge this time by making the practice more effective. Which of the techniques we described resonated most with you for your own class's needs?

   - Start from data
   - Know each sound . . . and defend it
   - Tap the power of visuals

4. In terms of having a fun—and effective—phonics lesson for your students, which of the strategies we identified would have the most impact for your class?

   - Precise praise
   - Game on!

- Chants and cheers

- Pacing

- Say it with your hands

CHAPTER 7: ANALYSIS AND ACTION

Questions for Discussion

1. Do you have a clear place to aggregate data for your assessments? If not, what would your ideal spreadsheet include? You'll find a sample assessment spreadsheet on the DVD.

2. What strikes you as particularly useful about the sample analysis and action plan we include in the chapter? What elements would you want to incorporate into your own data analysis?

3. What is the benefit of reviewing an action plan with an instructional coach or grade-level team?

Questions for Application

4. Making calendar space for assessments is one of the big rocks your team will want to tackle first. Where are the moments in your calendar that these can be woven into the school year? What strategies might you want to use to lighten the burden on the staff at these times?

5. Which aspect of data-driven instruction do you think will be most helpful for you to implement first?

- A calendar that supports assessment proctoring and grading

- A template for action planning from assessment data

- User-friendly mechanisms for collecting data

- A plan for meeting with an instructional coach to review data together

CHAPTER 8: GUIDED READING PLANNING

Questions for Discussion

1. It's important to see a guided reading lesson as fundamentally different from a comprehension skills lesson. What do you see as the chief distinctions?

2. Why do you think we chose to put the guided reading chapter right after the chapter on assessment?

3. What struck you as most powerful about the way Lauren Moyle plans? Was there something you're inspired to add or change in the way you plan?

4. Just because there are multiple possible "valid" inferences doesn't mean that every answer is acceptable. What, to you, distinguishes a valid inference from an invalid one?

5. What is the danger of "tipping" a text in your book introduction?

Questions for Application

6. The guided reading format is deliberately flexible to give you time with your students where they need you most. Considering what you know about your class, where do you think this will be?

7. On the basis of what you've learned in this chapter, how might you go about classifying guided reading texts for your class?

8. Which aspect of the guided reading lesson will you focus on first?

   - Prework
   - Before Reading
   - During Reading
   - After Reading

CHAPTER 9: GUIDED READING EXECUTION

Questions for Discussion

1. We refute the notion that the "magic" of the best guided reading lessons cannot be replicated by every dedicated teacher. What do you think are the critical moves to make this happen?

2. This chapter contains two real-life case studies of teachers who grew to become master educators. Do any of the problems they faced on their journey resonate with you?

Questions for Application

3. Try the prompting guide for yourself! Choosing a reading level and skill focus that would be useful for your class, see what questions you can develop by using the prompting guide. We recommend that you hold a simulation discussion with your team, then debrief what the experience felt like as students or as teachers.

4. This chapter discusses guided reading at various levels, but at each level, it demonstrates different aspects that could be useful in your room: data analysis, using the prompting guide, Common Core alignment. Which aspect of guided reading feels most immediately useful to you?

CHAPTER 10: INDEPENDENT READING

Questions for Discussion

1. What challenges do you face in making sure that your students are reading independently during the time you provide them? What approach in this chapter might help you push them?

2. Having read this chapter, how would you describe the goal of text selection for independent reading? Do you have a library designed to encourage students to choose the texts that are best for them? Are there library procedures to make sure this happens efficiently?

Question for Application

3. This chapter describes a series of steps you can take to hold students accountable when they read independently. Which do you think would make the biggest difference for your students?

CHAPTER 11: THE SCHEDULE

Questions for Discussion

1. What are the keys to building an effective reading schedule?

2. Which of the variations feels the most plausible for your school context?

Question for Application

3. Build your schedule for reading instruction throughout the day.

CHAPTER 12: COACHING TEACHERS

Questions for Discussion

1. Where does coaching normally fall apart in most schools?

2. Which are the levers that would add the most value to the coaching model in the school where you work?

Question for Application

3. Create a plan to implement high-leverage coaching for literacy teachers in your school.

Notes

Introduction

1. Chein, J. M., & Schneider, W. (2012). The brain's learning and control architecture. *Current Directions in Psychological Science, 21*(2), 78–84.

2. Ericsson, K. A., & Krampe, R. H. (1993). The role of deliberate practice in the acquisition of expert performance. *Psychological Review, 100*(3), 363.

3. Lesnick, J., Goerge, R., Smithgall, C., & Gwynne, J. (2010). *Reading on grade level in third grade: How is it related to high school performance and college enrollment?* Chicago: Chapin Hall at the University of Chicago. See also Kutner, M., Greenberg, E., Jin, Y., Boyle, B., Hsu, Y., & Dunleavy, E. (2007). *Literacy in everyday life: Results from the 2003 National Assessment of Adult Literacy.* (NCES 2007–480). Washington, DC: National Center for Education Statistics, Institute of Education Sciences, U.S. Department of Education. See also Harlow, C. (2003). *Education and correctional populations.* Bureau of Justice Statistics Special Report. Washington, DC: U.S. Department of Justice.

4. National Governors Association Center for Best Practices, Council of Chief State School Officers. (2010). *Common Core State Standards for English Language Arts & Literacy in History/Social Studies, Science, and Technical Subjects.* Washington, DC: Authors.

5. U.S. Department of Education. (2012). *The nation's report card: Reading 2011.* Retrieved from http://nces.ed.gov/nationsreportcard/pdf/main2011/2012457.pdf

6. Ambriz, M., & Sparling, C. (2012). *Annual report.* Newark, NJ: North Star Academy Charter School of Newark.

7. New Jersey Department of Education. (2012). *NJ ASK state data*. Trenton, NJ: Author.

8. ACT. (2006). *Reading between the lines: What the ACT reveals about college readiness in reading*. Iowa City, IA: Author. Retrieved from http://www.act .org/research/policymakers/pdf/reading_summary.pdf

9. Adams, M. J. (2010). Advancing our students' language and literacy. *American Educator, 34*(4), 3–11.

10. National Governors Association Center for Best Practices, Council of Chief State School Officers. (2010). *Common Core State Standards for English Language Arts & Literacy in History/Social Studies, Science, and Technical Subjects: Introduction: Key Design Consideration*. Washington, DC: Authors. Retrieved from http://www.corestandards.org/ELA-Literacy/introduction /key-design-consideration

Chapter 1

1. Luther, C. (2010, June 4). Coach John Wooden's lesson on shoes and socks. *UCLA Newsroom*. Retrieved from http://newsroom.ucla.edu/portal/ucla /wooden-shoes-and-socks-84177.aspx

2. Issacson, W. (2011). *Steve Jobs*. New York, NY: Simon & Schuster.

3. John Wooden: A coaching legend: October 14, 1910–June 4, 2010. (n.d.) Retrieved from http://www.uclabruins.com/sports/m-baskbl/spec-rel/ucla -wooden-page.html

Chapter 2

1. National Governors Association Center for Best Practices, Council of Chief State School Officers. (2010). *Common Core State Standards for English Language Arts & Literacy in History/Social Studies, Science, and Technical Subjects: Speaking & Listening: Introduction*. Washington, DC: Authors.

2. In the 1970s, Dolores Durkin conducted a study on comprehension. What she learned was that although comprehension was widely tested and thought to be important, an average of only six to seven minutes a day was spent in class teaching comprehension. Durkin, D. (1978). *What classroom observations reveal about reading comprehension instruction.*

Urbana-Champaign, IL: Center for the Study of Reading, University of Illinois at Urbana-Champaign. In 2002, a RAND report followed this up: not much had changed. RAND Reading Study Group. (2002). *Reading for understanding: Toward an R&D program in reading comprehension.* Santa Monica, CA: RAND.

3. You'll notice that the majority of the habits here apply to the CCSS for Speaking & Listening 1 and 6. Although the other standards are present in many reading clips, standards 2 and 3 occur primarily in read-aloud (see Chapter Four), and standards 4 and 5 are supported in social studies and science lessons.

4. Lemov, D. (2010). Technique 17: Ratio. In *Teach like a champion: 49 techniques that will put students on the path to college* (pp. 92–97). San Francisco, CA: Jossey-Bass.

5. Note that the CCSS don't differentiate very well into specific, isolated habits, especially at the higher grade levels. We have consolidated them into discrete habits that are teachable to students.

6. See previous note.

7. See note 5.

8. Note that the standards join a lot of skills together, especially at the higher grade levels. We have broken them down into the discrete habits that are teachable to students. So you'll note multiple habits listed in the chapter that are covered by only one standard in Common Core.

9. See previous note.

10. It is important to note that we recommend pressing beyond the CCSS language of "assigned roles" (for example, selecting one student to be the discussion "facilitator") and, rather, letting discussion groups guide themselves. This pushes more of the participants to be leaders and simulates real-world dialogue much more effectively.

11. This is another standard not explicitly addressed by Common Core. Beyond roles in a conversation, students should learn to lead all aspects of the conversation at one time.

12. Lemov, D. (2010). Technique 43: Positive framing. In *Teach like a champion: 49 techniques that will put students on the path to college* (pp. 210–213). San Francisco, CA: Jossey-Bass.

Part 2

1. Morrow, L. M. (2009). Literacy research and practice from the 1960s to the present. In *Literacy development in the early years: Helping children read and write* (pp. 23–28). Retrieved from http://www.education.com /reference/article/literacy-research-practice-recent/

2. Patterson, K., Grenny, J., Maxfield, D., McMillan, R., & Switzler, A. (2008). *Influencer: The power to change anything.* New York, NY: McGraw-Hill.

3. Wharton-McDonald, R., Pressley, M., & Rankin, J. L. (1997). Effective primary-grades literacy instruction = balanced literacy instruction. *Reading Teacher, 50*, 518–521. See also Pressley, M., Roehrig, A., & Bogner, K. (2002). Balanced literacy instruction. *Focus on Exceptional Children, 34*(5), 1–14.

Chapter 3

1. Jefferies, S. (2012, June 14). Keynote address, North Star Academy graduation, Newark, NJ.

2. Calkins, L., Ehrenworth, M., & Lehman, C. (2012). *Pathways to the Common Core.* Portsmouth, NH: Heinemann.

3. National Governors Association Center for Best Practices, Council of Chief State School Officers. (2010). *Common Core State Standards for English Language Arts & Literacy in History/Social Studies, Science, and Technical Subjects.* Washington, DC: Authors.

4. Three factors are mentioned for text difficulty level: qualitative evaluation (levels of meaning, structure, language conventionality and clarity, and knowledge demands); quantitative evaluation (readability measures and other scores of text complexity); and matching reader to text and task.

Chapter 4

1. Williams, J., Katz, C., & Seigel, B. (2003, September 17). Off their rockers: Wacky new rules for teaching class. *New York Daily News,* p. 5.

2. Langer, E., Blank, A., & Chanowitz, B. (1978). The mindlessness of ostensibly thoughtful action. *Journal of Personality and Social Psychology, 36,* 635–642.

Chapter 5

1. Helm, B. (2006, August 20). A boot camp for budding virtuosos. *Bloomberg Businessweek.* Retrieved from http://www.businessweek.com/stories/2006 -08-20/a-boot-camp-for-budding-virtuosos. See also Meadowmount School of Music of Society of Strings Inc. (n.d.). Retrieved from http://www .meadowmount.com/

2. Coyle, D. (2009). *The talent code.* New York, NY: Bantam Dell.

Chapter 6

1. Cunningham, P. M., & Cunningham, J. W. (2002). What we know about how to teach phonics. In A. E. Farstrup & S. J. Samuels (Eds.), *What research has to say about reading instruction* (3rd ed., pp. 87–109). Newark, DE: International Reading Association.

2. Lemov, D. (2010). Technique 19: At bats. In *Teach like a champion: 49 techniques that will put students on the path to college* (pp. 104–105). San Francisco, CA: Jossey-Bass.

3. Lemov, D. (2012). *Practice perfect: 42 rules for getting better at getting better.* San Francisco, CA: Jossey-Bass.

4. Lemov, D. (2010). Technique 44: Precise praise. In *Teach like a champion: 49 techniques that will put students on the path to college* (pp. 210–213). San Francisco, CA: Jossey-Bass.

5. Lemov, D. (2010). Improving your pacing: Additional techniques for creating a positive rhythm in a classroom. In *Teach like a champion: 49 techniques that will put students on the path to college* (pp. 225–234). San Francisco, CA: Jossey-Bass.

Chapter 7

1. Bambrick-Santoyo, P. (2010). *Driven by data: A practical guide to improve instruction*. San Francisco, CA: Jossey-Bass.

2. Ibid.

3. If you'd like more detail on that process, you'll find a thorough walkthrough on how to conduct data-driven planning meetings in *Driven by Data*.

Chapter 8

1. Rodriguez, B. (2012, July 3). Paper road maps fade in age of inexpensive GPS technology. *Anchorage Daily News*. Retrieved from http://www.adn.com/2012/07/03/v-printer/2529746/paper-road-maps-fade-in-age-of.html

2. At the time of this printing, we were still compiling lists of informational texts—a challenge for everyone in the early grades! EngageNY is a great resource for informational texts in the meantime.

Chapter 9

1. Boyles, N. (2012). *That's a great answer: Teaching literature response to struggling readers* (2nd ed.). Gainesville, FL: Maugpin House.

2. Fountas, I., & Pinnell, G. S. (2006). *Teaching for comprehending and fluency: Thinking, talking, and writing about reading, K–8*. Portsmouth, NH: Heinemann.

3. Martin, B., Jr., & Archambault, J. (1997). *Knots on a counting rope*. New York, NY: Square Fish.

Chapter 10

1. Campbell, J. (2008). *The hero with a thousand faces*. Novato, CA: New World Library.

2. Bradbury, R. (2001). In his words. Retrieved from http://www.raybradbury.com/inhiswords02.html

3. Booker, B. (2012, January 29). Children, authors to meet at book fair. *Philadelphia Tribune*. Retrieved from http://www.phillytrib.com/lifestyles articles/item/2522-children,-authors-to-meet-at-book-fair.html

4. Mol, S. E., & Bus, A. G. (2011). To read or not to read: A meta-analysis of print exposure from infancy to early adulthood. *Psychological Bulletin, 137,* 267–296. doi:10.1037/a0021890

5. Donahue, P. L., Voekl, K. E., Campbell, J. R., & Mazzeo, J. (1999). *NAEP reading report card for the nation and the states.* Washington, DC: U.S. Department of Education.

6. McNinch, G. W., Shaffer, G. L., & Campbell, P. (1998). Allocation of time in reading. *Reading Horizons, 39*(2), 123–130.

7. Beers, K. (2003). *When kids can't read, what teachers can do: A guide for teachers, 6–12.* Portsmouth, NH: Heinemann.

8. Duke, N. K. (2000). 3.6 minutes per day: The scarcity of informational texts in first grade. *Reading Research Quarterly, 35,* 202–224.

Part 4

1. Heath, C., & Heath, D. (2010). *Switch: How to change things when change is hard.* New York, NY: Broadway Books.

Chapter 12

1. As we've noted, identifying the highest impact feedback possible is in part a matter of experience; with practice, it becomes far easier. Yet some shortcuts exist. Studying the best literature around classroom instruction is a start. Doug Lemov's *Teach Like a Champion* (2010) and Jon Saphier's *The Skillful Teacher* (2008) were the most frequently mentioned resources by the leaders in this guide. In addition, Paul's *Leverage Leadership* includes a list of top ten action steps for coaching general teaching.

Appendix

1. CCSS SL 2 and 3 are embedded in read-aloud (see Chapter Four), and CCSS 4 and 5 are addressed in social studies and science classes.

Index

Bradbury, R., 244

Branson, M., 52

Branson-Thayer, M., 229

Bringing Words to Life, 114

Building off of the answers of others, 59, 64

Building the Framework for Your Curriculum (box), 93

Bus, A. G., 244

C

Calkins, L., 8, 83

Campbell, J. R., 243–244, 245

Campbell, P., 245

Carpet-square rugs, 35

Chairs, 34, 43

Chanowitz, B., 112

Chanting, 43, 159; and effective transitions, 41; and student enthusiasm, 41

Character motivation, identification of, 6

Cheers, 159

Chein, J. M., 3

Cited details, retell vs., 88

"Classmate-free" paths to/from library, 252, 259

Classroom habits, 27–44

Classroom setup, 43, 44; personal choices, 35; and student learning, 32; for transition, 31

Classroom transition, setting up for, 32–36

Close reading, and written responses, 210

Co-teaching, 304

Coach planning, 304–305

Coaching teachers, 287–307; growth mind-set, 288–291; observation, 292–295; professional development (PD), 292; reading teachers, developing, 307; self-assessment, 307; Valerie's story, 288–290

Coleman, D., 117

Coming prepared in writing, 63, 64, 73

Common Core State Standards (CCSS), 4–5, 114, 117, 210, *See also* Reading-by-Habit model; assessments, 85; bridging the rigor of, 12; complex texts, incorporating into

strong skill instruction, 15; content-area instruction, 13–15; curricular scope/sequence of, laying out, 5; dangerous myths about, 12–15; literacy block, 13; literary vs. informational texts, distribution of, 12–13; Reading Foundations, 146; and reading habits, 83; and text complexity, 87

Complex texts, incorporating into strong skill instruction, 15

Complexity of text, creating a staircase of, 19

Comprehension, 176; oral vs. written, 88, teacher assessment of, 53

Comprehension questions, 34; copies of, 43; types of, 213

Comprehension skills, 270; alternating between guided reading lessons and, 273; framework, 141–142; comprehension conversation, 208; I Do, 136–137, 141; improving comprehension instruction, 143; lesson prework, 132–136; lessons, 131; preparation, 141; self-assessment, 143; teaching, 78–79, 129–143; We Do, 137–139, 141–142; You Do, 139–140, 142

Comprehension Skills Workshop, 325–328; audience, 326; complete overview, 328; goal, 326; living the learning components legend, 328; when to use, 326; workshop preparation sheet, 327

Computer-based literacy program, purchasing, 257–258

Consistency, maintaining, 65

Content-area instruction, 13–15

Costanzo, K., 303, 304, 305

Coyle, D., 69, 130

Critical thinking, 213; building the habit of, 57–58

Cunningham, J. W., 146

Cunningham, P. M., 146

Curriculum: assessment bottom lines, 101; and assessments, 92–101; building the framework for (table), 93; samples, 95–100

H

I

Lisovicz, J., 151, 156, 158

Listening/talking only in turn, 55, 57, 66, 70

Literacy instructors, setup of spaces/resources, 32–33

Locked-in feedback meetings, 293

Luther, C., 27

M

Magical moments, making of, 167–169

Maintaining habits of discussion, 65–68

Mapmaking, 190

Martin, B., Jr., 239

Materials: on-hand, 34; paying attention to, before the lesson, 35

Maxfield, D., 77

Mazzeo, J., 245

McKeown, M. G., 115

McMillan, D., 45–46

McMillan, R., 77

McNinch, G. W., 245

Meaning of nonliteral phrases, vocabulary in context vs., 88

Michels, E., 1–3, 6, 60, 167, 220, 224, 235, 239–241, 240–241, 305–306

Midlesson transitions, 37

Mol, S. E.,, 245

Moyle, L., 104, 106, 115, 118, 120, 121, 136, 138, 139

Morrow, L. M., 77

Myers, W. D., 244

N

NAEP 1998 Reading Report Card for the Nation and the States, 245

Narrating the positive, 68

Narrative Guided Reading Prompting Guide, 224, 230, 231, 358–390; comprehension (400L), 230–231; comprehension (450L-500L), 235–237; comprehension (900L+), 240; figurative language (550L-600L), 238–239; symbolism (700L+), 239–241

Narrative Guided Reading Prompting Guide (North Star Academy Elementary School), 358–390; comprehension (50L-100L), 361–362; comprehension (100L-150L), 365; comprehension (150L-250L), 367; comprehension (250L-320L), 369; comprehension (320L-380L), 371; comprehension (380L-450L), 373–374; comprehension (450L-500L), 375–377; comprehension (500L-550L), 378–379; comprehension (550L-600L), 380–381; comprehension (600L-700L), 383–384; comprehension (700L-800L), 385; comprehension (800L-900L), 387–388; comprehension (900+), 390; comprehension skills framework, 352–353; comprehension (up to 50L), 359; concepts related to print and word solving (up to 50L), 358; vocabulary (700L-800L), 384; vocabulary (800L-900L), 386; vocabulary (900+), 389; word solving (450L-500L), 374; word solving (500L-550L), 377; word solving (600L-700L), 382; word solving and fluency (50L-100L), 360; word solving and fluency (100L-150L), 363–364; word solving and fluency (150L-200L), 366; word solving and fluency (250L-320L), 368; word solving and fluency (320L-380L), 370; word solving and fluency (380L-450L), 372

Narrative STEP assessment, 212

National Governors Association Center for Best Practices, 4, 13, 45, 89

National Reading Panel, 114–115

New Jersey Department of Education, 6

New vocabulary, learning, 114–115

95% Group Phonics Lessons, 147

No Hands habit, 62, 64, 72

Nonverbal cues, issuing, 68–69

Nonverbal prompts, 62

North Star Academy Elementary School, 8–9, See also Narrative guided reading prompting guide (North Star Academy

How to Use the DVD

SYSTEM REQUIREMENTS

PC with Microsoft Windows 2007 or later
Mac with Apple OS version 10.1 or later

USING THE DVD WITH WINDOWS

To view the items located on the DVD, follow these steps:

1. Insert the DVD into your computer's DVD drive.

2. A window appears with the following options:

    Contents: Allows you to view the files included on the DVD

    Software: Allows you to install useful software from the DVD

    Links: Displays a hyperlinked page of websites

    Author: Displays a page with information about the author(s)

    Contact Us: Displays a page with information on contacting the publisher or author

    Help: Displays a page with information on using the DVD

    Exit: Closes the interface window

If you do not have autorun enabled, or if the autorun window does not appear, follow these steps to access the DVD:

1. Click Start → Run.

2. In the dialog box that appears, type d:\start.exe, where d is the letter of your DVD drive. This brings up the autorun window described in the preceding set of steps.

3. Choose the desired option from the menu. (See step 2 in the preceding list for a description of these options.)

IN CASE OF TROUBLE

If you experience difficulty using the DVD, please follow these steps:

1. Make sure your hardware and systems configurations conform to the systems requirements noted under "System Requirements" listed earlier.

2. Review the installation procedure for your type of hardware and operating system. It is possible to reinstall the software if necessary.

To speak with someone in Product Technical Support, call 800-762-2974 or 317-572-3994 Monday through Friday from 8:30 AM to 5:00 PM EST. You can also contact Product Technical Support and get support information through our website at www.wiley.com/techsupport.

Before calling or writing, please have the following information available:

• Type of computer and operating system

• Any error messages displayed

• Complete description of the problem

It is best if you are sitting at your computer when making the call.

JB JOSSEY-BASS | Education

Jossey-Bass provides educators with practical knowledge and tools to create a positive and lifelong impact on student learning.

For more information about our resources, authors, and events please visit us at: www.josseybasseducation.com.

You may also find us on Facebook, Twitter, and Pinterest.

 Jossey-Bass K–12 Education

jbeducation

Pinterest jbeducation